河北省科普专项项目编号21557101K

The Food Industry Map for 2022
Winter Olympic Games
(Hebei Province)

迎冬奥
食品产业地图（河北省）

王晓茹　王颉　王浩勇　孙剑锋　主编

2022

化学工业出版社

·北京·

The Food Industry Map for 2022 Winter Olympic Games

Wang Xiaoru   Wang Jie   Wang Haoyong   Sun Jianfeng

内容简介

作为冬奥会主赛场地区，河北旅游资源丰富，食品产业呈集群式发展且特色鲜明。本书以科普读物的形式，展示了部分以河北为主的食品产业集群以及张家口和承德的风景名胜，对促进世界文化和产业交融，加速河北食品产业走向世界的进程具有重要意义。

本书中英文对照，方便中外运动员和观看冬奥比赛的观众阅读，也可供对河北省食品产业感兴趣的相关研究人员参考。

图书在版编目（CIP）数据

迎冬奥食品产业地图.河北省：英、汉/王晓茹等主编.—北京：化学工业出版社，2021.11
ISBN 978-7-122-40182-3

Ⅰ.①迎… Ⅱ.①王… Ⅲ.①食品工业-介绍-河北-英、汉 Ⅳ.①F426.82

中国版本图书馆CIP数据核字（2021）第223449号

责任编辑：李建丽　赵玉清　　　　　　　　装帧设计：王晓宇
责任校对：宋　夏

出版发行：化学工业出版社（北京市东城区青年湖南街13号　邮政编码100011）
印　　装：大厂聚鑫印刷有限责任公司
710mm×1000mm　1/16　印张16　彩插10　字数271千字　2021年11月北京第1版第1次印刷

购书咨询：010-64518888　　　　　　　　售后服务：010-64518899
网　　址：http://www.cip.com.cn
凡购买本书，如有缺损质量问题，本社销售中心负责调换。

定　　价：99.00元　　　　　　　　　　　　　　　　　版权所有　违者必究

迎冬奥食品产业地图（河北省）
The Food Industry Map for 2022 Winter Olympic Games

序

  2022年，第24届冬季奥林匹克运动会将在中国举办，其中雪上项目由河北省张家口市主办，这不仅是中国的盛事，更是河北省的荣耀。河北地处华北平原，东临渤海、内环京津，西靠太行山，北依燕山，是我国重要的农业大省，食品产业是该省的战略支柱性产业。河北省作为东方人类、华夏文明和农耕文明的重要发祥地，是新中国的诞生地，经过数千年的积淀，形成了丰富、独特的文化。

  河北省依托丰富的农产品资源，大力发展食品产业。2018年河北省规模以上食品行业营业收入2868.22亿元，占全省规模以上工业企业营业收入的比重为7.32%。拥有中国长城葡萄酒有限公司、石家庄君乐宝乳业有限公司、河北衡水老白干酒业股份有限公司、河北养元智汇饮品股份有限公司、今麦郎食品股份有限公司、金沙河集团等国内知名食品企业。金山岭长城、承德避暑山庄等历史遗迹均在河北省。

  在第24届冬奥会举办之前，河北农业大学编著的《迎冬奥食品产业地图》一书以中英文对照的形式介绍了河北省葡萄酒、乳品、粮食加工、饮品制造、马铃薯加工和白酒酿造等主要食品产业，以及冬奥会张家口赛区附近的风景名胜等旅游资源和河北省主要的食品相关高等教育机构。这为来自世界各地的友人在冬奥会观赛之余进一步了解河北、爱上河北打开了一扇窗，将对中国河北留下美好的记忆。

  在北京冬奥会举办之时，该书将作为礼物赠送给来自世界各地的运动员、裁判员等来华人员，这对于促进世界文化和产业交融，加速河北省食品产业走向世界具有积极的推动意义。

  希望该书的出版发行，为第24届冬奥会的举办增光添彩，并为河北省食品产业的发展提供更多、更好的机遇。

朱蓓薇

中国工程院院士

2021年10月8日

Foreword

The Food Industry Map for 2022 Winter Olympic Games

In 2022, the 24th Winter Olympic Games will be held in China, and Zhangjiakou City of Hebei Province will be the host city of the snow events. This is not only a great event in China but also the pride of Hebei Province. Hebei, surrounding both Beijing and Tianjin, is located in North China Plain, bordering the Bohai Sea to the east, Taihang Mountain to the west, and Yanshan Mountain to the north. The food industry is one of the strategic pillar industries of Hebei Province, Which is an important agricultural province in China. As one of the important birthplaces of the oriental civilization, Chinese civilization, farming culture, and also the New China, Hebei Province has accumulated abundant and distinctive culture through a history as long as thousands of years.

Hebei Province has been developing the food industry vigorously by means of exploiting the abundant agricultural products resources. In 2018 the operating income of the food industrial enterprises was CNY 286.7 billion, accounting for 7.32% of the operating income of all industrial enterprises. Well-known food enterprises include China Great Wall Wine Co., Ltd., Shijiazhuang Junlebao Dairy Co., Ltd., Hebei Hengshui Laobaigan Liquor Co., Ltd., Hebei Yangyuan Zhihui Beverage Co., Ltd., Jinmailang Mianpin Co., Ltd., Hebei Jinshahe Flour Manufacturing Group Co., Ltd., etc. Renowned historical sites are Jinshanling Great Wall, Chengde Mountain Resort and so on.

Before the 24th Winter Olympics, *The Food Industry Map for 2022 Winter Olympic Games* compiled by Hebei Agricultural University in both Chinese and English introduced major food industries in Hebei Province, including wine, dairy, food processing, beverage manufacturing, potato processing and liquor brewing industries, as well as tourist resources such as scenic spots near Zhangjiakou and major food-related higher education institutions in Hebei Province. This book may open a window for friends world-wide to learn more about Hebei and fall in love with Hebei, and the good memory may linger long on their mind.

At the Beijing Winter Olympics, this book will be presented as a gift to athletes, referees, and other foreign friends from all over the world. This book may play a positive role in promoting the understanding of different cultures and help them know more about the food industry in Hebei Province.

It is hoped that the publication of this book will make a good addition to the 24th Winter Olympics and provide more and better opportunities for the development of the food industry in Hebei Province.

Zhu Beiwei
Academician of Chinese Academy of Engineering
October 8, 2021

前 言

迎冬奥食品产业地图（河北省）
The Food Industry Map for 2022 Winter Olympic Games

第24届冬季奥林匹克运动会将于2022年2月4日至2022年2月20日在我国北京市和张家口市举行。该届冬奥会设7个大项，15个分项，109个小项，北京赛区承办所有冰上项目，延庆赛区和张家口赛区承办所有的雪上项目。届时将有一百多个国家和地区参加四年一度的冰雪盛会。2022年冬奥会共有12个竞赛场馆，其中北京赛区6个，延庆赛区2个，张家口赛区4个。

河北张家口是冬奥会主赛场之一，河北在冬奥会场馆附近旅游资源丰富，食品产业集群式发展，特色鲜明。据河北省统计局公布的数据，2018年，河北省规模以上食品工业企业1229个，营业收入2868.22亿元，占全省规模以上工业企业营业收入的7.32%，是河北省的支柱产业之一。例如位于北京西北80千米的怀来县，是中国第一瓶干白葡萄酒、第一瓶国际标准白兰地、第一瓶酒庄酒的诞生地，是中国县级最大的酿酒葡萄种植加工基地，葡萄酒生产企业41家，年葡萄酒生产能力15万吨，长城五星及桑干酒庄葡萄酒多年以来为国宴用酒，是葡萄酒中的"国家队"。由中国长城葡萄酒有限公司完成的"干白葡萄酒新工艺研究"和"长城庄园模式的创建及庄园葡萄酒关键技术的研究与应用"两项成果获国家科学技术进步二等奖。创立于1995年的君乐宝乳业集团，26年来始终专注于奶业发展，为消费者提供健康、营养、安全的乳制品。集团现有员工14000余人，业务范围包括婴幼儿奶粉、低温液态奶、常温液态奶、牧业四大板块，在河北、河南、江苏、吉林等地建有20个生产工厂、13个现代化大型牧场，销售市场覆盖全国。1994年成立，年销售额超200亿元的今麦郎集团，是横跨面品、饮品两大品类的大型食品企业集团。其产品覆盖方便面、挂面、面粉、饮品等。经过27年的发展，今麦郎已经成为集研发、生产、销售于一体的现代化大型综合食品企业集团。鉴于篇幅所限，本书只介绍以葡萄酒产业为主的30多个企业。此外，张家口的泥河湾遗址群、宣化古城、太子城遗址、承德的避暑山庄、外八庙、金山岭长城等，彰显了中华民族悠久的历史和灿烂的文化。

在第 24 届冬奥会举办之际，以中英文对照的形式，编辑出版《迎冬奥食品产业地图》，向世界展示部分以河北为主的食品产业集群以及张家口和承德的风景名胜，对促进世界文化和产业交融，加速河北食品产业走向世界的进程具有重要意义。

本书由王晓茹、王颉、王浩勇和孙剑锋主编。河北农业大学王晓茹编写第一篇第三章和第七章，参编第二篇和第三篇；怀来县葡萄酒局董继先、李斌、柯忻和河北农业大学王颉、刘亚琼、孙剑锋、赵文、王晓茹编写第一篇第一章；河北农业大学王颉、刘亚琼、锁然、牟建楼、王文秀、马倩云编写第一篇第二章、第六章，第二篇和第三篇；河北农业大学孙剑锋编写第一篇第五章；中国农业大学薛文通编写第一篇第四章；北京工商大学李秀婷参编第二篇；河北农业大学外国语学院王浩勇、聂宜欣翻译前言，郭海波、王立杰、成诗吟翻译第一篇第一章，王浩勇、聂宜欣翻译第一篇第二至七章，郭石磊、梁远馨翻译第二篇和第三篇。全书由河北农业大学王晓茹、王颉、王浩勇和孙剑锋统稿。

本书的出版得到了河北省创新能力提升计划科普专项（项目编号：21557101K）和河北省科协（学会能力提升计划）的大力支持，怀来县葡萄酒局和石家庄君乐宝乳业有限公司、中国长城葡萄酒有限公司、中粮长城华夏酒庄秦皇岛有限公司、晨光生物科技集团股份有限公司等企业为本书的出版提供了丰富的第一手资料，怀来县葡萄酒局和河北民族师范学院高俊虎为本书出版提供了精美的图片，在此一并致谢！

由于编者水平有限，书中不妥之处，敬请读者批评指正。

编者
2021 年 6 月 16 日

Preface

The Food Industry Map for 2022 Winter Olympic Games

The 24th Winter Olympic Games are to be co-hosted in Beijing and Zhangjiakou of Hebei Province in China from February 4 to 20, 2022. The 2022 Winter Olympic Games include 102 events in 7 sports. Ice events will be held in Beijing, and snow events will be held in Yanqing County of Beijing City and Zhangjiakou City of Hebei Province. It is estimated that more than 100 countries will attend the Olympic Games. There will be 12 venues in total: 6 in Beijing 2022 competition zone, 2 in Yanqing competition zone, and 4 in Zhangjiakou competition zone.

Zhangjiakou of Hebei Province is one of the host cities of the Winter Olympics. Hebei Province boasts abundant tourism resources and distinctive food industry clusters. According to the report of Hebei Provincial Bureau of Statistics, in 2018, there were 1,229 food industrial enterprises, with an operating income of CNY 286.8 billion, accounting for 7.32% of the operating income of all industrial enterprises, and the food industry was one of the pillar industries in Hebei Province. Huailai County of Hebei Province, about 80 kilometers northwest of Beijing, is the birthplace of the first bottle of dry white wine, champagne sparkling wine, international standard brand, and winery wine in China. Huailai County, also the largest county-level wine grape planting and processing base in China, owns 41 wine production enterprises and produces an output of 150,000 tons of wine annually. The Great Wall Five-Star and Sungod wine have been the wines for state banquets for many years and are "the national team" among wines. China Great Wall Wine Co., Ltd. has won the second prize of National Science and Technology Progress Award twice for two achievements: New Technology of Dry White Wine and Great Wall Manor Model and Key Technologies of Manor Wine. Junlebao Dairy Group, founded in 1995, has focused on the development of the dairy industry for 26 years, providing consumers with healthy, nutritious, and safe dairy products. The group has more than 14,000 employees, and its business covers infant milk powder, low-temperature liquid milk, normal temperature liquid milk, and husbandry. It has 20 factories and 13 large-scale modern ranches in Hebei, Henan, Jiangsu, and Jilin, and its products are sold all over the country. Jinmailang Group, established in 1994, has an annual sale of more than CNY 20 billion and has now become a large modern food company. Its products include instant noodles, dried noodles, flour, drinks, etc. After 26 years of development, Jinmailang has become a modern large-scale food enterprise integrating R&D, production, and sales. Due to the limited length, this book only introduces a little more than 40 wine and other enterprises. Besides, the cultural relics in Zhangjiakou as well as Chengde, show the long history and splendid culture of the Chinese nation. Notable cultural relics in Zhangjiakou include Nihewan site, Xuanhua Ancient City, and Taizicheng Resort, and the ones in Chengde include the Mountain Resort and the Eight Outer Temples, and Jinshanling Great Wall.

Before the 24th Winter Olympic Games, we write this book in Chinese and English. The aim is to show the world the food industry clusters in Hebei and the scenic spots in Zhangjiakou and Chengde which are in the vicinity of the sites of the Winter Olympics. It will promote the integration of world culture and industry, and accelerate the process of the opening to the world of Hebei food industry.

This book is edited by Wang Xiaoru, Wang Jie, Wang Haoyong and Sun Jianfeng, et. al. To be specific, Wang Xiaoru of Hebei Agricultural University wrote Chapter 3 and Chapter 7 of Part Ⅰ, and some parts of Part Ⅱ & Ⅲ; Dong Jixian, Li Bin, Ke Xin of Huailai County Wine Bureau, and Wang Jie, Liu Yaqiong, Suo Sun Jianfeng, Zhao Wen, Wang Xiaoru of Hebei Agricultural University finished Chapter 1 of Part Ⅰ; Wang Jie, Liu Yaqiong, Suo Ran, Mou Jianlou, Wang Wenxiu Ma Qianyun completed Chapter 2 and 6 of Part Ⅰ, Part Ⅱ and Part Ⅲ; Sun Jianfeng wrote Chapter 5 of Part Ⅰ; Xue Wentong of China Agricultural University completed Chapter 4 of Part Ⅰ; Li Xiuting of Beijing Technology and Business University joined in the writing of Part Ⅱ.

The translation task was completed by the teachers and MTI students of College of Foreign Languages, Hebei Agricultural University, including Wang Haoyong and Nie Yixin for the Preface; Guo Haibo, Wang Lijie and Cheng Shiyin for Chapter 1 of Part I; Wang Haoyong and Nie Yixin for Chapters 2-7 of Part I; Guo Shilei and Liang Yuanxin for Part II and Part III. The final compilation of this book was completed by Wang Xiaoru, Wang Jie, Wang Haoyong and Sun Jianfeng of Hebei Agricultural University.

The publication of this book is supported by Hebei Science Popularization Project of Innovation Ability Promotion Program (Project No.: 21557101K) and Hebei Association for Science and Technology (Academic Capability Enhancement Program). Huailai County Vine and Wine Administration, Shijiazhuang Junlebao Dairy Co., Ltd., China Great Wall Wine Co., Ltd., COFCO Greatwall Huaxia Wine (Qinghuangdao) Co., Ltd., Chenguang Biotech Group Co., Ltd. and other enterprises provided abundant first-hand materials. Huailai County Vine and Wine Administration and Gao Junhu of Hebei Normal University for Nationalities provided exquisite photos. Thank you all!

Due to the editors' limited level, there must be a lot to be improved in this book, and all the readers are welcome to provide suggestions.

Editors
June 16, 2021

目录 Contents

迎冬奥食品产业地图（河北省）
The Food Industry Map for 2022 Winter Olympic Games

第一篇　产业篇
Part I　Industry

第一章　葡萄酒产业 ················· 3
Chapter 1　Wine Industry ················· 97

1. 中国长城葡萄酒有限公司 ················· 5
1. China Great Wall Wine Co., Ltd. ················· 101

2. 中粮长城桑干酒庄（怀来）有限公司 ················· 9
2. COFCO Greatwall Huaxia Wine (Huailai) Co., Ltd. ················· 107

3. 怀来县贵族庄园葡萄酒业有限公司 ················· 11
3. Huailai County Nobility Chateau Winery Co., Ltd. ················· 110

4. 怀来中法庄园葡萄酒有限公司 ················· 12
4. Domaine Franco Chinois Wine Co., Ltd. ················· 111

5. 怀来容辰庄园葡萄酒有限公司 ················· 13
5. Huailai Ronchen Vineyard Co., Ltd. ················· 113

6. 河北沙城家和酒业有限公司 ················· 14
6. Hebei Shacheng Jiahe Winery Co., Ltd. ················· 114

7. 河北马丁葡萄酿酒有限公司 ················· 15
7. Hebei Martin Wine Co., Ltd. ················· 115

8. 河北沙城庄园葡萄酒有限公司 …………………………………… 16

8. Hebei Shacheng Villa Wine Co., Ltd. ………………………… 117

9. 河北怀来瑞云葡萄酒股份有限公司 ………………………………… 17

9. Hebei Chateau Nubes Co., Ltd. ……………………………… 118

10. 怀来红叶庄园葡萄酒有限公司 ……………………………………… 18

10. Huailai Chateau Red Leaf Co., Ltd. ……………………… 119

11. 怀来县誉龙葡萄酒庄园有限公司 …………………………………… 19

11. Huailai Yulong Winery Co., Ltd. ………………………… 121

12. 怀来赤霞葡萄酒有限公司 ………………………………………… 19

12. Huailai Chixia Wine Co., Ltd. …………………………… 122

13. 怀来德厚庄园葡萄酒有限公司 ……………………………………… 20

13. Huailai Dehou Manor Wine Co., Ltd. ……………………… 123

14. 怀来丰收庄园葡萄酒有限公司 ……………………………………… 21

14. Huailai Chateau Harvest Wine Co., Ltd. ………………… 123

15. 怀来县福瑞诗葡萄酒堡有限公司 …………………………………… 21

15. Huailai Fresh Wine Co., Ltd. …………………………… 124

16. 怀来县古堡葡萄酒庄园有限公司 …………………………………… 22

16. Huailai JinTuMu Wine Co., Ltd. ………………………… 125

17. 张家口怀谷庄园葡萄酒有限公司 …………………………………… 22

17. Zhangjiakou Huaigu Manor Wine Co., Ltd. ……………… 125

18. 怀来艾伦葡萄酒庄有限公司 ……………………………………… 23

18. Huailai Alan Chateau Co., Ltd. ………………………… 127

19. 怀来龙徽庄园葡萄酒有限公司 ……………………………………… 24

19. Huailai Dragon Seal Wine Co., Ltd. …………………… 128

20. 怀来迦南酒业有限公司 …………………………………………… 26

20. Huailai Canaan Winery Co., Ltd. ·································· 130

21. 叶浓（河北）葡萄酒业有限责任公司 ·································· 27

21. Yenong（Hebei）Winery Co., Ltd. ·································· 131

22. 河北龙泉葡萄酒有限公司 ·································· 27

22. Hebei Longquan Wine Co., Ltd. ·································· 132

23. 怀来葡缇泉葡萄籽科技开发有限公司 ·································· 28

23. Huailai OPC'S Life Technology Development Co., Ltd. ·································· 133

24. 张家口大好河山酿造有限公司 ·································· 29

24. Zhangjiakou Great Land Scape Winery Co., Ltd. ·································· 135

25. 张家口长城酿造（集团）有限责任公司 ·································· 30

25. Zhangjiakou Great Wall Winery（Group）Co., Ltd. ·································· 136

26. 怀来紫晶庄园葡萄酒有限公司 ·································· 33

26. Huailai Amethyst Manor Co., Ltd. ·································· 141

27. 利世 G9 国际庄园 ·································· 34

27. G9 Lee World Chateau ·································· 142

28. 中国怀来·世界葡萄酒之窗展览馆 ·································· 35

28. Huailai，China·Window of Global Wine Exhibition Hall ·································· 144

29. 中粮华夏长城葡萄酒有限公司 ·································· 36

29. COFCO Huaxia Greatwall Wine Co., Ltd. ·································· 145

30. 中粮长城华夏酒庄秦皇岛有限公司 ·································· 39

30. COFCO Greatwall Huaxia Wine（Qinhuangdao）Co., Ltd. ·································· 150

31. 朗格斯酒庄（秦皇岛）有限公司 ·································· 40

31. Bodega Langes（Qinhuangdao）Co., Ltd. ·································· 152

32. 河北夏都葡萄酿酒有限公司 ·································· 42

32. Hebei Xiadu Winery Co., Ltd. ·································· 155

第二章　乳品加工产业 44
Chapter 2　Dairy Processing Industry 158
石家庄君乐宝乳业有限公司 44
Shijiazhuang Junlebao Dairy Co., Ltd. 158

第三章　粮食加工产业 47
Chapter 3　Food Processing Industry 162
1. 今麦郎食品股份有限公司 47
1. Jinmailang Mianpin Co., Ltd. 162
2. 金沙河集团 48
2. Hebei Jinshahe Flour Manufacturing Group Co., Ltd. 164
3. 五得利面粉集团 49
3. Wudeli Flour Group 166

第四章　饮品制造产业 52
Chapter 4　Beverage Industry 169
1. 河北养元智汇饮品股份有限公司 52
1. Hebei Yangyuan Zhihui Beverage Co., Ltd. 169
2. 北京汇源饮料食品集团有限公司 54
2. Beijing Huiyuan Beverage & Food Group Co., Ltd. 173

第五章　马铃薯加工产业 57
Chapter 5　Potato Processing Industry 176
1. 雪川农业发展股份有限公司 57

1. SnowValley Agriculture Development Co.，Ltd. ……………… 176

2. 张家口弘基农业科技开发有限责任公司 ……………………… 61

2. Zhangjiakou Hongji Agriculture Science and Technology
Development Co.，Ltd. ……………………………………… 182

第六章　白酒酿造产业 …………………………………………… 62
Chapter 6　Liquor Brewing Industry ………………………………… 185

1. 河北衡水老白干酒业股份有限公司 …………………………… 62

1. Hebei Hengshui Laobaigan Liquor Co.，Ltd. ………………… 185

2. 河北雄安保府酒业有限公司 …………………………………… 64

2. Hebei Xiongan Baofu Winery Co.，Ltd. ……………………… 188

第七章　其他食品产业 …………………………………………… 66
Chapter 7　Other Food Industries …………………………………… 191

1. 保定槐茂食品科技有限公司 …………………………………… 66

1. Baoding Huaimao Food Technology Co.，Ltd. ……………… 191

2. 保定味群食品科技股份有限公司 ……………………………… 67

2. Baoding Way Chein Food Industrial Co.，Ltd. ……………… 193

3. 晨光生物科技集团股份有限公司 ……………………………… 69

3. Chenguang Biotech Group Co.，Ltd.（CCGB） ……………… 196

4. 秦皇岛市海东青食品有限公司 ………………………………… 71

4. Qinhuangdao Haidongqing Food Co.，Ltd. …………………… 198

5. 承德瑞泰食品有限公司 ………………………………………… 71

5. Chengde Ruitai Food Co.，Ltd. ………………………………… 199

第二篇　风土人情和名胜古迹
Part II　Local Customs and Places of Interest

1. 泥河湾文明	75
1. Nihewan Civilization	203
2. 黄帝城	79
2. Yellow Emperor City Ruins（Huangdi Cheng）	210
3. 鸡鸣山	80
3. Jiming Mountain	211
4. 宣化古城	81
4. Xuanhua Ancient City	213
5. 草原天路	81
5. Grass Skyline（Zhangbei Grassland Highway）	214
6. 太子城遗址	83
6. Taizicheng Relic	216
7. 御道口草原森林风景区	83
7. Yu Dao Kou Grassland and Forest Scenic Spot	218
8. 国家一号风景大道	84
8. First Scenic Boulevard	219
9. 承德避暑山庄	84
9. Chengde Mountain Resort	219
10. 承德避暑山庄外八庙	85
10. Eight Outer Temples	222
11. 磬锤峰国家森林公园	86

11. Qingchuifeng National Forest Park 223

12. 金山岭长城 86

12. Jinshanling Great Wall 223

第三篇　食品教育
Part Ⅲ　Food Education

1. 河北农业大学 91

1. Hebei Agricultural University 229

2. 河北科技大学 92

2. Hebei University of Science and Technology 232

3. 河北科技师范学院 93

3. Hebei Normal University of Science and Technology 234

第一篇

产业篇

第一章

葡萄酒产业

葡萄酒历史概述 中国葡萄酒酿造历史悠久,关于葡萄酒的较早中文记载,出自西汉时期的《史记》,其中的《大宛列传》写道:"宛左右以蒲桃(葡萄的古称)为酒,富人藏酒至万余石,久者数十岁不败。"及至唐宋,关于葡萄酒的诗词就有王翰的"葡萄美酒夜光杯,欲饮琵琶马上催"、白居易的"羌管吹杨柳,燕姬酌蒲萄(蒲萄是葡萄的古称)"、陆游的"如倾潋潋蒲萄酒,似拥重重貂鼠裘"等千古绝唱。在金元时期,元遗山的名篇《蒲桃酒赋并序》则详细记录了葡萄酒的酿造方法:"绞蒲桃浆封而埋之,未几成酒;愈久者愈佳。有藏至千斛者。"科学家对距今约7000~9000年的河南舞阳县的贾湖遗址的研究发现,人类至少在9000年前就开始酿造葡萄酒了,中国有可能是世界上最早酿造葡萄酒的国家,而且这一研究结果使世界葡萄酒的人工酿造历史推前了3000年。

中国葡萄酒的现代化酿造史,肇始于清光绪十八年(1892年),张弼士先生在烟台创办了张裕葡萄酿酒公司,正式开启了中国葡萄酒的工业化酿造时代,在城堡内装瓶,早于法国波尔多18年。张裕从光绪二十年(1894年)开始,就在酒庄内建造地下酒窖,历时11年经三次改建,于1905年初冬正式竣工,这意味着张裕至少在1906年就已经实现了"在酒庄内装瓶"。1907年的《商务官报》曾记载:"即此酒窖一项,振勋(张裕创始人张弼士别名)改图数次,始乃成功。而将成功时,各国工程师前来观者俱为诧异,竟谓中国人有此绝大本领焉。"亮相国际舞台,早于纳帕谷61年。1915年的旧金山世博会,来自中国张裕的"红玫瑰葡萄酒""雷司令白葡萄酒""可雅白兰地"和"味美思"一举荣获4枚金质奖章,震动了世界。

葡萄酒的分类方法 葡萄酒分类方法有很多,有按颜色分类的,有按含糖量进行分类的，有按酿酒工艺进行分类的。

按葡萄酒的颜色可分为以下几类。

红葡萄酒：红葡萄品种带皮发酵而成，酒色分为紫红、宝石红、石榴红等。

桃红葡萄酒：近几年来桃红葡萄酒在国际市场上也颇为流行，桃红葡萄酒颜色介于红葡萄酒和白葡萄酒之间。

白葡萄酒：用白葡萄或红葡萄榨汁后不带皮发酵酿造，颜色呈柠檬黄或金色，澄清透明，果香浓郁，风味独特。

按葡萄酒的含糖量可分为以下几类。

干型葡萄酒：亦称干酒，原料（葡萄汁）中糖分完全转化成酒精，残留糖分含量在 4 克/升以下，饮用时感受不到甜味，只有酸味和清怡爽口的感觉。

半干葡萄酒：含糖量 4～12 克/升。

半甜葡萄酒：含糖量 12～45 克/升，味略甜，是日本和美国消费较多的品种，在中国也很受欢迎。

甜型葡萄酒：葡萄酒含糖量超过 45 克/升，饮用时能感到明显的甜味。

按葡萄酒的酿酒工艺可分为以下两类。

平静葡萄酒：完全用葡萄为原料发酵而成，不添加额外的酒精及香料的葡萄酒。

起泡葡萄酒：这种葡萄酒中留有二氧化碳气泡。常被视为用于庆祝的酒，人们最熟悉的例子就是法国的香槟酒。其他的例子有西班牙的卡瓦（Cava）和意大利的普洛赛克（Prosecco）、莫斯卡托阿斯蒂（Moscato d'Asti），不过，起泡葡萄酒在世界各地都生产。

怀来县葡萄产业概述　　怀来葡萄栽培已有上千年历史。据《宣化府志》记载，怀来葡萄为宫廷贡品。据《怀来县志》物产篇果类中所记，怀来种有红、白两种葡萄，此志成书于清康熙五十一年（1712 年），说明 300 年前，葡萄在怀来已有种植，并颇具规模。

1993 年由河北文物研究所和张家口市宣化区文保所联合发掘的"下八里辽代壁画墓群"墓主人张世卿、张世本、张文藻、张匡正祭品中都存有已干枯的葡萄种子，后送交中国科学院植物研究所鉴定，属于欧亚种群葡萄。说明在辽代宣化葡萄已被"张家世族"所享用,张世卿为辽代银青崇禄大夫、检校国子监兼监察御史,终于元庆六年(1117年),可见这一产区的葡萄栽培历史在 900 年以上。

经考证宣化葡萄最早引种栽培时间应为唐代宗年间(公元 762~779 年),唐建武州城(宣化城),武军刺史刘怦,军驻武州,因无战事,在武州附近组织军民垦荒造田,营造园林,种植栗果,军中官兵由长安、洛阳招募而来,他们从中原引进葡萄、瓜果在军中和寺庙里试种,距今已有 1200 多年的栽培历史。

新中国建立后,怀来葡萄酒的酿造始于沙城酒厂。1960 年沙城酒厂自力更生建成年产 2000 吨的葡萄酒车间,以龙眼葡萄为主要原料,生产红、白甜葡萄酒,畅销全国各地。1976 年在沙城酒厂研制出了新中国首批干白葡萄酒,1978 年"干白新工艺的研究"被轻工业部列为重点科研项目。1979 年沙城酒厂干白葡萄酒获得国家金质奖,1983 年在英国伦敦第 14 届国际评酒会上获得银质奖,这是解放后我国酒类产品首次在国外获奖。"干白葡萄酒新工艺的研究"获得"国家科技进步二等奖"。该成果向葡萄酒行业全部推广,沿用至今。我国葡萄酒"由甜转干"的转型工作从此开始。

经过四十多年的发展,怀来县现有葡萄种植面积 12 万亩,其中酿酒葡萄 6.5 万亩,鲜食葡萄 5.5 万亩,葡萄年产量 13.1 万吨。怀来县被国家标准化委员会命名为"全国葡萄标准化种植示范县","沙城葡萄酒"被国家质监总局列入国家地理标志产品。全县共有中粮长城葡萄酒有限公司、长城桑干酒庄、中法庄园、容辰庄园、紫晶庄园、贵族庄园等 41 家葡萄酒加工企业,葡萄酒生产能力 15 万吨。先后打造"长城""中法""紫晶""坤爵"等名优品牌 30 多个,累计获得 800 多项国内外知名葡萄酒奖项。

1. 中国长城葡萄酒有限公司

中国长城葡萄酒有限公司位于河北省怀来县沙城镇,是世界 500 强企业中粮集团旗下全资子公司。

中国长城葡萄酒有限公司(以下简称公司)的历史可以追溯到"玉成明"缸房,1914 年"玉成明"缸房酿造的"红煮酒"在巴拿马国际名酒赛会上获金质奖章。1949 年,在原"玉成明"等六家私营酿酒缸房的基础上,成立了地方国营沙城酒厂。1960 年,沙城酒厂自力更生建成年产 2000 吨葡萄酒酿造车间。

1983年8月1日，由中国粮油食品进出口公司、香港远大公司和长城酿酒公司合资成立中国长城葡萄酒有限公司，为中外合资企业，张家口地区长城酿酒公司以所属全部葡萄酒产业资产（基地、技术、设备、厂房、人员等）出资，资产注入新合资公司。2003年中国长城葡萄酒有限公司成为中粮集团旗下全资子公司。自1914年"玉成明"缸房酿造的"红煮酒"获奖开始计算，长城葡萄酒已经有107年的历史。

截至2020年底，公司注册资本1.8亿元，占地面积20.8万平方米，建筑面积8.8万平方米，资产总额9.76亿元，固定资产7.49亿元。公司葡萄酒年综合产能8.8万吨，贮酒能力10万吨，成品仓储能力100万箱，单班日产量20万瓶，日发货能力7万箱，拥有橡木桶6526个，压榨、发酵、储酒、过滤和灌装等先进生产设备1200多台（套）。现有员工312人，其中，大专以上学历90人，国家评酒委员10人，国家资质品酒师23人，国家资质酿酒师11人。

公司设有国家认定企业技术中心、农业农村部酿酒葡萄加工重点实验室和河北省葡萄酒技术研发中心等国家和省部级研发平台，先后完成了原轻工业部"干白葡萄酒新工艺研究"科研项目和国家"七五"星火计划项目——香槟法起泡葡萄酒生产技术开发，研制生产出中国第一瓶干白葡萄酒和中国第一瓶香槟葡萄酒，填补了国内空白。1986年，"干白葡萄酒新工艺的研究"获轻工业部科技进步一等奖；1987年，"干白葡萄酒新工艺的研究"获国家科技进步二等奖；1990年，"香槟法起泡葡萄酒生产技术开发"获轻工业部科技进步三等奖；2005年，"长城庄园模式的创建及庄园葡萄酒关键技术的研究应用"获国家科技进步二等奖。

长城葡萄酒是中国最早按照国际标准酿造、生产的葡萄酒，是中国葡萄酒第一品牌，2004年"长城"商标被国家工商总局认定为中国驰名商标。长城旗下著名产品：星级系列、天赋葡园系列、长城桑干酒庄系列等，多次在巴黎、布鲁塞尔、伦敦等各个国际专业评酒会上捧得最高奖。1979年，长城干白获得国家金奖。1983年，长城干白葡萄酒在英国伦敦第十四届国际评酒会上荣获银质奖，人民日报刊文"这是近70年来，中国葡萄酒在国际上获得的最高荣誉"，并相继在1984年、1986年再获西班牙马德里、法国巴黎评酒会金奖。2019年，五星干红再获国际葡萄酒品评赛（IWC）伦敦特等金奖，为中国首款获此荣誉的产品，五星干红实现国际金奖大满贯。长城葡萄酒先后荣获国际、国家、省部级金、银、铜牌和优质产品等称号多达300余次，质量达到了国际先进水平，产品销售遍布全国，远销英国、德国、意大利、日本等 20 多个国家和地区，被欧美专家誉为"典型的东方美酒"。

公司独创的星级产品系列成为业内最优秀的系列产品之一，五星成为明星级超级单品，荣选为宴会用酒。长城葡萄酒以其卓绝的优秀品质，一直是钓鱼台国宾馆、人民大会堂、中国驻外大使馆、中国国际航空公司等窗口单位用酒，是北京奥运会葡萄酒独家供应商，亚洲博鳌论坛唯一指定用酒，北京亚运会标志产品，上海世博会、广州亚运会指定用酒，频频亮相 G20 中国系列峰会、"一带一路"高峰论坛、金砖系列峰会、上合峰会、亚太经济合作组织（APEC）会议等国宴餐桌。40 年来累计亮相各级别国家级宴会超过 800 场。2004 年，长城葡萄酒成为中国唯一荣登全球权威商业调查机构美国盖洛普"21 世纪奢华品牌榜之顶级品牌榜"的中国葡萄酒品牌。如今，"国事家宴，共享长城"的品牌理念已经深入人心，成为家喻户晓的中国葡萄酒代表品牌。

公司是农业产业化国家重点龙头企业、国家高新技术企业、国家技术创新示范企业、全国工业（葡萄酒）领军企业、国家级放心酒工程示范企业、国家重合同守信用企业、全国精神文明建设先进单位，荣获河北省政府质量奖等。

公司大事记

- 2020 年，长城五星成为中国女排官方合作葡萄酒。

- 2009～2019 年，长城葡萄酒连续十一年作为博鳌亚洲论坛会议用酒。

- 2019 年，长城五星赤霞珠干红葡萄酒在伦敦国际葡萄酒品评赛（IWC）荣获中国红葡萄酒首枚特等奖，是本届赛会亚洲唯一一枚奖牌也是中国首枚奖牌。

- 2018 年，技术中心被评定为农业农村部酿酒葡萄加工重点实验室。

- 2017 年，长城五星干红葡萄酒获得亚洲质量大赛金奖，荣获河北省政府质量奖，"一带一路"国际合作高峰论坛官方指定用酒，金砖国家会议指定用酒。

- 2016 年，明珠五星成功上市，被授予 G20 杭州峰会高级赞助商及指定产品的荣誉。

- 2015 年，长城桑干酒庄正式独立运营。

- 2014 年，APEC 会议及亚信峰会官方指定用酒，亮相索契冬奥会，欢迎美国第一夫人米歇尔宴会用酒；全面通过 ISO9001 \ FSSC22000 \ ISO14001 \ OH-

SAS18001管理体系独立认证，亮相索契冬奥会中国之家。

- 2013年，启动公司新成品库项目，占地面积72.44亩，欢迎冰岛总理宴会用酒，国家领导人在俄罗斯圣彼得堡G20峰会上款待墨西哥总统培尼亚阁下宴会用酒。

- 2011年，技术中心通过国家（CNAS）认可实验室认证，成为APEC工商咨询理事会欢迎晚宴用酒。

- 2010年，成为上海世博会唯一指定葡萄酒，广州亚运会指定用酒，中非合作论坛宴会用酒。

- 2009年，以长城庄园为基础成立长城桑干酒庄，技术中心被认定为"河北省葡萄酒工程技术研究中心"，欢迎美国总统奥巴马宴会用酒。

- 2008年，传统法起泡葡萄酒在珠峰庆功奥运圣火登顶珠峰，超越2008全球限量珍藏版葡萄酒被瑞士洛桑博物馆永久收藏，欢迎美国总统小布什、国际奥委会主席罗格宴会用酒，APEC财长会议晚宴用酒。

- 2007年，长城葡萄酒以125.87亿元品牌价值，入选2006中国品牌500强第67位，技术中心被国家发展改革委员会、科技部、财政部、海关总署和国家税务总局等国家五部委认定为"国家认定企业技术中心"。

- 2006年，长城葡萄酒被定为北京2008年奥运会葡萄酒独家供应商。

- 2005年，《长城庄园模式的创建及庄园葡萄酒关键技术的研究与应用》获得国家科技进步二等奖，国际标准白兰地（V·S·O·P）获得伦敦国际评酒会特别金奖。

- 2004年，"长城"商标被中国工商总局认定为"中国驰名商标"，欢迎法国总统希拉克宴会用酒。

- 2003年，中国长城葡萄酒有限公司成为中粮集团旗下全资子公司。

- 2002年，获得"中国名牌、国家免检产品"，首次通过"农业产业化国家重点龙头企业"认定。

- 1999年，完成国家二期"双加"工程，生产能力达到5万吨，星级系列产品正式上市。

- 1997年，研制成功中国第一瓶国际标准白兰地（V·S·O·P），科研中心被河北省轻工业厅认定为"河北省葡萄酒技术开发中心"。

- 1996年，完成国家一期"双加工程"，生产能力扩大到10000吨，全国同行业首批通过ISO9002质量体系认证，以技术中心为基础设立长城庄园。
- 1995年，科研中心被河北省经济贸易委员会认定为河北省首批"省级企业技术中心"。
- 1994年，设立中国长城葡萄酒有限公司科研中心。
- 1992年，长城香槟法起泡葡萄酒获首届曼谷名酒博览会特别金奖、香港国际食品博览会金奖。
- 1990年，研制成功中国第一瓶香槟法起泡葡萄酒，成为北京亚运会"标志产品"。
- 1987年，"干白葡萄酒新工艺的研究"获得国家科技进步二等奖，香槟法起泡葡萄酒成为款待美国前总统卡特宴会用酒。
- 1986年，法国巴黎获国际第十二届食品博览会金奖，成为人民大会堂供应用酒，迎接英国女王伊丽莎白二世宴会用酒。
- 1984年，长城干白获得西班牙马德里国际第三届酒类饮料评比会金奖。
- 1983年，中国长城葡萄酒有限公司成立，同年长城干白获得英国伦敦国际第十四届评酒会银奖。
- 1979年，长城干白葡萄酒获得国家金奖。

地理位置和联系电话

地理位置：河北省怀来县沙城镇

联系电话：0313-6232216

2. 中粮长城桑干酒庄（怀来）有限公司

中粮长城桑干酒庄（怀来）有限公司（以下简称中粮长城桑干酒庄）坐落于河北省张家口市怀来县沙城镇东水泉村东，距北京西北方向约100公里，地处燕山和太行山脉形成的怀涿盆地，处于桑干河、洋河交汇左岸。1978年，由轻工业部牵头、国家五部委联合考察，将中国葡萄酒的第一块试验田选定于怀涿盆地，在这里诞生了中国第一瓶干型葡萄酒，开启了长城桑干酒庄走向世界东方名庄的辉煌之路。

中粮长城桑干酒庄葡园占地1122.5亩❶，种植着著名酿酒葡萄十余种，如"雷司令""长相思""赛美蓉""霞多丽""白诗南"等白色品种；"赤霞珠""西拉""梅鹿辄""黑比诺""增芳德"等红色品种；"白玉霓""白福尔""鸽笼白"等白兰地酒用品种和"琼瑶浆"等甜白葡萄酒用品种。近年又引进"小芒森""马尔贝克""小味儿多"等酿酒用新品种和SO4、5BB砧木品种。长城桑干酒庄葡萄种植园已成为国内建园最早、规模大、树龄长、品种全、起点高的国际名优葡萄品种或株系的葡萄园区。

中粮长城桑干酒庄拥有9300平方米的生产车间以及8200平方米的地下酒窖，年发酵能力1000吨、储酒能力4000吨；配备3000瓶/小时全自动生产线。拥有2781平方米的科研楼、3000平方米的现代化苗木繁育中心，配套现代化分析设备，使得长城桑干产品在产品研发、成分研究、品质控制、质量保障、生态环保、旅游观光等方面都达到了国内、国际领先水平。

中粮长城桑干酒庄现有员工112人，其中各类专业技术人员25人，国家级评委5人，国家级酿酒师6人，国家级品酒师12人。主要产品有以赤霞珠干红、西拉干红葡萄酒、梅鹿辄/赤霞珠干红葡萄酒为主的高端干红产品系列；雷司令干白葡萄酒等高端干白产品系列；琼瑶浆甜白葡萄酒、传统法起泡葡萄酒、白兰地等其他葡萄酒产品。

2005年"长城庄园模式的创建及庄园葡萄酒关键技术的研究与应用"荣获国家科技进步二等奖；2007年通过了国家良好农业规范（GAP）认证；2012年被河北省林业厅评为"河北省林业龙头企业"称号；2015年被河北省农业厅认定为"河北省十佳现代休闲农业园"，成为"农村一二三产业融合试点项目"单位；2016年被评"张家口市农业产业化重点龙头企业"；2016年被评河北省五星级休闲农业园区。此外，国家认定企业技术中心、国家认可实验室、农业农村部酿酒葡萄加工重点实验室、河北省级葡萄酒工程技术研究中心等科研平台在酒庄设立。

长城桑干酒庄产品在2010～2017年间5次获得比利时布鲁塞尔葡萄酒大赛金奖，两次获得中国酒业协会新产品青酌奖金质奖，还两次获得亚洲质量大赛金奖。

---

❶ 1亩≈667平方米。

公司大事记

• 2019 年，第八届中国上市公司高峰论坛指定用酒，中国创业武林大会指定用酒。

• 2018 年，中非合作论坛北京峰会指定用酒，上海合作组织青岛峰会指定用酒。

• 2017 年，厦门金砖会晤指定用酒，"一带一路"高峰论坛指定用酒。

• 2016 年，G20 峰会指定用酒。

• 2009～2019 年，连续十一年成为博鳌亚洲论坛指定用酒。

• 2009 年，长城桑干 2002 年干红成为国宴特别专供酒，成为 2010 年上海世博会唯一指定葡萄酒。

• 2008 年，长城桑干酒庄"长城庄园超越 2008"全球限量珍藏版葡萄酒，被瑞士洛桑博物馆永久收藏。

• 2006 年，中粮长城桑干成为中国葡萄酒企业中第一个奥运会独家供应商。

• 2005 年，"长城庄园模式的创建及庄园葡萄酒关键技术的研究与应用"荣获国家科技进步二等奖。

地理位置和联系电话

地理位置：河北省怀来县沙城镇东水泉村东

联系电话：0313-6840294

3. 怀来县贵族庄园葡萄酒业有限公司

怀来县贵族庄园葡萄酒业有限公司（以下简称庄园）位于怀涿盆地风景秀丽的官厅湖畔土木堡外，毗邻长城桑干酒庄。是集葡萄种植、酿酒为一体的葡萄酒庄。2000 年，按国际标准建立酿酒名种葡萄种植园 1800 亩，栽培了"赤霞珠""美乐""西拉""马瑟兰"等酿酒专用葡萄品种。目前葡萄树龄 20 年，已进入酿造优质葡萄酒的树龄期。2008 年，按葡萄酒行业标准建厂，庄园建筑面积 6500 平方米，其中生产车间 3800 平方米，地下酒窖 1000 平方米，年生产能力 300 多吨。2009 年，注册资金 1100 万元，成立了怀来县贵族庄园葡萄酒业有限公司，推出了坤爵庄园系列干红葡萄酒；具有沙城产区特色的龙眼干白葡萄酒；美乐半干、半甜、原生态

5 度甜型等系列桃红葡萄酒。

公司大事记

- 2019 年，荣获中国国际马瑟兰葡萄酒大赛银奖、获第五届国际精品葡萄酒挑战赛（DSW）精品奖。

- 2018 年，坤爵龙眼干白葡萄酒获优质产品奖。

- 2017 年，坤爵龙眼干白葡萄酒在全球葡萄酒中国鉴评体系暨"河西走廊杯""香格里拉杯"国际葡萄酒大赛中获优质奖。

- 2016 年，与河北农业大学共建了研究生实习基地；坤爵龙眼干白葡萄酒在中国葡萄酒发展峰会上获年度最具潜力中国葡萄酒银奖；被张家口市委、市政府认定为高层次创新团队。

- 2015 年，坤爵珍藏赤霞珠红葡萄酒国际领袖产区葡萄酒质量大赛获优质奖；同年认定为河北省国际合作基地。

- 2014 年，庄园赤霞珠高级干红葡萄酒在国际领袖产区葡萄酒质量大赛中获优质奖；持有商标"坤爵"品牌被评为河北省著名商标，获河北省优质产品奖。

- 2013 年，赤霞珠干型桃红葡萄酒在国际领袖产区葡萄酒质量大赛中获特别奖，百大葡萄酒评选荣获 TOP100 铜奖。

- 2012 年，美乐桃红葡萄酒酿造技术研发项目获省科技进步三等奖；全国桃红葡萄酒挑战赛优质奖；被《中国葡萄酒》杂志评为中国魅力酒庄。

- 2011 年，坤爵牌葡萄酒产品荣获首届环京津食品工业展恰会银奖；同陕西科技大学建立了怀来县贵族庄园葡萄酒业有限公司教育培训基地。

- 2010 年，通过了 ISO 9000：2000 质量管理体系认证。

地理位置和联系电话

地理位置：河北省怀来县土木镇土木村

联系电话：0313-6802256

4. 怀来中法庄园葡萄酒有限公司

怀来中法庄园葡萄酒有限公司（以下简称中法庄园）的前身是中法葡萄种植与

酿酒示范农场。始建于 1999 年，是我国农业部、河北省政府以及法国农业部和法国国家葡萄酒行业组织（ONIVINS）共同组织实施的政府农业合作项目。

中法庄园见证了中法两国葡萄酒人对品质的不懈追求。1999 年，中法两国农业部长在巴黎正式签署"关于建立中法葡萄种植及酿酒示范农场"议定书。2000 年，"中法示范农场"正式开始建园，矢志成为中国葡萄酒行业的标杆。2001 年，"中法示范农场"正式建设完成，并从法国引进了 16 个葡萄品种及全套酿酒设备，其中包括首次引进的"马瑟兰"和"小芒森"，并于 2003 年酿酒。2005 年"中法示范农场"正式更名为"中法庄园"。

2010 年，中法庄园成为迦南投资集团旗下酒庄，与毗邻的迦南酒业成为姐妹酒庄。中法庄园地处怀来县东花园镇，注册资本 14000 万人民币，酒庄占地 33 公顷，葡萄园种植面积 23 公顷，年产优质葡萄酒 5 万～6 万瓶。

公司大事记

- 2021 年，中法庄园东花园干红葡萄酒 2015 获得中国葡萄酒发展峰会金奖。
- 2020 年，中法庄园小芒森甜白葡萄酒 2015 获得罗博之选年度国内产区白葡萄酒、品醇客世界葡萄酒大赛金奖。
- 2019 年，中法庄园珍藏干红葡萄酒 2014 获得国际葡萄酒品评赛金奖。
- 2015 年，中法庄园珍藏马瑟兰干红葡萄酒 2012 获得柏林葡萄酒大奖赛金奖。

地理位置和联系电话

地理位置：河北省怀来县东花园镇

联系电话：0313-6849666

5. 怀来容辰庄园葡萄酒有限公司

怀来容辰庄园葡萄酒有限公司（以下简称容辰庄园）位于河北怀来，是一家集种植、酿造、营销、旅游观光于一体的中美合资企业，始建于 1997 年，注册资金 6400 万元，占地 3000 亩。2001 年 3 月庄园被联合国教科文组织确定为"国际农村教育研究与培训中心联系基地"。葡萄园采取控产栽培技术（每亩产量控制在 500 千克以下）稳定葡萄产量，提高葡萄质量。容辰庄园包括葡萄园、容辰葡萄酒园和容辰庄园旅游区三部分。

葡萄园有"赤霞珠""梅鹿辄"等红葡萄品种和"霞多丽"等白葡萄品种，均属中晚熟品种，在怀涿盆地的自然气候条件和土壤水质条件下获得了良好的表现。2000年是庄园葡萄挂果的第一年，成熟后，葡萄的糖度达到195~226克/升，是生产高档葡萄酒的最好原料。

容辰葡萄酒园位于葡萄园东1公里，与葡萄园毗邻而居。主体建筑具有欧式风格，包括联合车间、灌装车间、地下酒窖、污水处理站、办公楼和宿舍楼等。

容辰庄园旅游区位于葡萄园内，庄园湖边，占地4公顷。周围群山环抱，湖水潋滟，风景秀美，四季气候分明，容辰庄园西有中原度假村、永定河峡谷漂流，北有卧牛山避暑山庄，东有天漠公园、康西草原、龙庆峡，是典型的人间仙境。2004年4月，容辰庄园被评为国家农业生态旅游示范点和省级AA级旅游区。

公司大事记

- 2005年，在伦敦国际评酒会（北京）上赤霞珠干红葡萄酒获得金奖，霞多丽干白葡萄酒获得银奖。

- 2003年，在新疆石河子市由中国食品工业协会组织的品酒会上，容辰庄园干红和干白葡萄酒分别获得大会最高荣誉和优质产品称号。

- 2002年，在烟台举行的有40余家葡萄酒厂参加、45种葡萄酒参评的活动中，国内60名品酒专家采取盲评方法，容辰庄园干红葡萄酒荣获第一名。

- 2001年，容辰庄园干白葡萄酒和干红葡萄酒在第四届北京希尔顿国际葡萄酒与食品展示会上获得国内干白第一名和干红第二名的好成绩。

- 2000年，容辰庄园以自产优质原料开始酿造第一批葡萄酒，在生产过程中，全新的工艺把葡萄的自然属性淋漓尽致地表现在葡萄酒中，2001年4月27日容辰庄园葡萄酒开瓶庆典活动在北京长城饭店举行。

地理位置和联系电话

地理位置：河北怀来小南辛堡乡小七营村

联系电话：0313-6215336

6. 河北沙城家和酒业有限公司

河北沙城家和酒业有限公司（以下简称家和公司）位于怀来县桑园镇夹河村。

公司成立于 2004 年，产能 6000 吨。家和公司从企业管理者到普通员工都坚守着"品质是企业生存之本"的理念，先后通过了 QS 认证、ISO9001 质量管理体系认证和 HACCP 体系认证、安全生产标准化认证、葡萄酒行业准入条件审核等。多次获得河北省或张家口市优质企业称号。2015 年，家和公司在石家庄股票交易所孵化板挂牌。

2015 年，家和公司由企业开创者的女儿接管，她 2014 年从法国波尔多葡萄酒商学院归国后，开阔的视野让她对家和的品质和产品的外观设计有了更高的要求和创新的思路，开启了家和葡萄酒文化之路，依托专业的葡萄酒酿造、品酒专家，资深的艺术设计人员、优秀的木艺创作人才，与北京多所艺术类院校达成校企合作意向，为公司注入年轻、新鲜的创作团队和设计理念，以创新前卫的思想为客户提供全方位、时尚个性的产品及专业服务。2019 年，家和公司限量版"绽放"美乐 2017 和"绽放"赤霞珠 2017 以及"似锦年华"干白混酿葡萄酒获得了业内的认可和奖项的见证。2019 年家和公司被认定为河北省高新技术企业。

地理位置和联系电话

地理位置：河北省怀来县桑园镇夹河村

联系电话：0313-6800119

7. 河北马丁葡萄酿酒有限公司

河北马丁葡萄酿酒有限公司（以下简称马丁酒庄）成立于 1997 年，占地面积 30 亩，建筑面积 10000 多平方米。酒庄地处河北省张家口市怀来县桑园镇，拥有两条葡萄酒生产线，酒庄酒生产线采用先进的粒选设备，年生产高端酒庄酒 300 吨，另外一条生产线，年产葡萄原酒 5000 吨。建有地下酒窖 1000 平方米。

马丁酒庄自有酿酒葡萄基地 500 多亩，种植了"龙眼""赤霞珠""蛇龙珠""黑比诺""梅鹿辄""马瑟兰""丹魄""霞多丽""雷司令""小芒森"等酿酒品种。酿造的葡萄酒在国内外比赛中屡获殊荣，并多次出口英国和奥地利。公司开放工业旅游，可以接待 20～30 人的团队参观品酒。

公司大事记

- 2021 年，在 IWSC 国际葡萄酒与烈酒大赛中获得 3 项大奖。

- 2020 年，马瑟兰干红获得国际领袖产区葡萄酒/烈酒质量大赛铂金奖。

- 2019 年，成为中国酒类流通协会精品葡萄酒酒庄联盟工作委员会常务副会长单位，同年，梅鹿辄干红、酒庄珍藏干红、龙眼干白分别获得中国河北葡萄酒大赛金奖。马瑟兰干红和小西拉干红获得年度中国十大葡萄酒，酒庄荣获年度最受欢迎中国精品葡萄酒酒庄的称号。

- 2018 年，成为中国酒类流通协会精品葡萄酒酒庄联盟会员单位，同年，马瑟兰干红获得布鲁塞尔大赛金奖。霞多丽干白获得 Decanter 世界葡萄酒大赛铜奖。

- 2017 年，通过了中国酒庄酒证明商标的审核，成为中国第一批合法使用中国酒庄酒证明商标的企业。同时成为中国酒庄旅游联盟理事单位，同年，小西拉干红和龙眼干白双双荣获 Decanter 世界葡萄酒大赛银奖，霞多丽干白荣获中国优质葡萄酒挑战赛质量金奖。

- 2016 年，赤霞珠干红入围上海葡萄酒发展峰会大师品鉴酒，小西拉干红获得"一带一路"国际葡萄酒大赛金奖。

- 2014 年，通过了国家地理标志保护产品"沙城葡萄酒"的认证。

- 2012 年，成为中国酒业协会会员单位。

地理位置和联系电话

地理位置：河北省张家口市怀来县桑园镇

联系电话：0313-6870326

8. 河北沙城庄园葡萄酒有限公司

河北沙城庄园葡萄酒有限公司（以下简称公司）创建于 1999 年，地处中国沙城葡萄产区，拥有先进的发酵、储存、灌装设备、地下酒窖及优良的葡萄基地。公司 2006 年通过 ISO9001 国际质量管理体系认证，2011 年通过了 HACCP 体系认证，2014 年获国家地理标志产品。

产品品种：干红葡萄酒、干白葡萄酒、桃红葡萄酒、甜白葡萄酒。

服务项目：葡萄种植、葡萄酒酿造、葡萄酒销售、葡萄酒定制、葡萄园定制、葡萄庄园旅游、葡萄酒品鉴体验等。

公司大事记

- 2020 年,第七届中国葡萄酒大会,桑洋河畔西拉干红,荣获 2019～2020 "明星大单品奖"和"消费者最喜爱产品奖"。

- 2019 年,获得一带一路甘肃宁夏国际葡萄酒大赛三项银奖;获中国河北葡萄酒大赛西拉干红金奖第一名。

- 2018 年,桑洋河畔西拉干红,获得沙城产区葡萄酒大赛金奖。

- 2016 年,桑洋河畔马瑟兰干红,荣获 RVF 中国优秀葡萄酒铜奖。

- 2014 年,获得国家地理标志保护产品。

- 2011 年,"沙庄"产品获得环京津食品工业展洽会金奖;通过了 HACCP 国际食品安全保障体系认证。

- 2010 年,在国家商标局注册"桑洋河畔"商标。

- 2006 年,通过 ISO9001 国际质量管理体系认证。

- 2003 年,中国质量万里行"全国产品质量满意服务过硬放心品牌";获中国食品工业协会"全国食品行业知名葡萄酒诚信产品"。

地理位置和联系电话

地理位置:河北省怀来县沙城镇地道桥南酒厂路

联系电话:400-612-6055,0313-6829888

9. 河北怀来瑞云葡萄酒股份有限公司

河北怀来瑞云葡萄酒股份有限公司(以下简称瑞云酒庄)创建于 1998 年,占地面积 725 亩,其中葡萄园占地约 600 亩。瑞云酒庄每年生产"赤霞珠"和"西拉"两个单一品种的酒庄酒,年产"赤霞珠"和"西拉"酒庄酒 6 万瓶。从葡萄种植、采收、发酵、陈酿到成酒灌瓶、贴标,所有工作均在酒庄内完成。为了保证葡萄酒质量上乘,瑞云酒庄只使用瑞云葡萄园自产的"赤霞珠"和"西拉"葡萄作为酿酒原料,采收及二次筛选均百分之百由人工完成,所有酒庄酒均经过橡木桶陈酿及地下酒窖瓶储,酒液色泽饱满明亮,果味突出,糖酸平衡,单宁及酚类物质含量高,适宜长期贮藏。

酒庄拥有多功能画廊三个，大型室内文艺活动空间一个，博物馆两个，各类展厅若干，以及一家精致自然的酒庄餐厅和一家酒庄民宿。瑞云酒庄开放工业旅游，不定期举办各类画展、音乐会、社区艺术联谊、田园观光团、艺术家驻地计划等活动，欢迎前来参观体验的各界人士。

地理位置及联系电话

地理位置：河北省怀来县东花园镇东榆林村

联系电话：400-088-9118

10. 怀来红叶庄园葡萄酒有限公司

怀来红叶庄园葡萄酒有限公司（以下简称红叶庄园）位于河北省怀来县东花园镇，成立于1998年，注册资金198万元，占地60亩，建筑面积4500多平方米，年综合生产能力1000多吨。

1998年4月公司租赁了东花园镇火烧营村和东湾村1350亩的荒地，在东花园镇建立了第一家葡萄庄园，种植了"赤霞珠""美乐""西拉""马瑟兰""霞多丽""琼瑶浆"等十多个优良酿酒葡萄品种。每年可生产优质酿酒葡萄300～400吨，为葡萄酒酿造提供了优质原料。

红叶庄园拥有先进的葡萄酒生产设备，原酒发酵、贮存能力3000多吨；有恒温恒湿的地下酒窖和优质橡木桶；有先进的3000瓶/小时全自动灌装生产线一条，实现了葡萄酒瓶清洗、消毒、过滤、灌装、压塞一体化和自动化。

红叶庄园自成立以来，积极同专业院校合作，提升技术水平和研发能力。2006年同北京农学院食品科学系进行技术合作，作为产学研实习基地，进行科研和学生校外实践。2009年红叶庄园被北京农学院评为"优秀校外实践教育基地"，2010年被北京市教育委员会评为"北京市高等学校市级校外人才培养基地"。

红叶庄园现已形成干、半干、半甜、甜型等20多个产品，"桑干河谷""红色恋人""佳露""金叶"等品牌系列葡萄酒产品在市场上享有较高的声誉。红叶庄园典藏赤霞珠美乐干红葡萄酒，在《中国葡萄酒》2012年葡萄酒评选中被评为"最佳国产葡萄酒"；红叶庄园出品的桑干河谷特选霞多丽干白葡萄酒荣获2018年布鲁塞尔国际葡萄酒大奖赛金奖。

地理位置和联系电话

地理位置：河北省怀来县东花园镇康祁公路北测（原东花园口林场）

联系电话：0313-6849598

11. 怀来县誉龙葡萄酒庄园有限公司

怀来县誉龙葡萄酒庄园有限公司（以下简称誉龙葡萄酒庄）成立于 2010 年，是一家以葡萄种植、葡萄酒、白兰地生产销售为一体的葡萄酒庄园。誉龙葡萄酒庄位于河北省怀来县桑园镇，拥有原料种植基地 1500 亩、先进的前处理生产线两条、容量为 60 吨的不锈钢控温发酵罐 60 个、全自动灌装线一条，年产葡萄酒 400 万瓶、年产白兰地 400 吨。誉龙葡萄酒庄有国家一级酿酒师 2 名，与国际葡萄酒产业相融合，创建国内首创地下音乐酒窖，培养打造"听音乐长大的葡萄酒"，产品备受国内外消费者青睐。

誉龙葡萄酒庄有"卡尔蒂尼""誉龙堡"两大品牌系列，其中"卡尔蒂尼"同时在法国境内注册，由子公司法国卡尔蒂尼葡萄酒贸易（香港）有限公司运营国际贸易。誉龙葡萄酒庄的葡萄酒被命名为国家地理标志保护产品。

公司大事记

- 2016 年，誉龙葡萄酒庄庄主游晓芳女士被中国农业联盟授予"红酒公主"荣誉称号。
- 2015 年，誉龙葡萄酒庄被国际食品安全协会授予国际食品安全典范企业。
- 2014 年，誉龙葡萄酒庄产品被授予国家地理标志保护产品。
- 2012 年，世界葡萄大会誉龙葡萄酒庄为主要赞助商。
- 2010 年，誉龙葡萄酒庄成立。

地理位置及联系电话

地理位置：河北省张家口怀来县桑园镇新响岭村北侧

联系电话：0313-6845572

12. 怀来赤霞葡萄酒有限公司

怀来赤霞葡萄酒有限公司（以下简称公司），成立于 1998 年，注册资金 130 万元，占地面积 6667 平方米，坐落于沙城产区，自有葡萄种植园 298.8 亩，主要种植葡萄品种为"赤霞珠"。公司一直以葡萄种植为产业链起点，从事果蔬汁饮料、葡萄酒及白兰地 3 个系列 20 余种产品的制造及销售。2017 年，公司新增了预包装食品的进出口业务，新增澳洲原瓶进口红酒约 20 种。

怀来赤霞葡萄酒有限公司自成立以来，始终坚持以质量管理为中心，产品创新为动力，安全生产为保障，建立了适合本公司实际的生产体系，并不断进行技术改造，走出了一条质量效益型的发展道路，欢迎各界朋友来参观指导。

公司大事记

- 2019 年，赤霞桃红葡萄酒、赤霞干白葡萄酒分别荣获中国河北葡萄酒大赛国产白葡萄酒组金奖和银奖。
- 2018 年，赤霞甜白葡萄酒荣获国际领袖产区葡萄酒质量大赛评委会特别奖。
- 2016 年，赤霞桃红葡萄酒荣获"一带一路"国际葡萄酒大赛金奖。

地理位置及联系电话

地理位置：张家口市怀来县沙城镇京张公路西大街北侧

联系方式：0313-6801162

13. 怀来德厚庄园葡萄酒有限公司

怀来德厚庄园葡萄酒有限公司（以下简称德厚庄园）成立于 2006 年，注册资本 100 万欧元，为中外合资的酿酒企业（中国与比利时），德厚庄园位于河北省怀来县东花园镇。

德厚庄园有 700 多亩的葡萄种植基地，主要种植"赤霞珠""美乐""马瑟兰"和"霞多丽"等酿酒葡萄品种，庄园以自种葡萄为主要原料，以生产庄园式高中档葡萄酒为主，年发酵葡萄酒能力为 200 吨，总储酒容量为 450 吨，有十几款不同档次的葡萄酒产品。

地理位置和联系电话

地理位置：河北省怀来县东花园镇西榆林村西

联系电话：0313-6849699

14. 怀来丰收庄园葡萄酒有限公司

怀来丰收庄园葡萄酒有限公司（以下简称丰收庄园），始建于 2008 年，由北京丰收葡萄酒有限公司投资兴建，注册资本 1200 万元，项目计划总投资 1.45 亿，建筑面积 65000 平方米。丰收庄园位于河北省张家口市怀来县瑞云观乡大山口村，以生产干红、干白葡萄酒为主。

北京丰收葡萄酒有限公司前身为北京南郊葡萄酒厂，始建于 1979 年。目前已发展成为以北京丰收葡萄酒有限公司为主，北京顺兴葡萄酒有限公司、怀来丰收庄园葡萄酒有限公司三家公司并行运营的模式。与燕京啤酒、红星二锅头同属北控集团参控股企业。

怀来丰收庄园是一座集葡萄酒生产与文化为一体的综合园区，其主要功能是承担高端葡萄酒酿造、灌装、市场推广及知识传播工作。预计项目完成后，储酒量达到 13000 吨，年产葡萄酒 6000 吨，其中精品酒庄酒 1000 吨。

公司大事记

- 2018 年，丰收西拉干红葡萄酒获中国酒业京津冀市场表现奖，成为中国葡萄酒品牌集群首批成员单位。
- 2017 年，第二届香格里拉杯国际葡萄酒大赛特别奖。
- 2016 年，国际领袖产区葡萄酒（中国）质量大赛特别奖。
- 2011 年，"克隆宾"杯第五届烟台葡萄酒大赛银奖。
- 2009 年，中国葡萄酒制造业十强企业。
- 2004 年，第一届亚洲葡萄酒质量大赛金奖。

地理位置和联系电话

地理位置：河北省怀来县瑞云观乡

联系电话：0313-6851000

15. 怀来县福瑞诗葡萄酒堡有限公司

怀来县福瑞诗葡萄酒堡有限公司成立于 2008，位于怀来县东花园镇西榆林村西南 1440 米处，占地面积 2677.29 平方米。公司经营范围：葡萄酒及果酒（原酒、加工灌装）生产及销售，葡萄种植，农副产品的种植及加工销售。主要产品为桃红葡萄酒、干红葡萄酒及干白葡萄酒，设计年产量为 100 吨。主产品有：福瑞诗桃红葡萄酒、福瑞诗干红葡萄酒、福瑞诗干白葡萄酒。

地理位置和联系电话

地理位置：河北省东花园镇西榆林村西南

联系电话：0313-6849690

16. 怀来县古堡葡萄酒庄园有限公司

怀来县古堡葡萄酒庄园有限公司（以下简称公司）始建于 2012 年，注册资本 100 万元，总投资 1000 万元，固定资产 400 万元，年产值 1000 万元。公司占地面积约 80000 平方米，建筑面积约 1000 平方米，主要生产经营葡萄酒，设计生产能力为 100 吨/年。

公司拥有葡萄园 150 亩，种植"赤霞珠""马瑟兰""小芒森""霞多丽"等酿酒葡萄品种，如今正值十多年的黄金树龄期。公司拥有较完善的基础设施和先进的生产设备，并配备恒温恒湿地下酒窖，公司有国家级酿酒师和品酒师 2 人，教授级高工 2 人。

地理位置和联系电话

地理位置：河北省怀来县狼山乡

联系电话：15831387892

17. 张家口怀谷庄园葡萄酒有限公司

张家口怀谷庄园葡萄酒有限公司（以下简称怀谷庄园）创立于 2013 年，怀谷庄园位于怀来县桑园镇张官营村北，占地面积 12500 平方米，葡萄酒年生产能力 1800 吨。

怀谷庄园在葡萄酒酿造技术传承和创新方面不断取得突破，先后研制出独具特色的小品种葡萄酒 11 种，酒庄特有技术半二氧化碳浸渍酿造技术赢得国际大金奖 2 枚、金奖 7 枚、银奖 9 枚、铜奖 8 枚，尤以 2018 年布鲁塞尔大金奖最为有名，累计获得各种奖项 30 个，受到国内外葡萄酒专家和消费者的赞誉。

公司大事记

- 2021 年，怀谷庄园金手掌西拉 2017 荣获第十届 WINE100 葡萄酒大赛银奖。

- 2020 年，怀谷庄园限量珍藏马瑟兰 2017 荣获布鲁塞尔国际葡萄酒大奖赛银奖；怀谷庄园四款限量珍藏马瑟兰荣获 DECANTER 世界葡萄酒大赛铜奖；怀谷庄园威代尔和限量珍藏马瑟兰分别荣获第十四届 G100 国际葡萄酒及烈酒评选赛银奖，怀谷庄园白兰地荣获铜奖。

- 2019 年，怀谷庄园限量珍藏马瑟兰 2017 荣获 WLA 世界美酒大奖赛年度马瑟兰金奖；怀谷庄园限量珍藏马瑟兰 2017 荣获中国国际马瑟兰葡萄酒大赛金奖；怀谷庄园限量珍藏 2017 马瑟兰和年年有余 2016 赤霞珠分别荣获世界沙漠国际葡萄酒大赛金奖，怀谷庄园金手掌 2017 赤霞珠荣获银奖；怀谷庄园限量珍藏 2015 梅鹿辄和年年有余 2016 马瑟兰分别荣获 DECANTER 亚洲国际葡萄酒大赛银奖，怀谷庄园限量珍藏 2015 马瑟兰和限量珍藏 2017 马瑟兰分别荣获铜奖；怀谷庄园年年有余赤霞珠荣获第十届亚洲葡萄酒质量大赛银奖。

- 2018 年，怀谷庄园年年有余 2016 马瑟兰荣获一带一路国际葡萄酒大奖赛大金奖；怀谷庄园限量珍藏级 2015 梅鹿辄荣获金奖；怀谷庄园限量珍藏级 2015 梅鹿辄荣获 DECANTER 亚洲国际葡萄酒大赛铜奖；怀谷庄园限量珍藏级 2015 赤霞珠荣获布鲁塞尔国际葡萄酒大奖赛大金奖。

地理位置和联系电话

地理位置：河北省怀来县桑园镇张官营村北

联系电话：0313-6851919

18. 怀来艾伦葡萄酒庄有限公司

怀来艾伦葡萄酒庄有限公司（以下简称艾伦酒庄）始建于 1998 年，是一家集葡萄种植、葡萄酒酿造、科研科普教育、旅游观光于一体的企业。艾伦酒庄仿佛一颗散发着神秘光辉的星辰镶嵌在美丽的官厅湖畔。艾伦酒庄南靠燕山，青帐别翠；北临官厅湖，景色迷人。在这片丰美富饶，人杰地灵的土地上艾伦葡萄种植园与酒庄交相辉映。

艾伦葡萄种植园地处沙城产区，是世界上葡萄种植的黄金地带，主要种植"赤霞珠""梅鹿辄""霞多丽"等各种酿酒葡萄，兼有红提、青提、黑提等鲜食葡萄品种。

艾伦酒庄坐落于葡萄种植园边，走进酒庄，路灯、铁椅、建筑、装饰、皆具欧式风格，酒庄的草坪、花池、喷泉、酒窖的设计仿佛将人带入古老而又神秘的欧洲古堡中。清晨置身于酒庄中，向毗邻的葡萄种植园望去是一望无际的绿色葡萄波浪，傍晚落日的余晖映红了天边，整个庄园都蒙上了一层酒红色的面纱。酒庄是如此古朴，如此静谧，仿佛脱离了尘嚣一般，让人不由深深沉醉。艾伦酒庄年产庄园酒 1000 吨以上。拥有 400 平方米的地下酒窖，可储藏葡萄酒 1000 吨。

2001 年 4 月，艾伦酒庄干白葡萄酒和干红葡萄酒在"第四届北京希尔顿国际葡萄酒与食品展示会"上获得国内干白第一名和干红第二名。2002 年在烟台举行的有 40 余家葡萄酒厂参加，45 种葡萄酒参评的品酒会上，艾伦酒庄干红葡萄酒荣获第一名。2003 年在新疆石河子市由中国食品工业协会组织的品酒会上，艾伦酒庄干红和干白葡萄酒双双获得大会最高荣誉。2005 年 1 月 20 日在 2005 伦敦国际评酒会（北京）上赤霞珠干红葡萄酒获得金奖，霞多丽干白葡萄酒获得银奖。这是由国际葡萄与葡萄酒组织（OIV，1978）举办的，世界最高级别的评酒活动。

2004 年，艾伦酒庄被批准为国家农业旅游示范点和国家级 AA 级旅游区。

2001 年，艾伦酒庄被联合国教科文组织确定为"国际农村教育研究与培训中心联系基地"。

地理位置和联系电话

地理位置：河北省怀来县小南辛堡镇小七营村

联系电话：400-003-0059

19. 怀来龙徽庄园葡萄酒有限公司

怀来龙徽庄园葡萄酒有限公司（以下简称龙徽庄园）是北京龙徽酿酒有限公司的全资子公司，于 2007 年在怀来县小南辛堡镇定州营村成立，注册资金 5000 万元，经营范围包括葡萄酒原酒生产和销售。龙徽庄园占地面积 145 亩，现有发酵酒罐、储酒罐 127 个，具有 5900 吨葡萄酒储存能力和 3000 吨葡萄酒发酵能力。

2018 年龙徽公司将北京公司的一条生产线搬迁至怀来龙徽庄园，2019 年怀来龙徽庄园顺利取得灌装生产许可证，以怀来珍藏干红葡萄酒、桂花陈酒、宫桂酒、起泡酒为代表的产品在各类比赛中屡获大奖。2020 年怀来龙徽庄园具备出口资质，并顺利完成了美国、缅甸、日本等国家的销售订单。

公司大事记

- 2019 年，龙徽桂花陈五年金装荣获 2019 年度酒类新品"青酌奖"。

- 2018 年，桂花陈金装 5 年陈酿获得 2018 一带一路（宁夏银川）国际葡萄酒大赛金奖；龙徽桂花露获得 2018 法国国际烈酒大奖赛银奖；比利时布鲁塞尔国际葡萄酒大奖赛，龙徽夏多内 2015 干白葡萄酒荣获银奖，中华桂花露酒（陈酿 40 度）荣获金奖。

- 2017 年，Decanter 亚洲葡萄酒大赛，龙徽起泡酒嘉许奖；怀来珍藏干红获得 2017 布鲁塞尔国际葡萄酒大赛银奖；比利时布鲁塞尔国际葡萄酒大奖赛，龙徽怀来珍藏 2015 干红葡萄酒荣获银奖。

- 2016 年，桂花陈金装 5 年陈酿获得 2016 一带一路（宁夏银川）国际葡萄酒大赛银奖。

- 2007 年，世界《葡萄酒报告》亚洲十大"品质杰出的葡萄酒"，龙徽怀来珍藏干红葡萄酒是唯一入选的中国葡萄酒，享有最佳"中国红葡萄酒"的美誉。

- 2006 年，法国酿酒师协会国际评酒会，龙徽美乐珍酿干红葡萄酒银奖。

- 2005 年，伦敦国际评酒会，龙徽赤霞珠干红葡萄酒获金奖；世界《葡萄酒报告》亚洲十大"品质杰出的葡萄酒"评选中，龙徽庄园葡萄酒是唯一入选的中国葡萄酒，龙徽庄园西拉干红葡萄酒获"亚洲最令人激动或非比寻常的发现"第一名。

- 2003 年，国际葡萄酒及烈酒大赛，龙徽夏多内获铜奖。

- 2002 年，中国国际葡萄酒及烈酒评酒会怀来珍藏金奖；中国国际葡萄酒及烈酒评酒会怀来珍藏最佳中国红葡萄酒。

- 2000 年，加拿大蒙特利尔世界葡萄酒大赛，龙徽起泡酒获银牌；法国波尔多国际葡萄酒大赛，97 年份龙徽怀来珍藏获铜牌。

- 1999 年，在香港国际葡萄酒大赛上，97 年份的龙徽赤霞珠荣获中国最佳红葡萄酒称号。

- 1996 年，在法国勃艮第世界夏多内葡萄酒大赛上，龙徽夏多内获银牌。

- 1994 年，龙徽干白葡萄酒在法国波尔多地区国际葡萄酒大赛上荣获金奖。

地理位置和联系电话

地理位置：河北省怀来县小南辛堡镇

联系电话：0313-6859952

20. 怀来迦南酒业有限公司

怀来迦南酒业有限公司（Canaan Winery）（以下简称迦南酒业）成立于 2003 年，注册资本 7645 万美元，酒庄于 2012 年正式建设完成。建筑面积 15000 平方米，设计生产能力 1500 吨，目前配有多套干白、干红生产设备以及不同规格发酵罐 140 余个，陈酿用橡木桶 3000 余支，可年产优质葡萄酒 50 万～60 万瓶。

2006 年迦南酒业聘请数十位国内外专家团队，历时两年时间选址怀来，自 2009 年迦南酒业从美国引进并试种下第一棵苗木，发展至今已种植有 275 公顷的葡萄园近 70 万株苗木，超过 40 个品种 70 余个品系，在平均海拔 500～1000 米的山丘、谷地拥有三处葡萄园，分别位于怀来县东花园镇、瑞云观乡和王家楼乡。

迦南酒业品牌名为"诗百篇"，出自唐代诗人杜甫作品《饮中八仙歌》，诗百篇葡萄酒多年来屡获业内及赛事大奖。

公司大事记

- 2021 年，诗百篇珍藏赤霞珠干红葡萄酒 2015 获得中国葡萄酒发展峰会金奖；诗百篇特选美乐干红葡萄酒 2015 获得第 28 届布鲁塞尔大奖赛金奖；诗百篇特选丹魄干红葡萄酒 2014 获得 WINE100 葡萄酒大奖赛黑金奖；诗百篇特选霞多丽干白葡萄酒 2018 获得中国葡萄酒发展峰会金奖。

- 2020 年，诗百篇珍藏西拉干红葡萄酒 2014 获得第十二届金樽奖评选赛金奖。

- 2016 年，诗百篇珍藏赤霞珠干红葡萄酒 2012 获得 RVF 中国优秀葡萄酒年度大奖赛金奖。

- 2016 年，迦南酒庄获得贝丹德梭年鉴年度十佳酒庄称号。

地理位置和联系电话

地理位置：河北省怀来县东花园镇

联系电话：0313-6849969

21. 叶浓（河北）葡萄酒业有限责任公司

2008 年怀来县经典长城葡萄酒有限公司成立，2020 年更名为叶浓（河北）葡萄酒业有限责任公司。

怀来县经典长城葡萄酒有限公司于 2008 年在怀来县官厅镇杏树洼正式成立，公司总占地面积 40 亩，厂区建设面积 12 亩，原酒发酵、贮酒能力达一千余吨。公司拥有顶级的酿酒师和优质的技术团队，采用先进的酿造工艺和设备，酿造生产"叶浓庄园"、"神漠"和"魔格"品牌葡萄酒。

公司大事记

- 2019 年，获得中国河北 2019 葡萄酒大赛评委会颁发的国产白葡萄酒银奖。
- 2016 年，获得 2016 "一带一路"国际葡萄酒大赛组委会颁发的特选级干红葡萄酒银奖。
- 2014 年，获得首届沙城产区赛酒会颁发的蛇龙珠组铜奖。

地理位置和联系电话

地理位置：河北省怀来县官厅镇杏树洼村东

联系电话：400-0313-960　13831393888

22. 河北龙泉葡萄酒有限公司

河北龙泉葡萄酒有限公司始建于 1995 年，2016 年 5 月由怀来龙腾葡萄酒有限公司股改而来。公司位于怀来县桑园镇，公司注册资本 500 万元，占地 13267 平方米，葡萄原酒生产能力 3000 吨，现有职工 30 多人。

公司拥有葡萄基地 734 亩，品种有"赤霞珠""梅鹿辄""霞多丽""西拉"等酿酒品种。本公司拥有自己的注册商标 4 个，分别为"黄金地带""龙盘庄园""雪漠""一棵藤"。主要生产陈酿系列、精选系列和庄园系列葡萄酒。

公司大事记

- 2021 年，获得 WINE100 铜奖。

- 2020 年，获得国际葡萄酒及烈酒大赛铜奖。
- 2019 年，获得中国河北 2019 葡萄酒大赛评委会颁发的国产葡萄酒金奖、银奖。
- 2015 年，获得沙城产区赛酒会颁发的蛇龙珠组金奖。

地理位置和联系电话

地理位置：河北省怀来县桑园镇后郝窑村

联系电话：0313-6878289

23. 怀来葡缇泉葡萄籽科技开发有限公司

怀来葡缇泉葡萄籽科技开发有限公司成立于 2009 年，是全国唯一的葡萄籽深加工企业，年处理葡萄籽 500 吨。公司引进葡萄籽冷榨技术及设备，将酿酒副产物葡萄皮渣加工成冷榨葡萄籽油、葡萄籽膳食纤维粉等数十种产品。葡缇泉公司成立以来，先后获得冷榨葡萄籽油生产许可及 ISO9001 质量体系认证；创建了中国自己的葡萄籽膳食纤维粉生产标准，为中国葡萄籽粉生产行业建立了准入机制。

公司整合周边葡萄种植园、葡萄酒庄和帝曼温泉资源，成立了亚洲首家葡萄籽抗氧化中心。包含葡萄主题餐厅、葡萄主题 SPA、葡萄文旅休闲农庄及葡萄主题康养课程。

葡萄主题餐厅

葡缇泉深度挖掘怀来本地的葡萄历史和文化，邀请国内外美食大师和营养师进行灵感碰撞，充分运用新鲜葡萄、葡萄酒、葡萄干、葡萄醋、葡萄叶、葡萄木等葡萄元素，搭配葡缇泉冷榨葡萄籽油和葡萄籽粉，匠心独具，成就亚洲首家葡萄主题餐厅。

创意西餐

每个月推出新的葡萄主题套餐，每个套餐包含 6～18 道精美的葡萄创意菜，搭配至少三款当地葡萄酒或自制无酒精葡萄饮品。例如每年一月份的德国传统新年套餐，将德国新年及圣诞节传统菜式和饮品，用怀来的葡萄食材呈现出来，例如葡萄籽油德式烤猪肘、葡萄籽粉圣诞树桩蛋糕、德式新年热红酒等。

怀来葡萄宴

挖掘怀来千年葡萄历史文化,巧妙运用各种葡萄相关食材,搭配葡缇泉冷榨葡萄籽油和葡萄籽粉,呈现独一无二的葡萄盛宴。2019年,葡缇泉名为"葡萄熟了"的葡萄宴,包含18道菜式,每道菜式都以葡萄籽油或葡萄籽粉烹调,并搭配其他葡萄元素,再与丰收主题古诗巧妙结合,曾获得由国家、省、市级评委和大众评委共同评选的怀来美食大赛最佳人气奖。名菜包括红葡萄酒和白葡萄酒腌制的象形葡萄鱼(月钩初上紫薇花)、用葡萄木烤制的猪排(满架蔷薇一院香)、葡萄叶蔬菜包(荷叶罗裙一色裁)、葡萄籽粉青蛙包(稻花香里说丰年)等。

公司大事记

- 2021年,被河北省科技厅评为"国际科技合作基地"。
- 2019年至今,被北京农学院评为"产学研基地"。
- 2018年,公司董事长荣获中国女企业家协会杰出创业女性荣誉称号;被河北省外国专家局评为河北省引才引智示范基地。
- 2017年,荣获十一届河北省品牌节一县一品荣誉称号;荣获河北省妇联巧手脱贫示范致富基地称号;荣获河北省四星级休闲农业园称号。
- 2015年,荣获九届河北省品牌节一县一品荣誉称号。
- 2014年,获得河北省外专局引进国外智力项目支持;荣获中国营养协会"明星企业家"奖杯;由河北省商务厅推荐参加广州召开的高交会。
- 2013年,获得国家外国专家局引进国外技术、管理人才成果示范推广项目支持;荣获河北省科技型中小企业称号。
- 2012年,获得国家科技部年度科技创新基金支持。

地理位置和联系电话

地理位置:河北省怀来县桑园镇

联系电话:0313-6878250

24. 张家口大好河山酿造有限公司

张家口大好河山酿造有限公司成立于1997年,地处河北省怀来县沙城镇。公司占地面积 9789 平方米，拥有职工近百人，其中各类技术人员占 20% 以上。公司生产和灌装车间设备先进，是集基地建设、葡萄栽培、科学研究、产品开发、规模生产于一体的葡萄酒庄园。

大好河山是公司的注册商标，取自张家口大境门门楣上大好河山四字。张家口大境门是张家口市标志性历史建筑，为将地域文化和产品品牌有机融合在一起，在打造品牌的基础上弘扬地方文化，使产品品牌和地方文化相得益彰、相互促进。

公司主要产品为大好河山干红、干白葡萄酒，金窑系列、沙酒系列两大优质白酒系列。

地理位置和联系电话

地理位置：河北省怀来县沙城镇工业街

联系电话：0313-6251399

25. 张家口长城酿造（集团）有限责任公司

张家口长城酿造（集团）有限责任公司前身为沙城酒厂，创建于 1949 年，为中国第一瓶干白葡萄酒诞生地，位于河北省张家口市怀来县沙城镇。公司占地 30 多万平方米，集沙城老窖白酒、沙城葡萄酒、沙城煮酒、各类果酒、饮料等多品类发展，为华北地区最大酿酒企业之一。

沙城老窖白酒至今有 800 年历史，源于元，壮于明，盛于清，为元、清两朝御酒，于清康熙三十五年被康熙皇帝赐名沙城沙酒。沙城煮酒三获巴拿马、费城等国际名酒赛会国际名酒大奖，1958 年沙城酒厂青梅煮酒再获全国第一名。公司白酒以浓香型为主，兼具清香、酱香多种香型，在浓香白酒"北斗工艺"实践推广、超低度白酒研究方面成绩卓著，沙城老窖在 1994 年获得"中国酒王"称号，是中国北方白酒生产的见证和活档案。

沙城葡萄酒源于 1917 年沙城兴办的全国第三家葡萄酒厂——裕华葡萄酒厂。公司于 1959 年响应国家号召新建果酒车间（现为中国第一瓶干白葡萄酒诞生地遗址），沙城葡萄酒 1975 年纳入全国葡萄酒发展规划，1976 年采用中国特有龙眼葡萄及自主技术，成功研发中国第一瓶干白葡萄酒。1978 年，国家重点科研项目"干白葡萄酒新工艺的研究"科研点设立在沙城酒厂，多项科研成果推动中国葡萄酒向干型转型。1979 年沙城干白葡萄酒获得"全国名酒"称号及"全国质量奖金奖"荣誉。沙城酒厂干白葡萄酒还被选定为外交部驻外使馆供应用酒，率先出口干型葡萄酒，建立首个干型葡萄酒国际酿酒名种母本园，率先出国考察交流，留下诸多民族品牌印记，沙城葡萄酒被誉为干酒之源。

公司大事记

- 2021年，沙城双龄409荣获中国酒业2020年度"青酌奖"；沙城双龄409、沙城老窖陶藏原浆20、沙城老窖特曲荣获美国旧金山世界烈酒大赛双金奖。

- 2020年，公司入选国家工业遗产，成为目前唯一白酒、葡萄酒双品类国家工业遗产项目。其中沙城老窖酒酿造技艺和沙城葡萄酒干白葡萄酒新工艺列入国家工业遗产核心物项。

- 2019年，企业成功改制，实施白酒、葡萄酒双轮驱动及沙城名酒复兴战略；《中国第一瓶干白葡萄酒诞生记》新书出版。

- 2010年，获"中国第一瓶干白葡萄酒"生产企业荣誉称号。

- 2009年，"沙城老窖酒酿造技艺"入选河北省非物质文化遗产项目。

- 2003年，公司将"中国长城葡萄酒有限公司"股权转让给中粮，转而以研发生产第一瓶干白的老沙城葡萄酒厂为基础扩建葡萄酒车间恢复沙城葡萄酒生产销售。

- 1999年，荣获全国食品工业科技进步优秀项目奖。

- 1998年，组建河北长城葡萄酒产业集团有限责任公司。

- 1996年，公司更名为张家口长城酿造（集团）有限责任公司，下设白酒厂、果酒厂、饮料厂、包装厂、热电厂等七大分厂和长城葡萄酒、长城生物饲料两个合资公司。

- 1994年，沙城老窖在中国国际名酒博览会上荣获"中国酒王"称号。

- 1993年，沙城老窖被评为"93"国际名酒（香港）博览会金奖；公司年综合生产能力8.5万吨，其中白酒3万吨，综合生产能力居全国第六位；公司在首届中国糖酒工业企业评价中被评为白酒制造业百强之一；国家统计局1993年主要经济指标排序中国行业一百强。

- 1992年，沙城老窖荣获首届曼谷国际名酒博览会国际名酒特别金奖；公司被核准为国有大型二档企业。

- 1991年，获国家一级企业档案管理合格证书。

- 1990年，沙城老窖获全国轻工业优质产品奖；中式鸡尾酒荣获河北省轻工业科技进步二等奖。

- 1989年，河北省人民政府授予公司"省级先进企业""节能先进企业""省级文明单位"称号。轻工部授予公司"推动企业技术进步金龙腾飞奖"。

- 1986年，酸枣可乐荣获河北省优秀新产品二等奖，酸枣系列产品荣获河北科技进步三等奖。1988年在首届中国食品博览会上，"54度沙城老窖""老龙潭牌青梅煮酒"获金奖；雪仙牌酸枣可乐、龙潭牌中国酸枣香槟酒获银奖；龙潭牌戈力麦花啤酒获铜奖。

- 1983年，经国家进出口管理委员会批准，公司以扩建的万吨葡萄酒车间等实物出资与中国粮油食品进出口总公司、香港远大公司三家合资成立"中国长城葡萄酒有限公司"，中粮、香港远大各持股25%，张家口长城酿造（集团）有限责任公司持股50%，生产销售长城葡萄酒。同年，干白葡萄酒在英国伦敦第十四届国际评酒会上荣获银奖，这是我国葡萄酒类70年来在国际名酒比赛中首次。

- 1981年，公司科研项目"干白葡萄酒新工艺的研究"荣获国家轻工业部科技成果三等奖。

- 1980年，自西德和美国引进13个品种（白8红5）54000株苗木在沙城酒厂母本园定植，成活率90%以上，这是我国首次多品种成批量引进国际著名酿酒葡萄品种。

- 1979年，沙城干白葡萄酒被评为"全国名酒"；同年与茅台、五粮液一道荣获"国家质量奖金奖"；半干葡萄酒荣获"中华人民共和国优质产品奖"；干白葡萄酒列为外交部驻外使馆用酒，出口美国英国等10多个国家。

- 1978年，轻工业部重点科研项目"干白葡萄酒新工艺的研究"的科研点设在沙城酒厂，共计16项科研课题，葡萄酒泰斗郭其昌为项目负责人，公司抽调22人组建科研团队；历时五年科研成果获鉴定通过并免费向行业推广，中国葡萄酒由甜型向干型转型。

- 1977年，公司被评为大庆式企业；同年与美国可口可乐公司签约干白葡萄酒出口美国；自主设计、扩建万吨葡萄酒车间。

- 1976年，中国第一瓶干白——沙城干白葡萄酒在公司诞生，填补了中国干型葡萄酒的空白。

- 1975年，国家五部委到怀来调研，将沙城酒厂高品质葡萄酒生产纳入全国发展规划。
- 1959年，自主设计新建果酒车间，生产甜型沙城葡萄酒和青梅煮酒，畅销全国10多个省市。
- 1957年，沙城酒厂扩建产能，产品遍销全国18个省市。
- 1949年，察哈尔省政府接收怀来县六家私营缸房等所有酿酒资源，成立华北第四十六公营酒厂，1950年更名为沙城酒厂。

地理位置和联系电话

地理位置：河北省怀来县沙城镇酒厂路

联系电话：0313-6256666

26. 怀来紫晶庄园葡萄酒有限公司

怀来紫晶庄园（以下简称庄园）为中外合资企业，成立于2008年。庄园位于河北省怀来县，自有葡萄园600亩，栽培有"赤霞珠""美乐""霞多丽""马瑟兰""小芒森"等酿酒品种。庄园拥有气囊压榨机、发酵和灌装设备、优质橡木桶，4000平方米的地下酒窖为葡萄酒提供了恒温恒湿储存条件。

紫晶美酒在比利时布鲁塞尔葡萄酒大赛、品醇客世界葡萄酒大赛及德国柏林葡萄酒大奖赛等国际国内重大赛事上荣获近200项大奖，并被《法国葡萄酒评论》杂志评选为"中国年度最佳酒庄"。2018年进入法国市场试销、进入以色列大使馆作为招待定制用酒。

公司大事记

- 2019年，在发现中国2019中国葡萄酒发展峰会上被评选为"年度最受欢迎中国精品葡萄酒酒庄"。
- 2018年，在中国葡萄酒市场年度风云榜中被评选为"2018中国葡萄酒市场年度风云品牌"。
- 2017年，获得"河北省优质产品"称号，推出新品"晶系列"，包含晶彩、晶灵、晶典、晶藏。在 RVF 中国优秀葡萄酒 2017 年度评选中被评选为"年度最佳酒庄"。

- 2016 年，获得河北省科技型中小企业称号，并被评为河北省著名商标企业。
- 2014 年，被评为农业产业化重点龙头企业。
- 2008 年，怀来紫晶庄园正式建立，开始在自有葡萄园中栽种精选的酿酒葡萄。
- 2007 年，怀来紫晶庄园开始筹划建立。

地理位置和联系电话

地理位置：河北省怀来县瑞云观乡

联系电话：0313-6850519

27. 利世 G9 国际庄园

利世 G9 国际庄园是由利世集团汇集国内外优质资源倾心打造的大首都产区的国际酒庄集群，一个以红酒、康养度假、文旅三大产业为主的高端国际交往平台。利世 G9 国际庄园坐落在京西北官厅湖北岸，与国家级湿地公园接壤，毗邻八达岭长城，总占地面积约 5000 亩，被燕山山脉环绕，属温带大陆性季风气候、四季分明、光照充足，是"中国葡萄之乡""中国葡萄酒之乡"。它的区域位置得天独厚，离北京只有 75 公里，驱车约一个半小时，乘坐高铁 20 分钟。项目处于怀来葡萄酒产区的中间位置，目前产区围绕着官厅湖已有 41 个酒庄，如长城桑干、迦南、中法庄园等，有着悠久的葡萄酒产业历史。

G9 项目是探索葡萄酒产业和庄园经济升级迭代，一、二、三产业联动的一个新的尝试。利世 G9 创造性地提出"大首都产区"的概念，学习和赶超世界葡萄酒产业发展。大首都产区要充分发挥首都消费群体的优势，满足日益增长的消费追求，同时也要在传统的产业上进行一、二、三产业联动。G9 的核心是依托首都北京，打造一个高端的国际交往平台，整合国内外顶级的品牌和 IP，联合多方进行资源合作，建成集葡萄酒生产、度假养生、休闲旅游、国际交往为一体的全产业链新型综合体，并将以突出的特色和国际优势，助力奥运。

项目涵盖千亩葡萄园、9 个国家顶级庄园：特色酒店、会展中心、康养中心、高端婚庆、酒庄博物馆、酒窖会议室、马球俱乐部、高端英管服务、钻石厅礼堂，以及其他休闲娱乐、活动空间等。

首开庄总占地约 100 亩，建筑面积约 12000 平方米，位于利世 G9 国际庄园地块西南，由法国凡尔赛宫历史建筑修复首席顾问让-皮埃尔（Jean-Pierre Errath）担任建筑设计师。G9 项目 2018 年 3 月正式启动，2020 年 9 月开始运营。

地理位置和联系电话

地理位置：河北省怀来县官厅水库国家湿地公园北侧

联系电话：19919911929

28. 中国怀来·世界葡萄酒之窗展览馆

中国怀来·世界葡萄酒之窗展览馆位于怀来县沙城镇东水泉村东，长城桑干酒庄北侧。建筑面积 7877 平方米，布展面积 4923 平方米。一层、二层为展览区，三层为河北省葡萄产业技术研究院。

世界葡萄酒之窗是以葡萄酒为核心，选取特色文化符号注入设计理念，集文化博览、品鉴交易、大型商贸、文娱活动、论坛培训、教育研学、餐饮服务等功能为一体的大型综合性展览馆。内部包含常设展馆、临时展厅、多功能厅、文创品牌店、餐饮区和办公室。

常设展馆勾勒世界与怀来葡萄酒产业的双版图，包括世界葡萄酒文化、中国葡萄酒文化、怀来葡萄酒和葡萄酒艺术四大主展厅。为葡萄酒酒品、葡萄酒人才技术、葡萄酒文化艺术搭建国际性的展示交流平台。通过先进的现代多媒体技术，充分调动视、听、触、嗅等多种感官功能，于趣味互动中带领参观者体验世界葡萄酒庄园的沉浸式环游之旅，感悟葡萄酒文化与产业的立体式诞生之路。

功能性展区坚持市场化运营，多维业态并举。定期举办主题展会、品鉴交流、商业展销、艺术展览、论坛培训等临时活动，汇聚世界级葡萄酒专业人才和葡萄酒爱好者。结合时下最为新颖有趣的流行趋势，带给参观者高品质、经济性的消费体验，国际化与前瞻性的审美赏鉴。

中国怀来·葡萄酒之窗的建成，将成为怀来县特色葡萄（酒）产业的展示窗口；结合恒大葡萄酒交易中心、G9 国际葡萄酒文化小镇，以及万亩葡萄园、桑干酒庄等现有资源成为葡萄产业引导与展示的平台，可以更好地展现怀来葡萄酒文化以及传承怀来葡萄酒历史，加速促进怀来葡萄产业产、学、研一体化发展。同时也可以推动葡萄产业高效种植、高品质酿造、高附加值发展，加快构建一、二、三产业融合发展的体系，不断提升怀来产区的知名度和影响力，打造中国知名葡萄酒产区的重要窗口。

地理位置和联系电话

地理位置：怀来县沙城镇东水泉村东

联系电话：15297329578

29. 中粮华夏长城葡萄酒有限公司

中粮华夏长城葡萄酒有限公司位于河北省昌黎县，注册资本 2.0 亿元，占地面积 80 万平方米，建筑面积 8.5 万平方米，拥有榨汁设备、发酵设备、储酒设备、过滤设备和灌装设备 1200 台套，固定资产原值 41000 万元；到 2014 年底，公司有酿酒葡萄基地 1340 公顷；葡萄酒年综合生产能力 5 万吨，贮酒能力 10 万吨。公司现有员工 234 人，其中：国家葡萄酒技术委员会顾问 2 名，国家葡萄酒技术委员会委员 2 名，国家级评酒委员 6 名，国家级品酒师 34 名（其中国家一级品酒师 16 名），国家级酿酒师 15 名（其中国家一级酿酒师 12 名），大专以上学历员工 86 名。

中粮华夏长城葡萄酒有限公司的历史可以追溯到成立于 1958 年的唐山地区昌黎果酒厂（1973 年后更名为河北省昌黎葡萄酒厂）。1955 年，为填补果露酒生产空白，河北省工业厅决定在昌黎县筹建全省首家果露酒厂。1956 年，河北省酿酒技师任桂源被派回家乡昌黎，在昌黎创建果酒发酵试验站，从事果酒试制和培训技术工人。在他的带领下，很快试制出了玫瑰香葡萄酒、龙眼葡萄酒和其他果露酒。试酿成功后，于 1958 年建立河北省昌黎葡萄酒厂。1964 年国家把昌黎葡萄酒厂作为科研试点单位，葡萄酒专家朱梅、郭其昌、杨子培、林文炳等先后与昌黎葡萄酒厂技术骨干一道完成了"河北省果酒稳定性试验项目"，解决了国内多项酿酒工艺难题。1966 年，该企业累计向国家上缴利税 600 多万元。1973 年，该厂用本地玫瑰香等葡萄开发出了一种红葡萄酒。为打开国际市场，聘请了国内著名葡萄酿酒专家郭其昌、严升杰担任项目负责人，研制国际流行的干红葡萄酒。1981 年 1 月，轻工业部食品发酵研究所与昌黎葡萄酒厂达成技术合作协议，签署了"酿酒原料优良葡萄品种选育研究任务书""间歇热处理果浆酿制干红葡萄酒设备试制研究合同""新工艺或新产品的科学研究合同"。轻工业部食品发酵研究所高级工程师郭其昌与河北省昌黎葡萄酒厂技术厂长严升杰分别代表双方在合同书上签字。1983 年 5 月，第一瓶"北戴河牌"干红葡萄酒在昌黎葡萄酒厂正式诞生。1987 年 12 月，中国粮油食品进出口总公司和昌黎葡萄酒厂正式成立"合营公司",总投资为 400 万元,生产规模为年产 500 吨,以生产干红葡萄酒为主,在昌黎葡萄酒厂开设一个高档葡萄酒生产车间,最初由 8 名员工生产长城牌干红葡萄酒。

1988 年 8 月 9 日,华夏葡萄酿酒有限公司正式成立。公司总投资 700 万元人民币,由中粮集团、昌黎葡萄酒厂和法国鹏利公司共同出资筹建,任命原昌黎葡萄酒厂技术厂长严升杰任总经理兼总工。2005 年 12 月更名为中粮华夏长城葡萄酒有限公司。

2008 年 6 月,建设完成了一座集葡萄栽培、酿造、研发、旅游观光于一体的千吨精品酒车间,总建筑面积 6272 平方米,同时引进 3000 瓶/小时全自动灌装生产线 1 条。公司建有 19000 平方米具有中国传统特色的"亚洲地下第一大花岗岩酒窖"(分为地下拱形酒窖、名人珍藏酒窖和精品圆形酒窖三部分),内存 2 万余只橡木桶。

中粮华夏长城葡萄酒有限公司拥有河北省酿酒葡萄工程技术研究中心、河北省 A 级研发机构、河北省企业技术中心等省级科研平台,先后承担国家级科研项目 7 项,省市级科研项目 32 项,获国家科学技术进步二等奖和河北省科技进步二等奖各 1 项。

中粮华夏长城葡萄酒有限公司开发了以"华夏葡园 A 区"为代表的国内高档产区酒,九二、九四、九五为代表的年份系列,亚洲大酒窖系列葡萄酒,以及个性化、具有典型地域风格的高品质酒庄酒,形成三大系列 60 个品种。

公司大事记

- 2020 年,在布鲁塞尔国际葡萄酒大赛中,华夏大酒窖珍藏级干红、华夏九二干红、华夏酒庄干红均获金奖。
- 2019 年,获伦敦国际挑战赛银奖一枚及推荐奖两枚;获品醇客国际葡萄酒大赛银奖一枚及推荐奖一枚。
- 2018 年,获品醇客国际葡萄酒大赛银奖、铜奖和推荐奖各一枚;伦敦国际挑战赛推荐奖两枚;布鲁塞尔国际葡萄酒挑战赛银奖两枚。
- 2017 年,获布鲁塞尔国际葡萄酒大赛银奖两枚、伦敦国际挑战赛铜奖及推荐奖各一枚。
- 2016 年,与西北农大葡萄酒学院合作完成的"中国葡萄酒产业链关键技术创新与应用"项目荣获国家科学技术进步奖二等奖。

- 2009年，自主创新和开发了中粮酒业产品追溯系统。
- 2008年5月，万吨高档葡萄酒灌装生产车间、千吨精品酒车间、废水综合利用及生态园建设工程等技改项目正式启动。
- 2006年，中粮酒业成为北京2008年奥运会葡萄酒独家供应商。
- 2005年，华夏葡萄酿酒有限公司更名为中粮华夏长城葡萄酒有限公司。
- 2003年，华夏葡园A区干红研发成功，并上市。
- 2002年，荣获科技部"科技创新型星火龙头企业"。
- 2001年，华夏首家开发了3000毫升、6000毫升装团体庆典专用超级容量"干红航母装"，打破了红酒界单一的750毫升"老面孔"，令人耳目一新。
- 2000年3月，华夏长城九二年份酒正式上市。
- 1999年5月，华夏正式成为中粮集团下属全资子公司。
- 1997年，公司被河北省科学委员会评为"高新技术先进企业"。
- 1996年，华夏葡萄酿酒有限公司的葡萄酒产品均获得中国绿色食品中心颁发的使用绿色食品商标标志证书。
- 1994年，华夏葡萄酿酒有限公司生产的桃红葡萄酒，被列入国家"八五"星火成果推广计划。
- 1992年，在首届香港国际食品博览会上，长城牌干红葡萄酒荣获金奖。
- 1991年，华夏长城牌高档干红葡萄酒在"七五"全国星火计划成果博览会上获得金奖。
- 1990年，华夏长城白标干红在法国第14届国际食品博览会上获得金奖；承担国家科委"七五"星火计划"高档干红葡萄酒"重点科研项目。
- 1989年，华夏长城白标干红荣获法国第29届国际评酒会特别奖。
- 1988年，华夏葡萄酿酒有限公司正式成立。
- 1986年，昌黎葡萄酒厂严升杰副厂长率团赴法国考察，引进"赤霞珠""品丽珠"品种。

地理位置和联系电话

地理位置：河北省秦皇岛市昌黎县城关昌抚公路西侧

联系电话：0335-7169969

30. 中粮长城华夏酒庄秦皇岛有限公司

中粮长城华夏酒庄秦皇岛有限公司（以下简称华夏酒庄）是依托中粮华夏长城葡萄酒有限公司的美酒工业旅游资源而建立起来的新兴工业、文化旅游景区。华夏庄园坐落于美丽的滨海小城——河北省秦皇岛市昌黎县，距京沈高速公路抚宁出口二十公里，交通便利。东临避暑胜地北戴河三十公里，南依中国最美的八大海岸之一黄金海岸仅十公里，山环海抱，天高云淡，风景秀丽，气候宜人，游人在这里坐享无限风光。

华夏酒庄，地处碣石山脚下，位于中国唯一"山海河"环绕的产区——秦皇岛碣石山产区的中心地带，属温带大陆性气候，日照充足，葡萄成熟度高。葡萄园中充满砾石和砂质的三层火山岩沉积土壤，富含矿物质与微量元素，利于葡萄积累更加丰富的香气物质。酒庄一直秉承华夏精神，以传承华夏文化为使命，以"创业华夏，创新华夏，人文华夏，科技华夏"为指导，用先进的种植理念和优异的酿酒技术，辛勤耕耘，尊重风土，酿出了一瓶瓶独具碣石山产区特色的华夏美酒。

2017年，聘请美国约翰逊·费恩建筑师事务所进行设计（美国纳帕溪谷标志性建筑作品一号的设计团队），集葡萄酒酿造、展销、会展、培训等多功能于一体。华夏酒庄设置财务部、综合管理部、旅游管理部、餐饮部、客房部，主要经营旅游接待、餐饮住宿、会议培训、商品销售等业务。华夏酒庄拥有总建筑面积14137平方米的葡萄酒展销中心，位于葡萄园之中，与华夏工厂相连，依山坡走势，在蜿蜒的建筑内可以看到葡萄园全貌。该中心一层建筑面积4765平方米，主要功能区分为红酒博物馆、零售区、仓储室、会议室、医务室、办公区、品酒包间、品酒大厅、储酒室、多功能区、客房、娱乐室等；二层建筑面积为6670平方米，主要为仓储室、会议室、多功能厅、客房、宴会包间、宴会大厅等；三层建筑面积2702平方米，主要为后勤服务空间、客房、教室等。是集旅游观光、餐饮住宿、会议培训、文化交流及商品销售等功能为一体的酒庄综合体。

华夏酒庄拥有国际名优葡萄品种、品系及30年以上树龄葡萄苗木母本园125亩，酿酒葡萄标准化生产示范园800余亩，拥有30吨贮酒罐22个、10吨贮酒罐9

个、5 吨贮酒罐 8 个，共计 39 个罐，储酒量可达 700 余吨。拥有现代化的灌装生产车间，全自动灌装生产线，每小时可生产葡萄酒 3000 瓶；凭借得天独厚的自然条件和地理优势，近三年累计接待党和国家领导人及国内外游客 15 万余人次，主营业收入近 3000 万元。

地理位置和联系电话

地理位置：河北省秦皇岛市昌黎县城关昌抚公路西侧

联系电话：0335-7169888

31. 朗格斯酒庄（秦皇岛）有限公司

朗格斯酒庄创始人朗格斯先生，是奥地利著名企业家施华洛世奇家族水晶传人，朗格斯先生的母亲曾对他说：水晶事业的成功，带来的是财富与奢华，你更应该用这笔钱做一些对人类健康有益的事情。自此，开启了朗格斯先生与葡萄酒的不解之缘，创建朗格斯葡萄酒庄园，酿造葡萄酒，让更多的人品尝到优质的葡萄酒，成了朗格斯执着的追求。

朗格斯团队遍访世界著名产区，1998 年来到河北昌黎。一路之上，多见葡园，至碣石山，见山势起伏，顶若覆钟，状如碣石。登之顶峰，遥望黄金海岸，深悟"东临碣石，以观沧海"之意。惊叹之余，流连忘返。经查昌黎县志，得知这里依山傍海，日照充足，昼夜温差大，无霜期亦长，有优越的自然生态条件，巨大的潜在葡萄酒市场，还有这里热情、质朴、勤劳的人民，使其决意斥资数亿，于碣石支脉的樵夫山下，削山劈石，填土开路，建立葡萄酒庄，并以其姓氏命名为朗格斯酒庄。

朗格斯酒庄（秦皇岛）有限公司（以下简称酒庄）创立于 1999 年，位于河北省秦皇岛市昌黎县碣石山产区，2018 年 5 月由秦皇岛宏兴钢铁有限公司并购，注册资本 2.48 亿元。酒庄总占地面积 2000 余亩，其中自营免灌种植管理酿酒葡萄基地 1800 余亩，年产优质酿酒葡萄 400 吨，贮酒能力 1000 吨。酒庄现有员工 130 人，其中：国家级酿酒师 8 人，大专以上学历的员工 49 人。

酒庄秉承"美好酝酿、自然品味"的理念，是国内率先采用自然重力酿造工艺的酒庄；跳动的音符，流淌的水晶，是国内首推给葡萄园、葡萄酒听音乐的酒庄。酒庄依山而建，欧式园林建筑风格掩映于蓝天碧野之中，是集葡萄种植、高档葡萄酒生产、葡萄酒文化展示、葡萄酒品鉴、会议接待和旅游观光于一体的高档综合型庄园，被誉为"中华第一人文绿色酒庄"。

公司大事记

- 2020年，河北省科学技术厅批准新建河北省葡萄酒产业技术研究院，朗格斯酒庄（秦皇岛）有限公司为依托单位；参加第21届国际葡萄酒节，荣获"碣石山产区名优酒庄"称号；科学技术部批准朗格斯酒庄（秦皇岛）有限公司认定为"高新技术企业"；荣耀2018小味尔多干红葡萄酒，荣获第23届Interwine葡萄酒与烈酒大奖赛铜奖；国际领袖产区葡萄酒烈酒质量大赛，黑山伯爵-B258西拉干红葡萄酒获得优质奖，赤霞珠特制干红葡萄酒获得铂金奖，马瑟兰特制干红葡萄酒获得优质奖。

- 2019年，第二十届中国秦皇岛（昌黎）国际葡萄酒节暨朗格斯酒庄20周年盛典在朗格斯酒庄召开并推出20周年纪念酒；珍藏马瑟兰干红葡萄酒获得中国国际马瑟兰葡萄酒大赛大金奖、小味儿多干红葡萄酒获得金奖。

- 2018年，朗格斯酒庄由宏兴钢铁成功并购；酒庄维欧尼干白葡萄酒荣获2018中国优质葡萄酒挑战赛"新酒优胜奖"。

- 2015年，被中国国际食品安全与创新技术展览会组委会评为"安全葡萄酒品牌"。

- 2013年，朗格斯酒庄应邀参加了2013年中国葡萄酒大会，并作了论坛发言；朗格斯酒庄被评为"中国五星级名庄"。

- 2011年，朗格斯酒庄推出珍藏版第五款2009年红色珍藏；朗格斯酒庄作为亚洲唯一一家获邀参展的酒庄，出席了瑞士Bad Ragaz国际葡萄酒节，酒庄2009年珍藏版干红被组委会授予特别荣誉奖。

- 2010年，朗格斯酒庄科研项目"国产橡木桶及贮存高档干红葡萄酒的研究"获河北省科技进步二等奖。

- 2008年，朗格斯酒庄推出珍藏版系列第三款2006年蓝色珍藏和珍藏版第四款2006年份西拉单品种1.5升包装十周年庆典版。

- 2007年，朗格斯酒庄推出珍藏版系列第二款2005年金色珍藏。

- 2005年，朗格斯酒庄首次推出珍藏版系列产品第一款2003年银色珍藏款；

中国葡萄酒庄联盟筹备会在朗格斯酒庄举行，同年 12 月中国葡萄酒庄联盟正式成立，朗格斯酒庄成为中国葡萄酒庄联盟首批八大酒庄之一。

- 2003 年，朗格斯酒庄第一瓶干红葡萄酒、第一瓶桃红葡萄酒正式面世。
- 1999 年，选址河北昌黎，春天正式开垦建立第一个葡萄种植园。
- 1998 年，朗格斯先生及其专家团队在中国考察选址。

地理位置和联系电话

地理位置：河北省秦皇岛市昌黎县两山乡段家店村北

联系电话：400-090-1999

32. 河北夏都葡萄酿酒有限公司

河北夏都葡萄酿酒有限公司位于河北省昌黎县，占地面积 80000 余平方米，注册资本 5000 万元，主导产品桃红葡萄酒，是集研发、生产、销售为一体的中国首家专业生产桃红葡萄酒企业，首个中国桃红葡萄酒技术研发中心。以"致力于酿造最适合中国人口感的葡萄酒"为经营理念，于 2007 年起草制定了《桃红葡萄酒企业标准》，成为国内首家葡萄酒行业中唯一的专业性企业标准，成为葡萄酒行业的一个标杆。

公司拥有"河北省工程技术中心"和"秦皇岛特色葡萄酒工程技术中心"两个企业技术中心，与中国科学技术大学、中国农业大学、河北农业大学、燕山大学、河北科技师范学院等院校取得了技术合作，共同研发，产学研一体化，研制出花楸干红系列酒、草莓冰酒、桑葚酒、起泡桃红等新产品。自主研发了低温复式发酵法、二氧化碳浸渍酿造法、热浸渍法、闪蒸技术等核心技术，多次荣获得河北省科学技术进步奖、河北省消费者信得过产品、河北省名牌产品，被授予"中国田园综合体＋美丽乡村特色小镇农业示范单位"。

公司大事记

- 2021 年，"盛世夏都"被河北省工业和信息化厅评为"河北省食品特色品牌"。
- 2015 年，国家质量监督检验检疫总局核准河北夏都葡萄酿酒有限公司使用"昌黎葡萄酒"中华人民共和国地理标志保护产品专用标识。
- 2014 年，河北夏都葡萄酿酒有限公司被河北省人民政府认定为"河北省农业产业化重点龙头企业",被评审为"河北省诚信企业"。

● 2014 年,河北夏都葡萄酿酒有限公司被河北省发展与改革委员会评价认定为"河北省企业技术中心"。

● 2013 年,河北省科学技术厅认定河北夏都葡萄酿酒有限公司为"河北省科技型中小企业"。

● 2011 年,河北省食品工业协会、河北省食品专家委员会授予河北夏都葡萄酿酒有限公司"河北第一"夏都桃红葡萄酒。

● 2010 年,盛世夏都牌 AAAAA 经典桃红葡萄酒荣获"克隆宾杯"第四届烟台国际葡萄酒大赛银奖。

● 2009 年,公司被授予"2009 年度最具投资价值葡萄酒企业"称号。

● 2008 年,夏都品牌获"普瑞特杯"2008 中国葡萄酒最具竞争潜力品牌。

● 2007 年,经中国酿酒工业协会组织专家鉴定,公司《桃红葡萄酒标准》通过专家鉴定,填补了中国桃红葡萄酒标准的空白,为中国葡萄酒行业创立了标杆。

地理位置和联系电话

地理位置:河北省秦皇岛市昌黎县昌黄公路北侧(张官庄)

联系电话:0335-2208999

第二章

乳品加工产业

石家庄君乐宝乳业有限公司

君乐宝乳业集团成立于1995年,是河北省最大的乳制品加工企业、农业产业化国家重点龙头企业、国家高新技术企业、国家乳品研发技术分中心。君乐宝乳业有限公司现有员工14000余人,在河北、河南、江苏、吉林等地建有20个生产工厂、13个现代化大型牧场。业务范围包括婴幼儿奶粉、低温酸奶、常温液态奶、牧业四大板块,建立起涵盖奶业全产业链的运营布局,上下游协同发展的格局,为消费者提供营养、健康、安全的乳制品。

为生产世界级的好奶粉,君乐宝乳业有限公司首创了两个模式:一是全产业链模式,即牧草种植、奶牛养殖、生产加工全产业链一体化生产经营,确保产品安全放心;二是"四个世界级"模式,用世界级的牧场、世界级的工厂、世界级的合作伙伴和世界级的质量管理体系,确保产品质量。

君乐宝婴幼儿奶粉在全球奶粉行业第一家通过了食品安全全球标准BRC A＋顶级认证,成为首个在香港、澳门销售的国产奶粉品牌;2017年以来,君乐宝旗帜奶粉连续三年蝉联世界食品品质评鉴大会特别金奖,并被授予国际高质量奖杯;2018年11月,君乐宝获中国质量奖提名奖,是中国乳品企业首次获得中国质量领域的最高荣誉。

君乐宝乳业有限公司拥有国家乳品专业研发中心、功能性乳酸菌资源及应用技术国家地方共建工程实验室等科技平台,承担国家和省部级科研项目30多项,其中国家级项目6项;获得科技奖励20余项,其中河北省科技进步一等奖4项;获得多项国际创新大奖,其中君乐宝舒适成长奶粉在世界食品科技大会上获得"全球食品工业创新大奖";2019 年 6 月,君乐宝乐铂 K2 儿童成长配方奶粉和悦鲜活牛乳获"2019 世界乳品创新奖"。

经过不懈努力,君乐宝乳业有限公司销售额增长率连续多年在全行业领先。君乐宝奶粉全国销量领先,增长速度领先行业数倍,全球增速第一;低温酸奶逆势成长,行业增速第一。

公司大事记

- 2020 年,君乐宝旗帜奶粉二期领航乳业年产 5 万吨奶粉生产线项目在张家口市察北管理区正式开工;君乐宝乳业有限公司入选"2020 中国制造业民营企业 500 强"。

- 2019 年,君乐宝乳业有限公司入选 2019 中国民营企业制造业 500 强;君乐宝乳业有限公司荣获"科学技术进步奖(企业技术创新奖)一等奖"。

- 2018 年,君乐宝乳业有限公司总裁魏立华入选由中央统战部和全国工商联推选的"改革开放 40 年百名杰出民营企业家";2018 年,全国人大代表、君乐宝乳业有限公司总裁魏立华出席第十三届全国人大一次会议。

- 2016 年,君乐宝白金装婴幼儿配方奶粉正式进入香港市场销售。

- 2015 年,君乐宝乳业有限公司荣获河北省科学技术进步奖一等奖;君乐宝乳业有限公司获批设立博士后科研工作站。

- 2014 年,中国营养学会-君乐宝婴幼儿营养合作研发中心成立;君乐宝乳业有限公司荣获河北省政府质量奖。

- 2013 年,君乐宝乳业有限公司获评 2013 国家地方联合工程实验室。

- 2012 年,君乐宝乳业有限公司获石家庄市政府质量奖荣誉称号。

- 2011 年,君乐宝乳业有限公司益生菌酸牛奶获得"国产保健食品批准证书"。

- 2010 年,君乐宝乳业有限公司荣获影响中国"2009~2010 年度新领军品牌奖"。

- 2009 年,君乐宝乳业有限公司被认定为国家乳品加工技术研发分中心。

- 2006 年,君乐宝乳业有限公司获得"河北省著名商标"荣誉称号。

- 2004 年,君乐宝乳业有限公司公司正式通过 ISO9001 质量管理体系、

ISO14001 环境管理体系双认证，公司荣获河北省民营百强企业称号。

- 2003 年，君乐宝乳业有限公司成为首批通过国家质检总局市场准入制审查，企业获得制品生产许可证。

- 2001 年，君乐宝袋装活性乳产品市场占有率位居行业首位。

- 1995 年，君乐宝乳业有限公司成立。

地理位置和联系电话

地理位置：河北省石家庄市鹿泉区

联系电话：0311-67362665

第三章

粮食加工产业

1. 今麦郎食品股份有限公司

今麦郎食品股份有限公司（以下简称今麦郎）创建于1994年，是国家级农业产业化龙头企业，中国民营企业500强，是集方便面、面粉、休闲食品、挂面、饮品生产于一体的现代化大型综合食品企业集团。今麦郎在全国有28个生产基地，员工2万余人。年处理小麦300万吨，方便面年产能140亿份，位居世界前三强，饮品年产能2000万吨，年产卤蛋5亿枚。拥有世界上最大的方便面生产基地、世界上最大的方便面单体车间、最快速的饮品生产线，年销售额超200亿元。

今麦郎拥有完善的全产业链优势，现有25万亩优质麦基地，形成了从农业种植、加工、包装、物流、信息技术、销售等闭环链条；拥有河北省认定企业技术中心、河北省中小企业集群技术服务中心、河北省方便食品创新中心、河北省面制品产业技术研究院等省级研发平台。今麦郎旗下的一桶半一袋半系列、辣煌尚系列、老范家非油炸系列均受到全国各地消费者的好评，产品远销美国、加拿大、澳大利亚、韩国、日本等海外50多个国家和地区。

公司大事记

• 2020年，投资超10亿元的今麦郎面品（河源）项目动工奠基，总投资10.2亿元的"世界首创新一代方便面项目"开工仪式在隆尧总部举行，总投资10.8亿元的面品智能化挂面高速生产线项目在济宁市兖州区开工，安阳华龙农庄面粉有限公司开业典礼成功举行；今麦郎一桶半一袋半销量突破50亿份，今麦郎凉白开销量突破24亿瓶。

- 2019 年，今麦郎广东河源基地签约，今麦郎云南曲靖基地签约；饮品北京工厂被工信部正式授牌为"国家绿色工厂"，老范家速食面馆面荣获"2018~2019 年度中国方便食品行业最佳创新产品"和"2019 年最受欢迎的方便食品"大奖。

地理位置和联系电话

地理位置：河北省邢台市邢台高新技术产业开发区华龙大街 1 号

联系电话：0319-6598888

2. 金沙河集团

金沙河集团起源于 1971 年沙河县青介人民公社善南村第二生产队的挂面房。经过 50 年的发展，金沙河集团拥有员工 6000 余名，日处理小麦 13500 吨，拥有 100 条挂面生产线，日生产挂面 5000 吨。挂面产销量全国排名第一，面粉产销量全国排名第五，是一家一、二、三产业融合发展的民营企业。

一产包括：邢台市南和区金沙河农作物种植专业合作社、河北红薯岭农业开发有限公司、沙河市佛照山荒山综合开发有限责任公司。

二产包括：河北金沙河面业集团有限责任公司、邢台金沙河面业有限责任公司、承德金沙河面业有限责任公司、廊坊金沙河面业有限责任公司、陕西金沙河面业有限责任公司、安徽金沙河面业有限责任公司、山东金沙河面业有限责任公司、新疆阿拉山口金沙河面业有限责任公司、河北金沙河饮品有限公司。

三产包括：金沙河主题生态餐厅、河北金沙河物流有限公司。金沙河集团开放工业旅游，游客可以到企业参观了解挂面和面粉的生产过程，观赏万亩油菜花，欣赏金沙河佛照山漫山红叶。

公司相继通过 ISO9001 质量管理体系认证、ISO14001 环境管理体系、HACCP 食品安全管理体系认证，2010 年被农业部评定为"农业产业化国家重点龙头企业"。2019 年金沙河农业合作社被评为国家级农业合作示范社。

金沙河集团总部位于冀鲁豫三省中心地带，地理位置优越，自然环境得天独厚，是国家优质小麦生产基地，为公司提供了优质的粮源，确保了产品品质。

金沙河始终坚持"为员工创造福利、为客户创造价值、为大众创造健康、为社会创造和谐"的使命，通过五十年的努力，金沙河已拥有 5000 余名客户，产品畅销全国各地，进入了沃尔玛、家乐福、大润发、华润万家、乐购等国际卖场，并远销欧洲、南北美洲、大洋洲、非洲等六十多个国家和地区。

公司大事记

- 2020年，全国农业产业化龙头企业100强及融合发展10强。
- 2019年，获国家级农民合作社示范社、全国放心粮油示范加工企业和河北省制造业单项冠军。
- 2018年，获河北省政府质量奖、河北省食品领军品牌和省级农民合作社示范社。
- 2017年，成为国家食物营养教育示范基地。
- 2016年，获邢台市政府质量奖。
- 2015年，全国主食加工示范企业。
- 2014年，获中国食品科学技术学会科技创新奖——技术进步奖。
- 2012年，获河南省科学技术进步奖。
- 2011年，获中国驰名商标。
- 2010年，农业产业化国家级重点龙头企业。
- 2007年，中国名牌产品。

地理位置和联系电话

地理位置：京深高速沙河道口东行200米

联系电话：400-063-9222

3. 五得利面粉集团

五得利面粉集团（以下简称五得利集团）始建于1989年，公司从一个日处理小麦能力不足15吨的作坊式小厂，发展成目前拥有6省18地18个子公司，日处理小麦55000多吨，员工5500多名的大型制粉企业，规模世界第一，2020年实现产值332.8亿元。自2003年以来，五得利集团产销量就领先于中国面粉加工行业，五得利集团的愿景是"做面粉行业提供安全、健康、美好享受的领跑者"，如今产品畅销全国，全国市场占有率18%，未来三年全国市场占有率将达到33%，连续荣列全国市场同类产品销量第一名。五得利集团获得"中国企业500强""中国制造业企业 500 强""中国驰名商标""最具市场竞争力品牌""农业产业化国家重点龙头企业""国家标准化良好行为企业""中国食品工业优秀龙头企业""中国小麦粉加工企业 50 强""中国粮油企业 100 强""面业之冠"等荣誉。

五得利集团投入巨资进行科技创新，提高面粉精度和出粉率，开发有中国人饮食特点的各类专用粉。目前五得利系列面粉共有 140 多个品种，面粉洁白细腻，麦香浓郁，品质好，质量稳，具有良好的蒸煮和烘焙特性，可广泛用于面包、饺子、拉面、面条、馒头、花卷、烙饼等面制品，是制作各种面制食品的上好原料，是家庭、食堂、宾馆、工厂面粉的理想选择，五得利产品以良好的成品效果和稳定性深受广大客户青睐。

公司大事记

- 2019 年，天麦然面业有限公司成立；日处理小麦 3000 吨的五得利邯郸公司投产；五得利集团 45000 吨的所有车间，通过了 ISO9001、ISO22000、FSSC22000、HACCP 质量和食品安全管理体系认证。

- 2016 年，五得利集团入选"中国企业 500 强"排名 487，及"中国制造企业 500 强"排名 253。

- 2015 年，五得利商丘公司第一车间 AB 线投产，五得利集团日处理能力首次达到 40000 吨。

- 2013 年，五得利新乡公司第四车间，日处理小麦 600 吨专用粉车间顺利投产。

- 2012 年，五得利深州公司第三车间投产，五得利集团日处理小麦能力首次达到 20000 吨。

- 2010 年，五得利雄县公司一车间顺利投产。

- 2009 年，五得利宿迁公司一车间顺利投产。

- 2008 年，五得利咸阳公司一车间顺利投产，五得利集团日生产能力首次达到 10000 吨。

- 2006 年，日加工挂面 80 吨的一车间投产。

- 2005 年，五得利集团荣获"中国制造企业 500 强"，排名 485。

- 2004 年，五得利集团被国家八部委评为"农业产业化国家重点龙头企业"。

- 2003 年，五得利集团成立。

- 2000 年，日处理小麦 500 吨的五厂顺利投产；日处理小麦 500 吨的深州公司第一车间顺利投产。

- 1999 年，日处理小麦 200 吨的四厂顺利投产。

- 1997 年，日处理小麦 200 吨的三厂顺利投产。

- 1996 年，日处理小麦 200 吨的二厂顺利投产。

- 1989 年，五得利集团的前身，日处理小麦 15 吨的"新市场面粉厂"在河北大名成立并顺利投产。

地理位置和联系电话

地理位置：河北省邯郸市大名县

联系电话：0310-6592569

第四章

饮品制造产业

1. 河北养元智汇饮品股份有限公司

河北养元智汇饮品股份有限公司（以下简称公司）始建于1997年，专注植物蛋白饮料核桃乳的研发、生产和销售。公司自成立以来，一直致力于核桃乳饮品的研发、市场培育和消费引导，引领核桃乳由风味型边缘饮料变身为"南北通喝、全国同饮"的主流饮料。2018年2月，养元饮品在上海证券交易所挂牌交易，成功登陆A股资本市场。

公司坐落于河北省衡水市经济开发区，注册资金12亿元。公司拥有三家全资子公司、五大生产基地、40条具有国际先进水平的核桃乳生产线，在职员工1842人，各类专业技术人员812人。公司核桃乳饮品在国内植物蛋白饮品市场占有率近10％，在细分的核桃乳饮品领域的市场占有率达80％，年综合产能已达200万吨，是国内产销规模最大的核桃乳企业。

养元饮品技术实力雄厚，不断突破行业技术壁垒。先后主导、参与起草了核桃乳饮料行业标准、核桃乳饮料国家标准；独创了核桃饮品生产工艺，解决了核桃乳"苦、涩、腻"难题；研发创新全核桃CET冷萃脱涩工艺，提升核桃营养利用率达97％以上；研发了五重细化研磨工艺，利用细胞破壁技术，实现核桃乳颗粒平均直径最小达80纳米，使核桃营养更易被人体吸收。

养元饮品不断引进先进的检验检测设备，为食品安全与产品质量提供坚强有力保证。公司检测中心拥有超高效液相色谱仪、气质联用仪、PE原子吸收分光光度计、福斯乳品快速分析仪、马尔文粒径分析仪、流氏细胞仪、凯氏定氮仪等检验检测设备，通过了 CNAS 国家实验室认可，具备国际互认资质。公司拥有河北省企业技术中心、河北省核桃饮品技术创新中心、河北省核桃营养功能与加工技术重点实验室、中国轻工业核桃饮品重点实验室、河北省植物源发酵饮品工程实验室。2018 年底，六个核桃院士工作站、博士后科研工作站成功启动。

公司先后荣获农业产业化国家重点龙头企业、全国农产品加工业示范企业、全国食品工业优秀龙头食品企业、中国食品产业（植物蛋白饮料行业）标杆品牌、中国驰名商标、中国饮料工业二十强、河北省政府质量奖、河北省名牌产品、河北省质量效益型企业、河北省轻工业排头兵企业、河北省重点龙头企业等殊荣。

公司大事记

- 2020 年，获"2019~2020 食品安全诚信单位""2019~2020 食品安全管理创新三十佳案例""第十八届中国食品安全大会社会责任领军企业"等三大奖项。

- 2019 年，公司与北京工商大学、河北医科大学联合共建的"河北省核桃营养功能与加工技术重点实验室"获得河北省科技厅批复建设。

- 2018 年，公司通过河北省科学技术厅、中共河北省组织部、河北省科学技术协会联合评定，成立"河北省院士工作站"；经人力资源和社会保障部全国博士后管委会批准设立"博士后科研工作站"。

- 2017 年，公司品牌"六个核桃"被"中国保护消费者基金会、中国食品报社"联合评为"最受消费者信赖的十大饮料品牌"。

- 2016 年，公司获得中华全国总工会颁发的"全国五一劳动奖状"，同年，被中国红十字会授予"中国红十字事业贡献勋章"；公司通过欧盟"BRC 食品安全全球标准"体系 A 级认证。

- 2015 年，公司被中国营养学会授予"营养促进贡献奖"；公司被中国饮料工业协会评为"中国饮料工业二十强"，"六个核桃"商标被国家工商总局依法认定为"驰名商标"；江西鹰潭养元智汇饮品有限公司正式成立。

- 2014 年，公司检测中心荣获"CNAS 国家实验室"资质；公司"河北省植物源发酵饮品工程实验室"建设项目通过河北省发改委审批。

- 2013 年，公司获"河北省政府质量奖"；公司总部占地 10 万多平方米的南厂项目落成投产。

- 2012年，公司获"河北省轻工业排头兵企业"；安徽滁州养元饮品有限公司落成投产。

- 2011年，公司获"年度全国食品工业优秀龙头食品企业"。

- 2010年，公司投入巨额资金，在央视等全国领先媒体开展品牌传播；公司技术中心获评"河北省企业技术中心"；"YANGYUAN及图"被国家工商行政管理总局商标局认定为驰名商标。

- 2009年，公司通过ISO22000食品安全管理体系认证；以顾客需求为出发点，确立"经常用脑，多喝六个核桃"品牌定位。

- 2008年，公司整体搬迁至开发区北区新厂。

- 2007年，公司获"中国食品产业最具成长性企业"。

- 2005年，创立全新核桃乳饮料品牌——六个核桃。

- 2004年，公司通过ISO9001质量管理体系认证。

- 2002年，以市场为导向，成立养元饮品销售公司。

- 1999年，养元核桃乳获"河北省轻工业科技进步奖一等奖""优秀新品奖一等奖"。

- 1997年，河北养元保健饮品有限公司（公司前身）成立；主导起草核桃乳饮料行业标准。

地理位置和联系电话

地理位置：河北衡水经济开发区北区

联系电话：0318-2215883

2. 北京汇源饮料食品集团有限公司

北京汇源饮料食品集团有限公司（以下简称北京汇源集团）成立于1992年，是主营果汁及果汁饮料的股份制现代化大型企业集团。从北京汇源集团分拆成立的中国汇源果汁集团有限公司于2007年2月在香港联交所主板上市。北京汇源集团在全国22个省区市创建了50个现代化工厂，链接了1000多万亩名特优、标准化水果生产基地，建立了遍布全国的销售服务网络，构建了一个全国性的果汁产业化经营体系。

北京汇源集团拥有近 200 条世界先进的果蔬加工、饮料灌装生产线。健全、实施了 ISO9001、ISO22000、OHSAS18000、ISO14001 等质量、安全、环境管理体系，并实施体系认证。引进消化吸收的水果原浆加工冷破碎、浓缩果汁加工超微过滤、饮料灌装超高温瞬时灭菌、无菌冷灌装、瓶坯干式灭菌、含气果汁饮料无菌碳酸化及含气果汁含气杀菌等工艺技术均处于世界先进水平，国产橙汁脱苦脱酸所采用的离心-吸附耦联技术为自主原创，该技术居国内领先水平。

北京汇源集团走产学研科技开发的研究模式，通过设备、工艺、功能性配料的引进，与国内外的先进公司合作，形成了解国际果汁科技发展的重要窗口。与中国农业大学、济南果品研究院、河北农业大学和中国农业科学院果树研究所等合作，开展专项研究，构筑产品开发和创新的交流平台。参与完成国家"十五""十一五""十二五"科技支撑计划各一项，承担国家"863"计划一项，参与"十三五"国家重点研发计划两项，"政府间国际科技创新合作"项目一项。2020 年，参与完成的"特色浆果高品质保鲜与加工关键技术及产业化"项目获得国家科技进步二等奖。

公司大事记

- 2018 年，进一步加速渠道优化，开启中国第一果汁品牌的新发展篇章。

- 2015 年，完成对上海三得利食品公司 100％ 股权收购，与三得利成立合资公司，将茶和咖啡饮料囊括进公司产品组合，实现产品组合多元化。

- 2013 年，上市公司收购集团果业子公司，将水果加工果浆制造业务并入上市公司，成功整合上下游产业链，进一步提升企业效率。

- 2010 年，调整内部架构，形成汇源果汁、汇源果业、汇源农业、汇源投资的经营管理体系和发展目标。

- 2006 年，引进法国达能和美国华平等战略和基金投资者，完成汇源果汁的海外重组，于 2007 年 2 月在香港联交所主板上市。

- 2003 年，通过中国饮料行业的"安全饮料认证"。

- 2001 年，引进亚洲首条 PET 无菌冷灌装生产线，推出 PET 包装"真鲜橙"果汁饮料。汇源先后被评为"中国驰名商标""中国名牌产品""国家农业产业化重点龙头企业"等多项殊荣。

- 1999 年，跻身中国果汁饮料行业十强。

- 1995 年，推出中国第一包 100% 纯果汁。
- 1994 年，将总部搬迁至北京。
- 1993 年，引进浓缩加工设备，安装中国第一条无菌冷灌装生产线。
- 1992 年，汇源集团成立。

地理位置和联系电话

地理位址：北京市顺义区北小营镇

联系电话：010-60483388

第五章

马铃薯加工产业

1. 雪川农业发展股份有限公司

雪川农业发展股份有限公司（以下简称雪川农业）位于河北省张家口市察北管理区，成立于2007年，注册资本8564.87万元。雪川农业是一家以马铃薯种业为核心，现代农业服务为延伸，食品加工为主，集育、繁、推、储、加、销为一体的马铃薯全产业链集团，集马铃薯新品种选育、品种和农业新技术IP（intellectual property）商业化、农业数据管理、农业金融服务、马铃薯食品开发和综合深加工等业务为一体的农业高新技术产业平台。

雪川农业是农业产业化国家级重点龙头企业、高新技术企业、农业农村部马铃薯良种繁育基地建设和示范单位、农业农村部首批种子质量认证试点单位、国家级和省级马铃薯良种攻关重点企业、中国种业信用骨干企业、中国种子协会副会长单位、马铃薯分会会长单位、农业农村部植物新品种保护能力提升试点单位。

公司旗下拥有5家种业子公司、2家种植业子公司、11个大型机械化农场、1家马铃薯冷冻食品加工子公司、1座马铃薯产业技术研究院及省级企业技术中心、1个博士后创新实践基地、1家农机服务子公司、1家贸易服务子公司和2家科技服务子公司。

核心种业——薯业芯片

雪川农业建有马铃薯组培车间5400平方米，智能化微型薯温网室47800平方米，马铃薯产业技术研究院17000平方米，加工车间25000平方米、智能化恒温储藏库 51500 平方米，建有现代化、机械化大型脱毒种薯繁育基地 16 万亩，每年生产不同品种与级别的种薯 15 万吨，销往全国各地。

2011 年雪川农业省级企业技术中心挂牌，2017 年获评河北省（张家口）马铃薯产业技术研究院，现有研发人员 84 名。雪川农业从 2008 年开始进行马铃薯新品种选育工作，先后从国内外引进、收集和自主创制马铃薯品种资源 400 余份，通过田间变异、室内杂交结合现代育种技术，开展马铃薯新品种选育。每年配制杂交组合 100~150 个，获得实生种子 30 万~50 万粒，后代选择圃试验面积 200 多亩，在国内不同生态类型区安排区域试验点 32 个，每年可选育出 3~4 个苗头品系。已育出"雪育"和"雪川"系列新品种及品系 40 多个，其中 10 个品种取得植物新品种权证书，7 个品种通过品种登记。"雪川"等多种马铃薯品种可适配国内不同生态类型种植，深受市场认可，累计推广种植达到了 280 多万亩。2020 年，"雪川"参与了载人飞船实验船项目，"雪川"马铃薯种子作为搭载物送入太空进行试验。从太空返回的实生种子已经进入种植试验环节，雪川农业也已踏出了育种研发创新的坚实一步。

薯食航母

根据国内马铃薯品种结构不平衡，鲜薯销售附加值低，经济效益差的特点，2012 年，雪川农业成立了雪川食品，2017 年，雪川农业投资 10 亿元建设雪川食品马铃薯加工 2 期项目，引进了世界先进的马铃薯冷冻薯条及零食生产线，建设了现代化的生物质能源供应中心、零排放环保中心、全自动立体冷库及相关配套设备设施，年处理马铃薯原料 40 万吨，年加工冷冻薯条 15 万吨、全粉 1 万吨。雪川食品旗下涵盖裹粉薯条、堂食薯条、直切细薯、直切粗薯、异形薯、马铃薯雪花全粉等多系列产品，目前拥有咔滋系列、雪峪剑系列、薯脆时光等多个产品品牌。雪川食品已发展成为国内冷冻马铃薯加工行业的领先供应者之一，是国内众多大型餐饮连锁企业、大型超市、酒店餐厅的优质薯条供应商，也是国内众多薯片、休闲食品的优质全粉供应商。雪川食品的销售网络已遍布全球，远销至东南亚、西亚、非洲等十几个国家。

2020 年，雪川食品获评高新技术企业和国家级绿色工厂认证，加工车间通过了业界高标准、严要求、认证通过率较低的 BRC-A＋和 BRC-AA 级认证，并通过清真食品认证、ISO9001—2015、GB/T 19001 质量管理体系认证、HACCP 食品安全体系认证，真正做到从种子到餐桌，呵护每一步。

产学研多方合作

雪川研究院承担农业农村部科技发展中心"农业植物新品种保护能力提升试点"等 5 项省部级项目，取得发明专利 1 项，实用新型专利 19 项，外观专利 10 项。雪川研究院与中国农科院蔬菜所、黑龙江省农业科学院、中国农业科学院农业环境与可持续发展研究所、华南农业大学、沈阳农业大学、荷兰瓦赫宁根大学等在内的国内外马铃薯领域高水平的共建单位合作，建立了市场化运作、成果共享的马铃薯科研平台。2018 年"黑龙江省马铃薯高产品种及栽培模式研究"项目，经黑龙江农科院、黑龙江八一农垦大学的多位专家联合测产，雪育系列马铃薯新品种亩产达 5.74 吨，打破黑龙江省马铃薯亩产历史记录。

安全溯源

雪川农业从成立即开始建设产品质量追溯体系，2008 年率先在国内通过了中国良好农业规范认证（China GAP），2009 年通过全球良好农业规范认证（Global GAP）、ISO9001 质量管理体系认证、ISO22000 食品安全管理体系认证，并通过了跨国连锁超市的供应商资质审核和 SGS、麦咨达的第三方审核，获得有机认证，鲜薯生产种植体系和产品质量管理体系均达到欧洲零售商联盟要求标准。

2011 年雪川农业被农业部国家农垦总局认定为农产品追溯体系建设单位，目前雪川农业是国内唯一通过中国良好农业认证、全球良好农业规范认证、ISO9001、ISO22000 以及"绿色食品"5 项认证的马铃薯公司，且是国内唯一一家单一作物全部通过全球良好农业规范认证且面积最大的企业。

雪川农业致力于以生态赋能农业，实现全产业链深度参与者的互惠互利，实现农业区域的现代化、信息化联动发展，开创全面共赢的新时代农业模式，助力国家马铃薯产业化发展，掌握粮食安全的主动权，以科技雪川，点亮中国"薯"光。

公司大事记

- 2020 年，国内首家"马铃薯企业博士后创新实践基地"落户雪川农业；雪川农业集团参与国家太空育种科研项目，将马铃薯实生种子送入太空，开启育种新篇章；雪川食品获评河北省优秀民营企业。
- 2019 年，雪川农业取得全国育繁推一体化农作物种子生产经营许可证。
- 2018 年，河北省（张家口）马铃薯产业技术研究院通过论证，被列入省产业技术研究院。

- 2017 年，马铃薯产业技术研究院落成。

- 2016 年，公司马铃薯技术研发中心建设项目开工，马铃薯加工生产线扩产竣工。

- 2015 年，雪川农业发展股份有限公司创立大会暨第一次股东大会召开。

- 2014 年，雪川农业成功引入新一轮投资，注册资本增至 6570 万元。

- 2013 年，雪川食品公司马铃薯薯条加工项目一期工程进行生产调试；雪川食品通过 QS 认证；雪川马铃薯被认定为绿色食品 A 级产品；雪川农业被认定为农业产业化国家级重点龙头企业；河北省国营察北牧场加工型脱毒马铃薯良种繁育基地续建项目开工。

- 2012 年，张家口雪川食品有限公司注册成立；雪川食品马铃薯薯条加工项目一期工程生产线开始安装。

- 2011 年，在内蒙古赤峰市巴林右旗投资建设雪川西拉木伦农场；克什克腾雪川农牧业科技有限公司注册成立；公司企业技术研发中心被认定为河北省省级企业技术中心。

- 2010 年，张家口雪川农机服务有限公司注册成立；张家口雪川农业发展有限公司北京科技分公司注册成立；张家口雪川农业发展有限公司 100% 收购控股内蒙古雪原马铃薯种业有限公司；张家口雪川农业发展有限公司被河北省政府评为省级农业产业化重点龙头企业；"雪川"马铃薯种薯获河北省名牌产品。

- 2009 年，锡林浩特塞纳雪川农业发展有限公司注册成立。

- 2008 年，张家口雪川农业发展有限公司注册资本增至 5000 万元。

- 2007 年，张家口雪川农业发展有限公司注册成立，注册资金 1000 万元；张家口市马铃薯产业化示范项目立项，计划总投资 8.5 亿元；与世界最大的马铃薯育种公司荷兰 HZPC 公司正式签署合作协议，共同合作在中国地区开展马铃薯新品种选育项目。

地理位置和联系电话

地理位置：河北省张家口市察北管理区雪川工业园区

联系电话：400-851-6000

2. 张家口弘基农业科技开发有限责任公司

张家口弘基农业科技开发有限责任公司成立于2008年，是一家集马铃薯种薯繁育、商品薯种植、智能化储存、全粉加工为一体的农业产业化国家重点龙头企业和全国农产品加工业示范企业。现有员工300多名，年营业收入近2亿元。公司所在地距离北京260公里，毗邻内蒙古、山西和京津地区，交通便利。公司拥有马铃薯全粉加工生产线和马铃薯种薯繁育体系，马铃薯全粉加工能力及市场占有率位居全国前列。公司的主要产品为马铃薯雪花粉、土豆饼预拌粉、燕麦和藜麦。

公司现有3万亩种植基地，年种植马铃薯1.5万亩，轮作作物燕麦、藜麦、荞麦等1.5万亩。年生产1万吨马铃薯雪花全粉，脱毒马铃薯种苗5000万株、培育微型薯1亿粒，年产4万吨优质脱毒马铃薯种薯；拥有总仓储能力9万吨的马铃薯恒温恒湿气调库、占地6000平方米的马铃薯全粉加工生产车间、3800平方米组培中心、10000平方米日光温室和400个温网棚。公司起草并参与制定了马铃薯全粉国家行业标准（SB/T 10752—2012）、马铃薯种薯流通规范国家行业标准。"弘基"马铃薯雪花全粉为河北省著名商标，2017年获得第十五届国际农产品博览会金奖，被指定为张家口2019~2020"一带一路"国际滑雪系列赛事特许供应商。

公司与中国农业科学院、河北农业大学、张家口市农业科学院等单位建立了密切的科研合作关系，与河北农业大学、河北北方学院合作建立了河北省马铃薯加工技术创新中心。

公司大事记

- 2012年，弘基马铃薯良种繁育中心投产。
- 2011年，年产1万吨马铃薯全粉生产线建成投产，公司被认定为第五批农业产业化国家重点龙头企业。
- 2010年，张家口弘基马铃薯良种繁育中心有限责任公司注册成立。
- 2008年，张家口弘基农业科技开发有限责任公司注册成立。

地理位置和联系电话

地理位置：河北省张家口市塞北管理区榆树沟管理处

联系电话：0313-5755901、0313-5755000

第六章

白酒酿造产业

1. 河北衡水老白干酒业股份有限公司

河北衡水老白干酒业股份有限公司（以下简称公司），是河北衡水老白干酿酒（集团）有限公司的控股子公司，起源于 1946 年衡水的十八家传统私营酿酒作坊收归国有组建的"冀南行署地方国营衡水制酒厂"，是新中国第一家白酒生产企业，2002 年在上交所上市，是中国白酒骨干企业、老白干香型国家标准起草单位。2018 年经中国证监会核准，公司成功并购丰联酒业，成为拥有五家企业，涵盖三大香型（老白干香型、浓香型、酱香型）的白酒上市公司，开创了中国白酒上市公司中多香型、多品牌、多渠道的先河。目前，公司总占地面积 4000 余亩，现有员工 5000 余人，优质白酒年生产能力 12 万吨。

公司主导产品衡水老白干酒迄今已有 2000 多年悠久历史，据文字记载，兴于汉，盛于唐，名于宋，正式定名于明代，1915 年荣获巴拿马万国博览会最高奖——甲等大奖章，享誉世界。衡水老白干酒采用小麦中温大曲、地缸发酵、混蒸混烧老五甑工艺，具有醇香清雅、醇厚丰满、甘洌挺拔、诸味谐调、回味悠长的风格特点。近年来，公司及产品先后荣获中国驰名商标、中华老字号、中国白酒老白干香型代表、国家级非物质文化遗产等荣誉，2018 年衡水老白干荣获拉斯维加斯世界烈性酒大赛最高奖——"双金奖"，并被评为"全场最佳"。2019 年公司荣获国家级世界性奖项——"全国质量奖"。2020 年衡水老白干 1915 荣获世界食品品质评鉴大会最高奖——"特级金奖"，同时十八酒坊 15 年获得"金奖"。

公司大事记

- 2015年，衡水老白干荣获巴拿马万国博览会甲等金质大奖章100周年。

- 2013年，衡水老白干荣获"河北省政府质量奖"。

- 2010年，在上海世博会期间被认定为河北馆唯一指定参展白酒，同时荣获联合国相关组织的千年金奖。

- 2008年，衡水老白干传统酿造工艺被评选为"国家级非物质文化遗产"，衡水老白干酒业股份有限公司的"十八酒坊"品牌荣膺"中国驰名商标"，公司从此同时拥有两个"中国驰名商标"。

- 2006年，衡水老白干被商务部认定为"中华老字号"。

- 2005年，公司被国家旅游总局批准为全国第一批工业旅游示范点。

- 2004年，衡水老白干酒的注册商标及图案被国家工商管理总局认定为"中国驰名商标"，成为河北省首家获此殊荣的白酒品牌；由衡水老白干倡导并发起的"老白干香型"定型工作获得成功，成为中国"老白干香型"的鼻祖和品鉴代表。

- 2002年，以衡水老白干酒业公司为主发起人的河北裕丰实业股份有限公司在沪（上海证券交易所）上市，成为河北省白酒行业目前唯一一家上市公司。

- 1996年，河北衡水老白干酿酒（集团）有限公司正式成立。

- 1994年，率先在河北省通过ISO9001产品质量认证和质量管理体系认证，取得了出口贸易的通行证。

- 1993年，改名为"河北衡水老白干酒厂"；衡水老白干获双金奖新闻发布会在北京人民大会堂召开。

- 1992年，衡水老白干荣获香港国际食品博览会金奖；衡水老白干获中国名优酒博览会金奖，为河北省唯一金奖。

- 1991年，衡水老白干在中国食品工业十年新成就展览会上被授予"优秀新产品"奖牌和证书。

- 1989年，"老桥牌"注册商标被河北省工商行政管理局评为河北省著名商标。

- 1988年，衡水老白干酒在中国首届食品博览会上获得金奖。

- 1946 年,"冀南行署地方国营衡水制酒厂"正式成立。
- 1915 年,荣获巴拿马万国博览会最高奖——甲等大奖章。

地理位置和联系电话

地理位置:河北省衡水市

联系电话:0318-2992385

2. 河北雄安保府酒业有限公司

河北雄安保府酒业有限公司历史源远流长,其前身"万泉涌"创建于清光绪年间,现古烧锅遗址,位于河北雄安新区容城县。李俊山,容城县东四庄村人,清光绪年间秀才,曾任教于私塾,后辅助收盐及烧锅税,创办"万泉涌",善于经营,鼎盛时有 9 个发酵池,1 个烧锅,20 多个伙计,一天一宿投粮食 4000 斤,酿酒 800 斤,在县城、保定府设有分号,销售分布西到易县,南到安国,东到天津,北至北平。1937 年"七七事变",民不聊生,烧锅停业,毁于抗日年代,未能存续,发酵池遗址、古烧锅遗址、古井遗址部分保留。

1996 年,李俊山之重孙李宏涛,遍访民间酿酒艺人,收集酿酒古方,2009 年在"万泉涌"原址创办河北保定府酒业有限公司,2018 年经雄安新区管理委员会批准更名为河北雄安保府酒业有限公司。

河北雄安保府酒业有限公司位于雄安新区容城县容城镇,注册资本 1.68 亿元,占地面积 200 余亩,建筑面积 5.8 万平方米,拥有粮食粉碎、发酵蒸馏、酒窖储酒、勾调灌装等一系列现代化设备,总资产 2.29 亿元,年产原酒 1000 吨。

公司历经 20 载发展壮大,现已成为以白酒酿造和营销为核心,由文化旅游、酒店餐饮、金融担保、系列商贸、中央厨房等六大板块组成的集团化公司,拥有原创品牌"百年保定""千年大计"等白酒产品,被评为"河北省著名商标企业""河北省质量诚信 AAAAA 品牌企业""河北省放心酒产销示范基地""国家级放心酒工程示范企业"。其核心产品"百年保定"酒被评为"河北省优质产品""河北老字号",在保定 2006 年度首届行业展示会上被授予"最受欢迎家乡品牌",成为地产白酒典范,产品销售目前已覆盖 10 余个省、市,畅销 15 年,蝉联保定区域最畅销地产酒。

公司依靠创新求发展,与江南大学共同创建白酒创新中心,并于 2018 年 8 月签约原水井坊总工程师、国家级酿酒大师赖登燧先生为总工程师，改造提升老五甑酿酒工艺，提升产品研发水平，实现企业跨越式健康发展，公司先后被评定为"科技型中小企业""国家高新技术企业"。

公司在深入挖掘雄安新区地方悠久历史、人文典故的基础上，结合企业自身发展历程及行业特点，投资兴建了"雄安酒文化博物馆"，形象生动地展现了雄安地区悠久的历史文化传承和"老五甑"酿酒工艺的独特魅力，同时兴建了保定府经典故事"十大酒局"主题公园及万泉涌酿酒作坊遗址、玉井甘泉遗址、咖啡厅、荷塘、廊桥、酒神尧帝广场等，实现了现代化酿酒企业与优雅园林景区的完美结合，被评定为"国家AAA旅游景区"。

公司大事记

- 2019年，成立河北千年大计酒业有限公司。
- 2018年，河北保定府酒业有限公司更名为河北雄安保府酒业有限公司。
- 2016年，成立河北今元康食品有限公司。
- 2010~2012年，在金融、酒店、旅游开发、园林绿化、系列商贸等辅助行业成立专营公司，构建综合性集团化企业。
- 1998年，成立保定百年酒业有限公司。
- 1996年，成立河北保定府酒业有限公司。

地理位置和联系电话

地理位置：河北省雄安新区容城县容城镇

联系电话：0312-5608222

第七章
其他食品产业

1. 保定槐茂食品科技有限公司

"槐茂"的历史可以追溯到公元1671年,浙江绍兴赵氏夫妇到保定创业,成立"槐茂"号,经过不断积累,逐渐成为了北方酱业发展的引领者之一,与"北京六必居""临清济美""济宁玉堂"并称为北方四大酱园。1956年,在原"槐茂"等保定二十七家酱园的基础上,成立了保定国营酱菜厂;1983年,为使"槐茂"字号得到延续,公私合营后"槐茂"字号的继承者保定国营酱菜厂更名为保定槐茂酱菜厂,并注册"槐茂"商标,于1999年改制为股份制公司——河北保定槐茂有限公司。"槐茂"在2006年被中华人民共和国商务部首批认定为"中华老字号",2007年"槐茂酱菜制作技艺"被河北省人民政府、河北省文化厅认定为"省级非物质文化遗产",在发展过程中河北保定槐茂有限公司和"槐茂"品牌获得了诸多荣誉,"最受欢迎中华老字号品牌奖""中华人民共和国商务部优质产品奖""河北名牌""河北畅销品牌""河北省商业名牌企业"等,并进入"国际精品批发中心"批发体系。2013年,河北保定槐茂有限公司为打破发展瓶颈决定迁址另建,并注册全资子公司——保定槐茂食品科技有限公司。自1671年"槐茂"建立开始计算,保定槐茂已有350年的历史。

保定槐茂食品科技有限公司位于河北省定兴县金台经济技术开发区,注册资本1.5亿元,占地300亩,建筑面积64000平方米,是一家综合性的调味品生产企业,主产品为"槐茂甜面酱""槐茂酱油""槐茂酱菜""槐茂香醋"等,拥有投料提升设备、连续蒸煮设备、发酵设备、压榨设备、储存设备、清洗设备、腌制设施和灌装设备500多套,资产总值5.2亿元。年设计产能:甜面酱30000吨,酱油20000吨,醋20000吨,酱菜5000吨,其他调味产品30000吨,储存能力20000

吨。公司现有员工 160 人，其中国家级调味品行业专家 1 人，高级工程师 2 人，具有大专以上学历的员工 36 人。

公司设有专门的科研和质检机构，2000 年成立食用调味品技术研发中心，2019 年河北省科学技术厅批准建设"河北省甜面酱及酱渍菜技术创新中心"。2018 年与河北农业大学共同完成的金丝枣醋酿造关键技术研究项目，技术水平达到国际领先水平，获得河北省科技进步二等奖。

公司通过标准运营获得了 GB/T 19001—2016/ISO9001—2015 质量管理体系、危害分析与关键控制点（HACCP）体系双认证，2021 年被河北省科学技术厅认定为"科技型中小企业"，并被市场监督管理局认定为食品安全管理教育示范基地，在质量管理及技术创新等方面走在了行业前列。

公司大事记

- 2018 年，保定槐茂食品科技有限公司生产运营。
- 2013 年，保定槐茂食品科技有限公司成立。
- 2007 年，"槐茂酱菜制作技艺"被河北省人民政府、河北省文化厅认定为省级非物质文化遗产。
- 2006 年，"槐茂"被中华人民共和国商务部首批认定为"中华老字号"。
- 1999 年，河北保定槐茂有限公司成立。
- 1995 年，"槐茂"被河北省工商行政管理局认定为"河北省著名商标"。
- 1983 年，保定国营酱菜厂更名为保定槐茂酱菜厂，并注册"槐茂"商标。

地理位置和联系电话

地理位置：河北省定兴县槐茂路 6 号

联系电话：0312-5875606

2. 保定味群食品科技股份有限公司

保定味群食品科技股份有限公司位于河北省保定市，始建于 1991 年，总占地面积 12 万平方米，近三十年来致力于调味品、固体饮料、方便食品的生产和销售。公司总部位于保定国家高新技术产业开发区，下辖两个分公司生产基地。拥有员工

600 余人，注册资本 8150 万元，年综合产值达 3.6 亿元。

保定味群食品科技股份有限公司第一分公司，位于保定市莲池区莲池南大街 1630 号，占地 30 亩，为公司主要的固体饮品、方便食品的生产基地。生产涵盖果饮、茶饮、冰饮、热饮、点心、西式浓汤、烘焙预拌粉及拼配茶制品等 12 个系列的 250 余种产品。厂区设有固体饮料、方便食品、茶等三大独立生产线，年均产能达 1.3 万吨，主要供应中西餐、休闲餐饮、水吧等。

保定味群食品科技股份有限公司第二分公司，位于保定市清苑区新华东路 167 号，占地 130 亩，为公司主要的调味品生产基地。主要生产发酵酱油粉、水解植物蛋白粉、复合调味料粉等产品。厂区设有喷雾干燥、水解、混拌、包装等多条生产线，年均产能达 4.2 万吨。该基地主要原料来源于东北非转基因大豆豆粕及玉米蛋白，年消耗量折合大豆 3500 吨、玉米 4 万吨。

味群食品建立了从原材料验收、产品检测直至运输配送等各环节的质量保证系统。公司分别于 1998 年、1999 年和 2003 年在同行业中率先通过了 ISO9001 质量管理体系、ISO14001 环境管理体系和 HACCP 食品安全管理体系的认证，被收录进中国食品行业建国五十年"中国的一百个第一"中。

味群食品设有自主研发中心和国家实验室认可实验室，具备国家实验室同等检测效力，为稳定的产品质量和有效的产品输出做出了保证。凭借其自主研发技术开发的发酵酱油粉、水解蛋白粉、复合调味粉等九大系列一百余种产品适应了国内、国际市场的需求，填补了国内市场的空白。目前销售网络覆盖全国 30 多个省市自治区，远销东南亚、美国、加拿大、澳大利亚等 32 个国家和地区，销售业绩稳定增长，在国内外同行业中居领先地位。目前，已成为国际食品行业五百强企业最重要的调味品供应商。

2014 年，味群食品正式在全国中小企业股份转让系统有限责任公司挂牌，是河北首家挂牌的台资公司。2015 年被河北省科学技术厅评定为高新技术企业、科技小巨人企业。先后被省市政府机关和科研单位评为纳税先进单位、先进技术型企业、AA＋级信用客户，由于企业信用情况优良，2018 年获得了中国人民银行颁发的景气调查定点企业。

公司大事记

- 2015 年，被河北省科学技术厅评定为高新技术企业。

- 2014 年，正式在全国中小企业股份转让系统有限责任公司挂牌（证券简称：味群食品，证券代码：830915）；通过了 ISO22000 体系认证。

- 2010 年，通过了菲律宾 IDCP 体系认证。

- 2006 年，保定味群食品科技股份有限公司成立，同时设立两个分公司。

- 2005 年，通过了英国 BRC 及印尼 MUI 体系认证。

- 2004 年，实验室通过了中国 CNAS 认可。

- 2003 年，通过了 HACCP 食品安全管理体系的认证，同年通过了 HALAL 认证。

- 2002 年，清苑宏笙味群食品工业有限公司成立，保定味群通过了 KOSHER 体系的认证。

- 1999 年，通过了 ISO14001 环境管理体系认证。

- 1998 年，通过了 ISO9001 质量管理体系认证。

- 1992 年，保定味群食品工业有限公司成立。

地理位置和联系电话

地理位置：河北省保定市天鹅中路 178 号

联系电话：0312-2124937，0312-2132158

3. 晨光生物科技集团股份有限公司

晨光生物科技集团股份有限公司是一家专注于植物有效成分提取的高科技型上市企业，在中国、印度、赞比亚等地建有 30 多家子（分）公司。产品涵盖天然色素、天然香辛料提取物和精油、天然营养及药用提取物、保健食品、天然甜味剂、油脂和蛋白质六大系列上百个品种。如今晨光生物已成为中国植物提取行业领军企业、全球重要的天然提取物生产供应商。

晨光生物是农业产业化国家重点龙头企业、国家高新技术企业、国家"守合同重信用"企业、全国制造业单项冠军示范企业；建有国家认定企业技术中心、院士工作站、博士后科研工作站、国家地方联合工程实验室等科研平台；拥有 200 多项国家授权专利技术、荣获 59 项省部级以上科技奖励；2013 年荣获河北省政府质量奖；2014 年和 2017 年获 2 项国家科技进步二等奖。

公司现有员工 800 多人，本科学历占比 50% 以上。以博士生、硕士生为核心、大学生为骨干、庞大专业人才为主体的开拓型、创新型、学习型人才队伍，再加上先进的工艺设备和科学高效的技术创新管理体系，使晨光生物的技术水平和产品品质稳居国际前沿。创业二十一年来，晨光生物依靠自身实力提升了中国辣椒红色素生产在世界上的地位，使中国一跃成为世界辣椒红色素生产强国，为中国增加了一个世界第一的产业。如今，晨光生物已成为世界天然色素行业领军企业，国际重要的天然植物提取物生产供应商，促进了我国植物提取物行业的再度升级，进一步提升了"中国制造"的国际影响力。

公司大事记

- 2020 年，荣获中国工业大奖表彰奖。
- 2019 年，晨光生物科技（美国）有限公司成立。
- 2018 年，荣获全国智能制造试点示范企业。
- 2017 年，荣获制造业单项冠军企业；再获国家科技进步二等奖。
- 2016 年，叶黄素产销量成为世界第一。
- 2014 年，辣椒油树脂产销量世界第一，荣获国家科学技术进步二等奖。
- 2012 年，第一家海外子公司——晨光生物科技（印度）有限公司成功试车。
- 2010 年，在深交所创业板上市，证券代码：300138。
- 2008 年，辣椒红色素产销量世界第一。
- 2006 年，在新疆成立第一家子公司——新疆晨光天然色素有限公司。
- 2002 年，签订第一笔出口创汇订单 3500 美元。
- 2000 年，筹资 38 万元，正式改制为股份制公司——曲周县晨光天然色素有限公司；销售收入 187.8 万元。

地理位置和联系电话

地理位置：河北省邯郸市曲周县

联系电话：0310-8859030

4. 秦皇岛市海东青食品有限公司

秦皇岛市海东青食品有限公司成立于 2000 年,是一家集水产养殖、加工、冷藏、冷链物流仓储、水产品进出口贸易、休闲渔业为一体的现代化科技型民营企业,也是河北省农业产业化重点龙头企业。主导产品熟制真空蛤出口国外。

公司现有职工 500 多人,有专业的研发机构和技术研发管理中心,研发试验室面积 300 多平方米,配有先进检验检测研发设备设施。

公司大事记

- 2020 年,被评为河北省食品特色品牌。
- 2017 年,获批河北省"真空食品研发中心"。
- 2016 年,获批"河北省引才引智示范基地"。
- 2015 年,荣获"河北省科学技术进步一等奖"。
- 2014 年,获批河北省农业产业化"重点龙头企业"。
- 2010 年,获批"科技成长型企业"。
- 2008 年,荣获食品安全放心工程"先进企业"。

地理位置和联系电话

地理位置:河北省秦皇岛市海港区

联系电话:0335-3352212;13513365850

5. 承德瑞泰食品有限公司

承德瑞泰食品有限公司是一家专注山楂系列健康食品的企业,公司产品涵盖山楂果脯蜜饯食品、山楂罐头饮品、山楂保健红酒、山楂膳食纤维、原花青素等 70 余种产品,是全国山楂大健康食品第一品牌。

2015 年公司成立以来,已荣获"河北省省级农业产业化龙头企业""河北省扶贫龙头企业"等荣誉称号;公司设有"院士工作站""河北省山楂产业技术研究院""河北省农业创新驿站"等省级研发平台 4 个;公司深入挖掘山楂"药食同源"潜力,与中国农业科学院、中国科学院、河北农业大学等 10 所高校启动研发课题 21

项，拥有专利 14 项，自主研发品牌 13 个，公司的山楂膳食纤维提取技术经过中国农科院查新鉴定填补了 4 项国际空白。

公司现有员工 120 多人，本科学历占比 50％以上。以硕士生为主体的人才队伍，再加上先进的工艺设备和科学高效的技术创新管理体系，使瑞泰山楂供不应求，形成了"山楂种植、加工、研发、销售、旅游观光"一体的"三园一平台"的产业链条，辐射带动县域 4000 多名农户。

公司大事记

- 2020 年，被评为省级农业产业化重点龙头企业。
- 2019 年，被评为省级扶贫龙头企业。
- 2018 年，成立河北（承德）山楂产业技术研究院；被评为河北省同行业领军品牌企业。
- 2017 年，成立院士工作站。

地理位置和联系电话

地理位置：河北省承德市兴隆县兴隆镇北区（河北兴隆经开区内）

联系电话：0314-5606222

第二篇

风土人情和名胜古迹

1. 泥河湾文明

泥河湾遗址群，位于河北省阳原县东部，桑干河北岸，化稍营镇泥河湾村境内，地处桑干河上游的阳原盆地。距今约 177 万年前，远古的人类就活动在这片土地上，泥河湾标准地层记录了第三纪晚期至第四纪地球演化和生物、人类进化的历史，受到国内外地质、古生物、古人类及史前考古专家的极大关注。泥河湾盆地东西长 60 余公里，南北宽约 10 公里。在 200 多万年前，这里是一个较大的湖泊，湖泊的周围，是古动物的世界。当时盆地周围的山地森林密布，气候温暖潮湿，野生动物密集，同时也是远古人类理想的生活场所。早在二十世纪二三十年代，中外科学家就在这一带发现了许多双壳蚌化石和哺乳动物化石。新中国成立后，我国地质及古生物工作者多次到这里考察，发现了数以百计、种类繁多的动物化石以及许多旧石器时代文化遗址。在时代上，从 100 多万年到 1 万年旧石器时代早、中、晚期每个阶段的遗址都有，且内容十分丰富。其中百万年以上遗址就有 18 处，这在世界上是独一无二的。

泥河湾遗址群以其丰富的哺乳动物化石和人类旧石器遗迹而闻名于世。对泥河湾马圈沟遗址的发掘研究，使泥河湾遗址的年代有了巨大突破，把亚洲文化的起源推进至距今 200 万年前，从而在东非奥杜威峡谷之外找到了地球上第二个 200 万年前的古人类活动遗迹，向"非洲唯一人类起源论"提出了具有决定意义的挑战。同时，还发现了世界旧石器考古发掘中极为罕见的距今 200 万年前的可以复原的远古人类的进食场景。可以说，这一遗址群直接改写了世界关于人类起源和人类文明发展的历史，成为人类寻根问祖的圣地。

1924 年 9 月，法国古生物学家德日进和桑志华在考察内蒙古萨拉乌苏的返回途中来到张家口，会同美国地质学家巴尔博在泥河湾进行了短暂的地质考察。在科学报告中，巴尔博将盆地内的河湖沉积物命名为泥河湾层，从而拉开了泥河湾盆地科学研究的帷幕。

从那一刻起至今 90 余年，经过 20 多个国家和地区的 500 多位专家、学者的考古发掘和研究，在东西长 82 公里、南北宽 27 公里的桑干河两岸区域内，发现了含有早期人类文化遗存的遗址 80 多处，出土了数万件古人类化石、动物化石和各种石器，几乎记录了从旧石器时代至新石器时代发展演变的全部过程。在我国已经发现的 25 处距今 100 万年以上的早期人类文化遗存中，泥河湾遗址群就占了 21 处。

泥河湾早期文化遗存的密度之高，年代之久远，不仅在国内绝无仅有，在世界上也极为罕见。特别是2001年马圈沟遗址的发掘，首次发现了距今约200万年前人类进餐的遗迹，这是迄今为止我国发现的最早的人类起源地。泥河湾向人们昭示，人类不仅从东非的奥杜威峡谷走来，也有可能从中国的泥河湾走来。泥河湾是我国以至世界上独具特色的旧石器考古研究基地，泥河湾盆地有国际地质考古界公认的第四纪标准地层，泥河湾盆地、泥河湾地质剖面、泥河湾动植物群和泥河湾文化遗址已成为世界古人类文化等多学科研究的宝库。1978年中国考古工作者在泥河湾附近的小长梁东谷坨发现了大量旧石器和哺乳类动物化石，其中包括大量的石核、石片、石器以及制作石器时废弃的石块等。

1997年，泥河湾成为河北省第一个省级地质遗迹保护区，1998年被评为全国十大考古发现之一，第五批全国重点文物保护单位。

1994年，我国著名地质学家和古生物学家、"北京猿人"的发现者之一贾兰坡院士和他的同事们，在泥河湾盆地小长梁遗址发现了大量的世界上最早的细小石器。这些石器大多重在5~10克之间，最小的不足1克。可分为尖状器、刮削器、雕刻器和锥形器等类型，共约2000件。这些石器经过古地磁专家的测定，证明距今约有160万年。贾兰坡院士说，小长梁遗址年代的测定"是最详细可靠的"。而令人难以理解的是，泥河湾盆地小长梁遗址发现的这些细小石器"竟是如此之多如此之早，加工技术又如此精细、进步"，而且世界上尚未见有记录。1957年，贾兰坡院士观察了"北京人"制作石器已很进步，能使用和控制火，因而推断说，距今五六十万年前的"北京人"绝不是最早的人类，"北京人"不是第一。这次细小石器的发现，确证"泥河湾期的地层才是最早人类的脚踏地"，于是贾兰坡院士认为，在160万年前，就有如此进步的石器，证明人类起源比过去的认识要早得多，说400万年前有了人类并不夸张。

1995年8月至1998年9月，在以往发掘的基础上，河北省文物研究所和北京大学考古系合作发掘，在于家沟遗址找到了华北地区极为难得的更新世末至全新世中期的地层剖面和文化剖面，该项发掘入选1998年度"全国十大考古新发现"。1996年6~8月，美国印第安大学和河北省文物研究所等单位组成的中美联合考古队，对泥河湾遗址进行过为期两个月的发掘研究工作，获得了一大批较为珍贵的动物化石和旧石器等实物资料，进一步证实泥河湾盆地是中国人类起源的摇篮，是古人类发祥地之一，是一座有待深入研究、开发利用的巨大科学宝库和世界文化遗产。2001年10月，在泥河湾马圈沟遗址发现了层位最低、时代最早的遗址，发掘出的几百件石制品、动物骨骼，将泥河湾盆地旧石器的年代向前推进了数十万年，达到距今 200 万年左右。鉴于泥河湾遗址在史前文化中具有的重要地位和价值，2001 年 3 月入选"中国 20 世纪 100 项考古大发现"，被国务院列为全国重点文物保护单位。2002 年初，泥河湾地质遗迹晋升为国家级自然保护区。

泥河湾遗址群：马圈沟遗址、小长梁遗址、侯家窑遗址和虎头梁遗址

马圈沟遗址 地处泥河湾盆地东部，桑干河南岸的大田洼台地北部边缘区，距岑家湾村约 1000 米处。这里是旧石器时代早期文化遗址的集中分布区。由于水流的作用，这里的泥河湾层发育了数条南北向的巨型冲沟，马圈沟遗址正是其中的一条冲沟。在这一带存在着一条北东—南西向的基岩正断层，马圈沟遗址位于该断层的上盘，距断层面非常近。马圈沟遗址发现的石制品种类有石核、石片、石锤、刮削器等，从 1993 年以来开始对马圈沟进行小面积发掘，2000 年以来连续五年又进行了发掘，马圈沟遗址中发现的动物骨骼化石种类有象、犀、鹿、马、啮齿类等。在第三文化层发现了极为难得的人类祖先餐食大象的场景，敲骨吸髓、餐食大型动物已成为人类的生存行为，在全世界的旧石器考古发掘中是唯一的一例。马圈沟遗址的意义，不仅将泥河湾盆地旧石器遗址的年代向前推进了数十万年，达到 180 万～200 万年左右，成为迄今为止，东亚地区发现的最早的具有确切地层的人类活动遗址，更重要的是对人类起源于非洲埃塞俄比亚的一元论提出了挑战。2014 年 7 月，河北省文物研究所在泥河湾遗址群马圈沟遗址新发现两个文化层，专家将其命名为马圈沟 IA、IB 文化层，依据地层对比可以确认其时代在 132 万～155 万年之间。2015 年 7 月 20 日，泥河湾考古发掘工作取得了新进展，河北师范大学泥河湾考古研究院在距今约 150 万～160 万年的石沟遗址发现了古人类的用餐场面，这是继马圈沟遗址发现人类餐食大象之后的又一餐。

小长梁遗址 位于桑干河南岸官厅村的一道土梁"小长梁"。1978 年 8 月 21 日，中国科学院古脊椎与古人类研究所在大田洼台地进行第四纪地质调查时，在官厅村北小长梁的早更新世地层中发现了石制品和哺乳动物化石。同时他们在小长梁遗址的东侧找到了同层的后石山遗址。这是泥河湾盆地首次在早更新世地层中发现距今 100 万年以前的旧石器时代文化遗物，对于泥河湾盆地旧石器考古研究而言，这一发现具有划时代的意义。经过多次发掘，发现了大量的哺乳动物化石，可以鉴定的种类有貂、古菱齿象、中国三趾马、三门马、披毛犀、鹿、羚羊、牛类等。三趾马是第三纪的标志动物，可延续到第四纪早期，在泥河湾各遗址中，只有小长梁遗址发现了这种古老动物化石。在小长梁遗址出土的石器以小型为主，有石核、石片、石器 1000 多件，同时还有打击骨片。小长梁遗址形成于湖滨相沉积层中，遗

物几乎未受到扰动，属于原地埋藏。小长梁遗址的发现，意味着早期人类就生活在小长梁一带。作为人类活动最北端的见证，被镌刻在北京中华世纪坛的青铜甬道上。

侯家窑遗址　位于泥河湾盆地西北部，1974年发现了该遗址。遗址的年代距今10.4万～12.5万年，属于旧石器中期遗址的典型代表，出土了数以千计的石球，是该遗址的代表性器物。人类化石的发现是该遗址发掘的重要收获之一，发现人类化石材料18件，枕骨2块、顶骨11块。有一例头骨的顶骨的后部有一个直径9.5毫米的孔，孔缘已经愈合，愈合时间至少有两个星期以上，这可能是发现的最早的外科环钻手术。

虎头梁遗址　位于阳原县东部25公里处。1965年中国科学院科学家首先发现。1972～1974年中科院在虎头梁一带进行调查发掘，在遗址中发现的动物化石数量较多，可鉴定的化石有：蛙、鸵鸟、似布田鼠、蒙古黄鼠、中华鼢鼠、变种仓鼠、狼、野马、野驴、鹿、牛、普氏羚羊、鹅喉羚、转角羚羊和野猪，在遗址附近还发现了披毛犀和纳玛象化石。虎头梁遗址出土的石锤和石砧共7件，其中石锤5件，石砧2件。出土盘状和龟背状石核16件，楔形石核共236件，柱状石核17件，出土两极石片10件，出土的圆头刮削器221件，同时出土的有13件扁珠装饰品。虎头梁遗址的地质时代为更新世晚期之末，文化时代为旧石器时代晚期的较晚阶段。在虎头梁的于家沟遗址中发现了夹砂黄褐色陶片和哺乳动物化石，对研究旧石器时代向新石器时代过渡，以及农业起源、制陶起源等具有重要意义，填补了华北旧石器时代文化系列中的一个空白，被评为1998年全国十大考古新发现之一。

泥河湾遗址群考古价值　在世界上可见的泥河湾层有两处，另一处在维拉佛朗期，这两处相比，中国泥河湾是剖面最多、保存最完好、国际公认的第四纪标准地层。泥河湾遗址群没有年代断层，有200万年的马圈沟遗址；136万年小长梁遗址；136万年的葡萄园广梁遗址；100万年的有山祖庙咀、麻地沟、东谷坨、飞梁、霍家地、许家坡、东梁、照坡、后土山和岑家湾遗址；78万年的有马梁、雀遗址儿沟遗址；12万年的有山兑、细弦子遗址；10万年的侯家窑、漫流堡遗址；7.8万年的板井子遗址；2.8万年的上沙嘴、新庙庄遗址；1.16万年的有虎头梁、油房、西沟、西白马营遗址；4000年的有周家山、九马坊、榆条沟等；3000年的有丁家堡垒泥泉等，总共达130多处。现存战国、汉、辽墓葬124座，因而这里成为"世界天然博物馆"；泥河湾是研究百万年以来古地层、古生物、古地理及新构造运动等学科的著名地区。泥河湾对外开放是在1988年，当年应中国科学院邀请，美国加利福尼亚大学的学者前来考察，拉开了泥河湾开放的步伐。1990年，经国务院批准的中美合作泥河湾考古项目，成为新中国成立以来的第一个中外合作考古项目。至此，已接待了30多个国家和地区的500多名学者和专家，发表了有关泥河湾的论文700多篇。由此而言，泥河湾的历史、科学、文化、旅游、经济价值不可估量。

泥河湾遗址群是我国以至世界上独具特色的旧石器考古研究基地，从1924年西方学者巴尔博在这里发现大量古生物化石并命名为泥河湾层后，已有20多个国家的500多名考古专家前来考察和研究，我国一批知名专家更是经常涉足。他们认为"在一两个县的范围内，发现这么多遗址，在全世界是首屈一指"，"无论地质还是旧石器时代考古，泥河湾都是极为理想的场所"，充分说明泥河湾是东亚地区人类文明的起源地，是世界人类及其文化起源的中心，保护开发泥河湾遗址群的价值不可估量。泥河湾遗址群的保护和开发，不仅对人类考古研究有重要意义，而且对于推动当地经济发展有巨大带动作用。

2. 黄帝城

黄帝城，位于涿鹿县矾山镇西2公里处。黄帝城遗址呈不规则正方形，长宽各500米，城墙系夯土筑成。现存城墙高3～5米，南、西、北城墙尚在，东城墙浸于轩辕湖中。黄帝城遗址内，有大量陶片，除少量夹砂泥质粗红陶外，大部分是泥质灰陶和黑陶。器物残件和陶鼎腿、乳状鬲足、粗柄豆栖等，到处都可拣到，有时还可拣到完整的石杵、石斧、石凿、石纺轮、石环等。涿鹿之野的黄帝城，这座残破的5000年前的古城堡，中华民族这个东方伟大的民族就从这里起步，最初的文明就从这里开始创立。

黄帝泉，即古之阪泉，位于黄帝城东0.5公里处。传说黄帝当年常在此泉"濯浴龙体"，故又称"濯龙池"。黄帝泉为自流泉，水自平地涌出，潴而成池，池围97.2米，直径31米，北有一出水口，潺潺流向千年形成的天然河道，足供矾山镇十多个村庄万余民众饮用。据国家水利部门专家测定，黄帝泉水为地下1700～5000米的深层水，水色清澈，泉涌如注，冬不结冰，夏不生腐，久旱而不竭。水不仅是生命之源，而且人类的文明生活也离不开水。水利学家说，黄帝在涿鹿一带的统一战争，就是由寻找水源开始的。当我们手掬这水质甜润的黄帝泉水时，会自然想到，涿鹿这一带能够成为始祖文化的诞生地和中华民族的发祥地，是否与这里丰富的水资源有关呢？

在轩辕湖以东、黄帝泉以北200米处，原来建有黄帝祠（现不存，改建为"中华三祖堂"），传说与黄帝城同建于黄帝时代。黄帝祠是我国历代帝王将相祭祀怀古的殿堂。秦始皇、东晋司马德宗、清乾隆等，都曾不远千里，风尘仆仆，前往拜谒。著名的南宋爱国将领文天祥曾写道："我瞻涿鹿郡，古来战蚩尤。黄帝立此极，玉帛朝诸侯。"黄帝城，是中华民族的精神家园，走近这座城，你会感悟到，中华民族的伟大精神为什么会千年不泯，这座最古老的城堡，是一处极具真实性，极富特色，极有深意地揭示中华民族文化渊源的宝地。

3. 鸡鸣山

鸡鸣山位于张家口市下花园区境内，占地17.5平方公里，海拔1128.9米，是塞外最高的孤山，有"飞来峰"之美称，元朝诗人郝经曾用"一峰奇秀高插空"的诗句来形容鸡鸣山的高峻。此山景观峻秀，伟岸挺拔，如巨人参天，又如天然屏障。每当夏秋之际，白云环腰，景色宜人，似大海波浪逶迤而动，令人叹为观止。

鸡鸣山原有庙宇112间，建筑面积1300多平方米，塑像200余尊，是高僧念佛讲经、祈福社稷吉祥的历史文化圣地。鸡鸣山的最高点为顶峰玉皇阁旁的平石台，登临其上，宇净天澄，如置仙境。

鸡鸣山自古即为名山，北魏文成帝、唐太宗、辽圣宗、萧太后、元顺帝、明英宗等历代帝王都先后登临鸡鸣山，观赏北国风光。鸡鸣山顶存有清乾隆四十六年（公元1781年）的古碑，碑文中有："唐太宗驻跸其下，闻雄啼而命曰鸡鸣"，即是说鸡鸣山为唐太宗所命名。清圣祖玄烨自康熙三十五～四十五年（公元1696～1706年）的十年间，曾四次驾临下花园，两次登临鸡鸣山。他休息过的"卧龙石"至今仍静"卧"小道旁，让游人遐想无限。

从山门沿碎石铺成的"之"字形小路盘旋而上，依次可观赏到三楼四柱牌坊、山神庙、萧太后亭、鸣鸡、观音院、龙骨岩、永宁寺、五指峰、骆驼岩、寿龟峰、朱砂洞、锁路门、避风桥、南天门、玉皇阁、西顶碧霞元君殿（俗称奶奶庙）、东顶观日台等几十个景点。其中永宁寺始建于辽圣宗太平四年（公元1024年），这座寺院由天王殿、大雄宝殿、三圣殿组成，是经河北省宗教主管部门批准开放的寺院，可满足居士、香客做各种佛事活动的需要，也是大德高僧修行之场所。近年来，慕名来鸡鸣山拜佛的京、津等地的居士源源不断。

鸡鸣山的最高点为顶峰玉皇阁旁的平石台，登临其上，宇净天澄，如置仙境。举目四望，四周绚丽景色尽收眼底。山上的奇峰怪石淹没于云雾之中，如同大海上的礁石在波涛中时隐时现，百态千姿，别致有趣。置身于顶峰与断崖之间的避风桥上，凭栏四顾，脚下云雾缭绕，身似悬空，仿佛来到了蓬莱仙境。桥面上有块巨石，俗称避风石，人立其上，即使山风劲吹也不觉察。鸡鸣山的灵气、鸡鸣山的独特风情，凡曾到此游览的人无不对其由衷赞美。

4. 宣化古城

战国、秦汉时，天下分三十六郡，宣化属上谷郡。唐代始置武州和文德县（州县同治），明代为宣府镇，清朝改为直隶省宣化府。之后，曾属察哈尔省，置宣化市，后改属河北省，直到 1963 年改市为区，属张家口市至今。

宣化曾是京西的政治中心。历代帝王常来宣化巡视。清康熙皇帝七次北巡、西征均在宣化府整顿军队，筹集粮草。康熙三十六年（1697 年）二月，康熙皇帝第二次亲征噶尔丹，十二月驻宣化，赐口北道尹诗一首，赐宣化总兵"媲训练"匾一块，赐宣化知府"亲民"匾一块。

宣化是省级历史文化名城。宣化古城旅游区现有国家重点文物保护单位 3 处：清远楼、镇朔楼及辽墓壁画；省级重点文物保护单位 6 处：拱极楼、察哈尔省民主政府旧址、五龙壁砖雕、旧城垣、时恩寺及辽代壁画墓群二区。此外，还拥有一批如立化寺塔、大北街的马宅和都司街的南宅四合院、六中院内的"武庙"大殿、按院街内的张自忠将军故居、慈清西行时的行宫等极具开发价值的人文旅游资源。

5. 草原天路

草原天路，位于张家口市张北县和崇礼区的交界处，西起尚义县城南侧的大青山（国家级森林公园），东至崇礼区桦皮岭处，是连接崇礼滑雪区、赤城温泉区、张北草原风景区、白龙洞风景区、大青山风景区的一条重要通道，也是中国大陆十大最美丽的公路之一。草原天路，全长 132.7 公里，犹如一条蛟龙，盘踞于群山峻岭之巅，蜿蜒曲折、跌宕起伏，绵延百余公里。蓝天与之相接，白云与之呼应，行走在天路之上，就像是漫步在云端，故而得名"天路"。草原天路公路沿线蜿蜒曲折、河流山峦、沟壑纵深、草甸牛羊、景观奇峻，展现出一幅百里坝头风景画卷，分布着古长城遗址、桦皮岭、野狐岭、张北草原等众多人文、生态和地质旅游资源。

草原天路沿线分布着古长城遗址、苏蒙联军烈士陵园、桦皮岭、大圪垯石柱群等大量人文、生态和地质旅游资源。虽然草原天路只是张北坝上的一条柏油公路,但海拔也有千米左右,深色柏油路与黄实线本身就是一条美丽的风景。百里之间,左右徘徊曲折,剧烈地跌宕起伏、静谧深远,仿佛通向梦的彼岸。

桦皮岭 夏季桦皮岭,翠生生野花遍布山头,秋季桦皮岭,层林尽染秋意浓浓。桦皮岭年均气温只有4℃,位于海拔2128米的坝头主峰,因山上有千亩桦树林而得名。背坡原始桦木葱葱郁郁,各种山花野草有一米多高。夏季山花烂漫,蓝天如洗;秋季,漫山遍野五颜六色,美丽至极。桦皮岭气候宜人,这里空气含氧量达到27%,含负氧离子较高,被誉为"天然氧吧",是理想的避暑胜地。冬季的桦皮岭更为壮阔,这里降雪期可达120多天,年降雪量达到700毫米,为滑雪、滑冰等提供了条件。

阎片山 距桦皮岭入口约15公里路边有一处制高点——阎片山,很突兀地矗立在草原天路一侧平缓浑圆的丘陵中。阎片山位于大囫囵镇南端,百里坝头风景线由此经过,是崇礼与张北的中点站。村庄周围峦山围绕,环境优美,自然环境保护得力,负氧离子含量高,是名副其实的"天堂氧吧"。此外,其原始的村容村貌、古朴浓郁的民俗风情,与奇秀壮丽的阎片山景区形成得天独厚的地理环境,为发展乡村旅游奠定了良好的基础。

梯田 梯田是北方不多见的风光之一,如果不是草原天路,不知道还要跑多远才能看到这样的美景。夏天的颜色还只有翠绿色的单一,但依然能看得见分明的层次。秋天塞北梯田最有看头的,除了缤纷的色彩、纵横交错的线条,还有那收割后成垛、成堆、成行码放的各种庄稼。塞北梯田,是一个有着故事的地方,这里的景色如同这里的人一样,真实而未经修葺。一层层的梯田,静静地躺在大自然的怀抱中,呼吸着最纯净的空气,沐浴着最灿烂的阳光,享受着与世无争的氛围。

风力发电塔 风力发电机,俗称风车,一座座高高耸立沿着天路蔓延开来,占满了人整个视线。白色的风车,蓝天白云,还有绿色草原相得益彰,构成天路最经典的风景之一。

花海 天路沿线,野罂粟、苜蓿、土豆花、向日葵和油菜花,各种颜色的花朵点缀在草原之上,五彩缤纷,漫山遍野,随风摇曳,仿佛置身童话里。

空中草原 南泥河空中草原位于张北县小二台镇,为百里坝头代表性景观"百花草坪"之一,海拔在1600米以上,夏秋凉爽,花艳草深,蝶舞蜂飞,微风吹拂,气象万千。

沽源滦河 从桦皮岭出到丁字路口左拐沿沽源方向走,可以到达沽源滦河。闪电河,是滦河的源头,越山林,过湖泊,迤逦前行,在沽源辽阔的湿地草原上恣意流淌,九曲回折,意韵悠长。滦河神韵,形成了沽源又一标志性景观。

6. 太子城遗址

崇礼金代太子城遗址位于河北省张家口市崇礼区四台嘴乡太子城村村南,西距崇礼县城20公里。遗址四面环山,南、北各有一河流自东向西绕城而过后在城西汇合西流。

太子城遗址经勘探确认为一座平面为长方形的城址,出土遗物以各类泥质灰陶胎的筒板瓦、龙凤形脊饰等建筑构件为主,白釉瓷器中已发现15件印摩羯纹碗盘底有"尚食局"款铭文,进一步佐证了太子城遗址的皇家性质。

该遗址位于北京2022年冬奥会张家口赛区太子城奥运村项目占地范围内,为做好遗址文物保护工作,河北省组成联合考古队,于2017年5~11月对太子城遗址进行了全面测绘、勘探与发掘,取得重要收获。从出土遗物分析,太子城遗址时代为金代中后期。根据相关史籍记载以及太子城遗址发掘结果,太子城有可能是《金史》中记载金章宗驻夏的泰和宫。

2018年2月26日,该遗址入围2017年度全国十大考古新发现终评项目。太子城遗址经勘探确认为一座平面为长方形的城址,南北400米、东西350米,总面积14万平方米。现东西南三面城墙存有地下基址,北墙基址被河流破坏无存,残存三面墙体外均有壕沟,另钻探发现城址西墙有2道,东西间距50米。道路系统方面,钻探确认城内主街道基本呈T字形分布,有南门与西门各1座,门外均有瓮城。城内钻探共发现建筑基址28座,其中南北中轴线上有3组:南部正对南门的9号基址,中部1、2、3号组成的中心基址群,北部25号基址,另东西向大街的南北两侧有大量建筑基址。各种迹象表明该城址为一处金代皇室行宫遗址。

7. 御道口草原森林风景区

御道口牧场草原森林风景区位于承德市围场满族蒙古族自治县的内蒙古高原——坝上高原地区,1982年被国务院批准为国家级风景名胜区;1998年建立御道口草原风景区;1999年被河北省政府定为河北省生态旅游示范区;2005年被评为国家 AAAA 级旅游景区；2006 年被评为中国最佳旅游风景区。著名景点有神仙洞、月亮湖、大峡谷、龟山、桃山湖、红泉谷和图尔根草原。

景区总面积一千平方千米，位于内蒙古坝上高原，海拔 1230～1820 米，寒温带大陆性季风气候，年平均气温 3℃。景区内有原始草原 70 万亩，湿地 20 万亩，天然淡水湖 21 个，泉水 47 处（多为矿泉），河流 13 条，是滦河发源地之一。有植物 50 科 659 种，野生动物 100 多种，山野珍品几十种，具有典型的生物多样性，真正是"水的源头，云的故乡，花的世界，林的海洋，珍禽异兽的天堂"。成为人们草原观光、观鸟、骑马、垂钓、游船、篝火娱乐、越野赛车、科考探险、休闲度假、会议、滑冰滑雪、狩猎等生态旅游的绝佳去处。这里交通方便，距北京 400 公里，距承德 220 公里，距围场 100 公里，主干公路直通景区。

这里与最大的皇家园林承德避暑山庄遥相辉映，成为京承黄金旅游线的重要组成部分。这里曾是清代皇家猎苑木兰围场的一部分，康熙练兵台、御泉、卧牛盘、天梯梁、古御道等历史遗迹蕴涵着丰富的清代皇家文化内涵，神仙洞、桃山湖、太阳湖、月亮湖、百花坡、大峡谷和龟山等景点令人叹为观止，流连忘返。

御道口草原森林风景区居于中国经典自驾路线——国家 1 号风景大道的起点，东部、北部与塞罕坝森林公园相连，西部与内蒙古多伦县接壤，交通便利。这里视野开阔，植被丰富，自古以来就是一处纵马弯弓的天然猎苑，曾是清朝康熙、乾隆年间的皇家避暑、狩猎胜地。

8. 国家一号风景大道

国家一号风景大道东起围场塞罕坝森林小镇，西至丰宁大滩，全长 180 公里。国家一号风景大道是我国首条国字号景观路，是一条连接森林、草原、湿地和花海的风景秀丽的自驾线路。沿途有塞罕坝国家森林公园、御道口风景区、五道沟、滦河神韵、京北第一草原等著名景区。一路上苍翠连绵，绿草如茵，野花芬芳斗艳。这里是云的故乡，水的源头，花的世界，林的海洋。

9. 承德避暑山庄

承德避暑山庄（以下简称避暑山庄）又名"承德离宫"或"热河行宫"，是世界文化遗产、国家 AAAAA 级旅游景区、全国重点文物保护单位、中国四大名园之一。避暑山庄位于河北省承德市中心北部，武烈河西岸一带狭长的谷地上，是清代皇帝夏天避暑和处理政务的场所。

避暑山庄分宫殿区、湖泊区、平原区、山峦区四大部分。避暑山庄始建于1703年。1961年3月，避暑山庄被公布为第一批全国重点文物保护单位，1994年12月，承德避暑山庄被列入《世界遗产名录》。

避暑山庄从康熙四十二年（1703年）至康熙五十二年（1713年），开拓湖区、筑洲岛、修堤岸，随之营建宫殿和宫墙，使避暑山庄初具规模。康熙皇帝选园中佳景以四字为名题写了三十六景。乾隆六年（1741年）至乾隆十九年（1754年），乾隆皇帝对避暑山庄进行了大规模扩建，增建宫殿和多处精巧的大型园林建筑。乾隆仿其祖父康熙，以三字为名又题了三十六景，合称为避暑山庄七十二景。

1961年国务院将避暑山庄及周围寺庙中的普宁寺、普乐寺、普陀宗乘之庙、须弥福寿之庙列为第一批全国重点文物保护单位。从1976～2006年，国务院先后批准实施了三个《避暑山庄外八庙十年整修规划》，明确了以"抢救和整修"为主的保护原则，国家和地方政府相继投入几亿元专项资金用于古建维修和园林整治，并投入大量资金用于文物保护区周围环境的综合整治。

承德避暑山庄的七十二景　避暑山庄是中国三大古建筑群之一，它的最大特色是山中有园，园中有山，大小建筑有120多组，其中康熙以四字组成三十六景，乾隆以三字组成三十六景，这就是避暑山庄著名的七十二景。

康熙朝定名的三十六景　烟波致爽、芝径云堤、无暑清凉、延薰山馆、水芳岩秀、万壑松风、松鹤清樾、云山胜地、四面云山、北枕双峰、西岭晨霞、锤峰落照、南山积雪、梨花伴月、曲水荷香、风泉清听、濠濮间想、天宇咸畅、暖流暄波、泉源石壁、青枫绿屿、莺啭乔木、香远益清、金莲映日、远近泉声、云帆月舫、芳渚临流、云容水态、澄泉绕石、澄波叠翠、石矶观鱼、镜水云岑、双湖夹镜、长虹饮练、甫田丛樾、水流云在。

乾隆朝定名的三十六景　丽正门、勤政殿、松鹤斋、如意湖、青雀舫、绮望楼、驯鹿坡、水心榭、颐志堂、畅远台、静好堂、冷香亭、采菱渡、观莲所、清晖亭、般若相、沧浪屿、一片云、萍香泮、万树园、试马埭、嘉树轩、乐成阁、宿云檐、澄观斋、翠云岩、罨画窗、凌太虚、千尺雪、宁静斋、玉琴轩、临芳墅、知鱼矶、涌翠岩、素尚斋、永恬居。

10. 承德避暑山庄外八庙

外八庙是河北承德避暑山庄东北部八座藏传佛教寺庙的总称。先后于清康熙五十二年（1713）至乾隆四十五年（1780）间陆续建成。当时，北京、承德共有四十座直属理藩院的庙宁，京城三十二座，承德八座，因承德地处北京和长城以外，故称外八庙。外八庙包括溥仁寺、溥善寺（现已不存）、普宁寺、安远庙、普陀宗乘之庙、殊像寺、须弥福寿之庙和广缘寺，是汉、蒙、藏文化交融的典范。承德外八庙建筑雄伟，规模宏大，反映出清代前期建筑技术和建筑艺术的成就。

1982年，外八庙作为河北承德避暑山庄外八庙风景名胜区的组成部分，被国务院批准列入第一批国家级风景名胜区名单。1994年12月，外八庙与避暑山庄一起被列入《世界文化遗产名录》。

11. 磬锤峰国家森林公园

磬锤峰国家森林公园环抱承德市区，与驰名中外的避暑山庄和外八庙风景名胜镶嵌相融，国家AAAA级景区。总面积15.9万亩，距市区约2.5公里。公园自然景观奇特，以千岩竞秀、异峰峥嵘的丹霞地貌著名，温带季风气候，磬锤峰索道为目前全国最长的吊椅式索道。景区内有一挺拔峭立的石柱擎天而立直插云端，石柱高59.42米，其上粗下细，形如洗衣用的棒槌，故康熙皇帝赐名"磬锤峰"，俗称"棒槌山"。磬锤峰半山腰有棵树龄达300余年的桑树，名蒙桑，虽生长在石缝间，却长得枝繁叶茂，结白桑葚。

12. 金山岭长城

金山岭长城，位于河北省承德市滦平县境内，与北京市密云区相邻，距北京市区130公里。金山岭长城始建于明洪武元年（公元1368年），为大将徐达主持修建。隆庆元年（公元1567年）抗倭名将蓟镇总兵官戚继光、蓟辽总督谭纶在徐达所建长城的基础上续建、改建。是万里长城的精华地段，素有"万里长城，金山独秀"之美誉。障墙、文字砖和挡马石是金山岭长城的三绝，素有"摄影爱好者的天堂"之美誉。金山岭长城是全国重点文物保护单位、国家级风景名胜区、国家4A级旅游景区，并列入《世界文化遗产名录》。

金山岭长城西起历史上著名的关口古北口，东至高耸入云的望京楼，全长10.5公里，沿线设有关隘5处，敌楼67座，烽燧3座，因其视野开阔，敌楼密集，景观奇特，建筑艺术精美，军事防御体系健全，保存完好而著称于世。

金山岭海拔700米，登山北观群山似涛，东望司马台水库如镜，南眺密云水库碧波粼粼。长城依山凭险，起伏跌宕于山水之间，形势极为雄奇。尤其此处敌楼密集，构筑精巧，形式多样，是八达岭、山海关、嘉峪关等地长城难以媲美的，为万里长城中正在开发的旅游胜境之一。

金山岭长城作为长城的组成部分于 1987 年列入世界文化遗产，1988 年列入第三批全国重点文物保护单位名单。金山岭长城还是国家级风景名胜区、国家 4A 级旅游景区。"金山岭-司马台长城"被 2010 年第 11 期《中国国家地理》评为中国十大秋色的第七名。文章中写到：长城是世界上最奢侈的山际线，是最唯美的观景台，也是最深刻的历史废墟。看长城之美有太多的角度，它的美，多少文字也难以尽言。

金山岭长城是现保存最完好的一段明长城，被专家称之为明长城之精华。依山设险，凭水置塞，雄城起伏似钢墙铁壁。碉楼林立，如甲兵护卫，"一夫当关，万夫莫开"，以其视野开阔、敌楼密集、建筑防御体系功能奇特而著称于世。

这里的长城构筑复杂，敌楼密布，一般 50～100 米一座，墙体以巨石为基，高 5～8 米，形式多样，各具特色。有砖木结构的，也有砖石结构的，有单层的，也有双层的，既有平顶，也有穹隆顶、船篷顶、四角钻天顶和八角藻井顶，可谓一楼一式，被誉为"万里长城，金山独秀"。金山岭长城的军事防御体系，设有障墙、垛墙、战台、炮台、瞭望台、雷石孔、射孔、挡马墙、支墙和围战墙等，层层设防，可谓固若金汤。登上金山岭长城倾心感受古长城的壮美与雄浑，便可体会一个民族的伟大与豪迈。

这里春天山花烂漫，浓郁飘香；盛夏万木葱茏，云雾缥缈；金秋漫山红遍、层林尽染；严冬银装素裹、白雪皑皑。在这如诗如画的天地间，处处是美景，处处有奇观，实在令人叫绝。

第三篇

食品教育

1. 河北农业大学

河北农业大学是河北省人民政府与教育部、农业农村部、国家林业和草原局共建的省属重点骨干大学，国家大众创业万众创新示范基地，全国深化创新创业教育改革示范高校，教育部卓越工程师、卓越农林人才教育培养计划实施高校，河北省"双一流"建设高校。

学校创建于1902年，是我国最早实施高等农业教育的院校之一，也是河北省建立最早的高等院校，先后经历了直隶农务学堂、直隶高等农业学堂、直隶公立农业专门学校、河北省立农学院、河北农学院、河北农业大学等历史时期。20世纪50年代，学校的森林系、畜牧兽医系、农田水利系参与组建了北京林学院（现北京林业大学）、内蒙古农牧学院（现内蒙古农业大学）、武汉水利水电学院（现与武汉大学合并）。1995年与原河北林学院合并组建为新的河北农业大学。2000年原河北水产学校、原河北畜牧科技学校并入河北农业大学。

百年积淀，河北农业大学形成了鲜明的办学特色。学校坚持"农业教育非实习不能得真谛，非试验不能探精微，实习试验二者不可偏废"的教学原则，秉承"崇德、务实、求是"的校训，开创了享誉全国的"太行山道路"，培育了"艰苦奋斗、甘于奉献、求真务实、爱国为民"的"太行山精神"，多次受到党和国家的肯定与表彰，涌现出了以李保国教授为代表的一批扎根基层、服务"三农"的知名专家教授，成为高等教育的一面旗帜。

学校的学科专业以服务农业现代化的生物应用技术、信息技术、智能装备设计与制造为优势特色，"农、工、管、理、经、文、法、艺术"等多学科交叉融合、协调发展，具备学士、硕士、博士完整的人才培养体系。有8个博士后科研流动站；11个一级学科博士点，1个专业学位博士点；24个一级学科硕士点，12个专业学位硕士点。其中，1个学科列入河北省世界一流学科建设序列，3个学科列入河北省国家一流学科建设序列；有1个国家重点（培育）学科，3个部级重点学科，4个河北省强势特色学科，16个河北省重点学科；农业科学、植物与动物科学2个学科进入ESI全球排名前1%。设有93个本科专业，其中15个国家级一流本科专业建设点，26个省级一流本科专业建设点。先后培养毕业生40多万名，涌现出了一批批兴业英才、学术骨干、管理才俊，如董玉琛、刘旭、杨志峰、赵春江、郭子建等11名院士，塞罕坝优秀毕业生群体，还有许多干事创业的优秀代表。

学校紧紧围绕国家农业重大需求开展科学研究，在承担科技创新项目数量、经费总量和获奖等级、数量上一直名列省内高校前茅。作为依托单位，建有国家级、省部级重点实验室（技术创新中心、基地、试验站、协同创新中心、产业技术研究院等）68个，拥有国家级现代农业产业技术体系专家20名、省级62名。学校始终以服务国家重大战略和区域经济发展为己任，不断深化拓展"太行山道路"，全力服务河北省乡村振兴和农业农村现代化。创建了"太行山农业创新驿站"，引起了社会广泛关注，受到省部领导充分肯定，入选了全国产业扶贫典型案例、全球减贫案例征集活动最佳案例，并在全省推广。广泛开展校地、校企合作，在全省六大生态类型区建立教学、科研、生产"三结合"基地347个，太行山农业创新驿站50个，区域综合试验站9个，现代农业教育科技创新示范基地41个，"十三五"以来，推广新成果、新品种和新技术1000余项，有力促进了地方经济社会发展。

河北农业大学食品科学与工程学科始于1931年，1987年成立食品科学系，2000年成立食品科技学院，拥有该学科一级博士学位授权点和博士后科研流动站，是国家首批一流本科专业建设点，河北省重点建设的一流学科。该学科1985年开始招收本科生，1998年开始招收研究生，2002年入选河北省重点学科，2005年获二级学科博士学位授予权，2017年获一级学科博士学位授予权，2019年获批博士后科研流动站，2019年入选首批国家一流本科专业，是河北省食品科学与工程人才培养的摇篮。

2. 河北科技大学

河北科技大学是河北省重点建设的多科性骨干大学。学校紧紧围绕"致力于人的全面发展，服务于区域经济建设和社会进步"的办学宗旨，坚持"区域性、应用型、国际化"的办学特色定位，抢抓机遇，加快发展。2007年以"优秀"的成绩通过教育部本科教学工作水平评估，2011年入选教育部"卓越工程师教育培养计划"高校。2016年入选河北省重点支持的国家一流大学建设高校。

学校占地面积2760亩，建筑面积80多万平方米，固定资产总值32.5亿元；现有全日制本科生、研究生、留学生共23000多人，教职工2400余人，双聘院士1人、外籍院士2人、百千万人才工程国家级人选2人、享受国务院政府特殊津贴专家、省高端人才、省管优秀专家等各类高层次人才140人次，国家优秀教师2人，省级教学名师45人。

学校设有16个本科专业学院，79个本科专业，25个硕士学位授权一级学科，3个硕士学位授权二级学科，15个专业硕士学位授权类别。学科专业涉及工、理、文、经、管、法、医、教育、艺术等九大门类，与河北省产业转型升级和战略性新兴产业发展高度契合。现有9个省级重点学科，1个省级重点发展学科，河北省世界一流学科建设项目1个，河北省国家一流学科建设项目2个。工程学学科位于ESI世界排名前1%。

学校坚持走与区域社会发展深度融合的特色之路，不断增强科学研究和服务社会能力。学校曾获国家科技进步奖二等奖1项，全军科技进步一等奖1项，全国高等学校技术发明二等奖1项。近五年，承担了国家重点研发计划、科技重大专项课题在内的省部级以上科研课题2000多项，授权专利2500多项，获省部级奖励70余项，其中省部级一等奖5项、二等奖18项，连续三年获得省级自然科学一等奖。学校建有省级以上各类科研平台96个。河北科技大学技术转移中心是科技部认定的"国家技术转移示范机构"，在省内产业聚集区建立了13个技术转移分支机构，与377个地方政府及行业组织、研究单位建立了科技教育合作关系。

河北科技大学食品与生物学院始建于1980年，其前身为河北轻化工学院轻工工程系；1996年更名为河北科技大学轻工工程系；1998年更名为河北科技大学生物科学与工程系；2001年更名为河北科技大学生物科学与工程学院；2021年更名为河北科技大学食品与生物学院。

河北科技大学食品与生物学院设有生物工程、食品科学与工程、生命科学3个教学系，现有生物工程、食品科学与工程、食品质量与安全、生物科学、生物技术5个本科专业，其中食品质量与安全专业为国家级特色专业，食品质量与安全、食品科学与工程和生物工程专业入选河北省一流专业，食品科学与工程专业通过国家工程教育认证。拥有4个硕士学位授权学科及生物与医药专业硕士授权领域，其中生物工程、食品科学与工程、生物学为一级硕士学位授权学科，生物化工为二级硕士学位授权学科。学院建有"河北省发酵技术创新中心""河北省功能食品技术创新中心""河北省生物科学与工程实验教学中心"等省级平台，发酵工程学科为河北省重点学科。

3. 河北科技师范学院

河北科技师范学院是河北省教育部首批全国重点建设职教师资培养培训基地、科技部国家级科技特派员创业培训基地、农业部现代农业技术培训基地、中国科协首批全国科普教育基地。

学校始建于 1941 年，1975 年开始举办高等教育，1977 年开始招收本科生，2006 年获得硕士学位授予权。1949 年昌黎农业职业学校更名为河北昌黎高级农业学校；1958 年河北昌黎高级农业学校升格为昌黎农学院；1960 年昌黎农学院改建为昌黎农业高等专科学校；1962 年昌黎农业高等专科学校改建为河北昌黎高级农业学校；1972 年河北昌黎高级农业学校更名为唐山地区农业学校；1975 年唐山地区农业学校改建为华北农业大学（唐山分校）；1975 年华北农业大学（农机专业）并入华北农业大学（唐山分校）；1977 年华北农业大学（唐山分校）更名为河北农业大学（唐山分校）；1984 年河北农业大学（唐山分校）更名为河北农业大学（昌黎分校）；1985 年河北农业大学（昌黎分校）升格为河北农业技术师范学院；1998 年河北农业技术师范学院更名为河北职业技术师范学院（秦皇岛）；2000 年秦皇岛煤炭工业管理学校并入河北职业技术师范学院；2003 年河北职业技术师范学院（秦皇岛）更名为河北科技师范学院；2006 年秦皇岛教育学院并入河北科技师范学院。

河北科技师范学院现有 7 个省级重点学科和重点发展学科，拥有 6 个学术学位硕士授权一级学科，17 个二级学科的学术学位硕士授权点；5 个专业学位 15 个授权领域。学校设有 75 个本科专业，涵盖农、教育、工、理、文、法、经济、管理、艺术等 9 大学科门类。建有 1 个国家级专业综合改革试点专业，20 个省级一流本科专业建设点，3 个省级本科教育创新高地、6 个省级品牌特色专业。获批教育部首批卓越农林人才教育培养计划改革试点。

河北科技师范学院食品科技学院前身是 1993 年设立的食品工程系，学科建设始于 1987 年建立的农产品贮运与加工专业，2009 年设立食品科技学院。2021 年 4 月获批教育部首批现代产业学院——葡萄酒学院。学院拥有食品科学与工程一级学科学术学位硕士授权点和农业硕士食品安全领域学位硕士授予权。设有食品科学与工程、食品质量与安全、酿酒工程、生物工程 4 个本科专业，有食品科学与工程一级学科硕士点和食品加工与安全等专业领域硕士授权点。

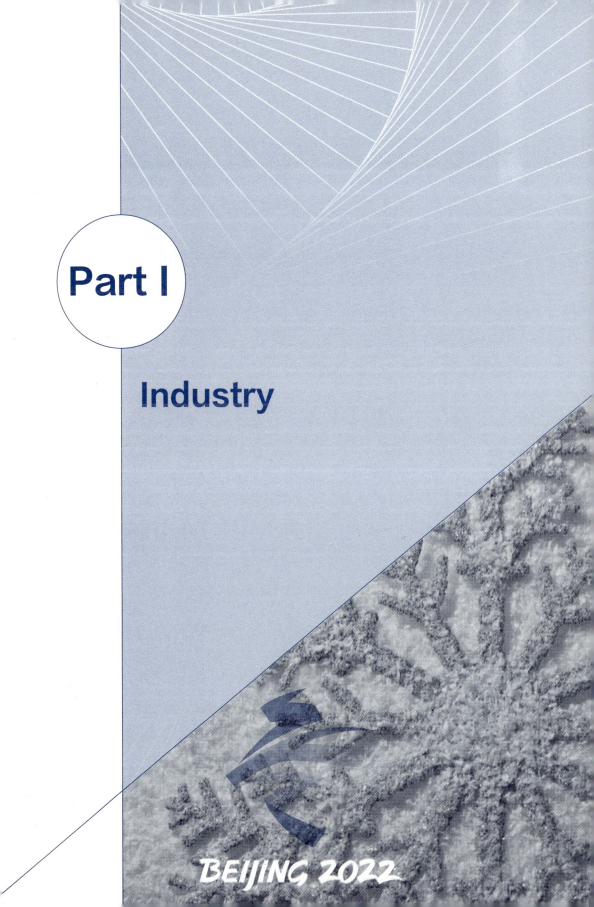

Part I

Industry

BEIJING 2022

Chapter 1
Wine Industry

Overview of wine history

China has a long history of wine brewing. The early Chinese records of wine originated from the Grand Scribe's Record in the Western Han Dynasty. Dawan Commentary Section of Grand Scribe's Record wrote: "Around Wanzhou, syzygium jamboo (the ancient name of grapes) is used as wine. The rich store wine to over 10,000 kilograms, which have been preserved for decades." In the Tang and Song dynasties, poems about wine included Wang Han's "With wine of grapes the cups of jade would glow at night, Drinking to pipa songs, we are summoned to fight. (translated by Xu Yuanchong) ", Bai Juyi's "The Qiang flute blows willows, Yanji drinks syzygium jamboo (another ancient name for grapes) wine", Lu You's "Like pouring glistening wine; like holding heavy mink and fur coat" and other eternal swan songs. During the King and Yuan dynasties, Yuan Yishan's famous article "Verses and essays of grape wine" recorded the brewing process of wine in detail: "Smashed grape pulp is sealed and buried, and the wine was fermented quickly; The storage time is longer, the taste of the wine would be better. Some wine is stored for thousands of years." The Jiahu site in Wuyang County, Henan Province, about 7,000-9,000 years old. Chinese and American scientists found that people in Jiahu site started brewing wine at least 9,000 years ago. China might be the first country in the world to brew wine, and this result of the research pushed forward the artificial brewing history of wine in the world by 3,000 years.

Modern brewing history of Chinese wine began in the 18th year of Guangxu period in the Qing Dynasty (1892). Mr. Zhang Bishi, founded Changyu Grape Brewing Company in Yantai, officially opening the era of industrial brewing of Chinese wine, bottling in castles 18 years earlier than Bordeaux in France. Since the 20th year of Guangxu period (1894) in Qing Dynasty, Changyu has built an underground wine cellar in the winery. It took 11 years to rebuild the wine cellar three times and was officially completed in the early winter of 1905, which means that Changyu has already realized "bottling in the winery" at least in 1906. In 1907, the Business Official once recorded: "The wine cellar was built successfully only after Zhen Xun (another name of Zhang Bishi, founder of Changyu) changed the map several times. When it was successful, engineers from all over the world came to visit and were surprised to say that the Chinese mastered such great skill." It appeared on the international stage 61 years earlier than Napa Valley. At the 1915 San Francisco World Expo, Chengyu's "Red Rose Wine", "Riesling White Wine", "Kaya Brandy" and "Vermouth" from China won four gold medals, shocking the world.

Wine Classifications   Many means can be used for wines classification including by its color, sugar content and wine-brewing technique.

According to the color of wine:

Red wine: Red grape varieties are fermented with skins, and their colors are purplish red, ruby red, pomegranate red, etc.

Rose wine: In recent years, rose wine is also quite popular in the global market. The color of rose wine is between red and white.

White wine: White grape or red grape is made for wine without skin. After fermentation, the wine is lemon yellow or gold, clear and transparent with a rich fruit aroma, unique flavor.

Classified by sugar content:

Dry wine: Also known as dry wine, the sugar in raw materials (grape juice) is completely converted into alcohol, and the residual sugar content is below 4g/L. When drinking, it doesn't taste sweet but sour, clear and refreshing.

Semi-dry wine: sugar content is between 4-12g/L.

Semi-sweet wine: The sugar content is between 12-45g/L, and the taste is slightly sweet. It is a variety consumed much more in Japan and the United States, and is also very popular in China.

Sweet wine: The sugar content of wine is over 45g/L, and it tastes obviously sweet when drinking.

Classified by wine-brewing technique:

Calm wine: Wine fermented entirely from grapes without adding extra alcohol and spices.

Sparkling wine: It has carbon dioxide bubbles left in it. Such a wine is often used for celebration. The most familiar sparkling wine is French champagne. And other wines are Spain's Cava and Italy's Prosecco and Moscato d'Asti, though sparkling wines are produced all over the world.

Overview of grape industry in Huailai county

Huailai grape cultivation has a history of thousands of years. According to the *Records of General Information in Xuanhua*, Huailai grapes are used for court tributes. According to the fruit category of *Huailai County Records*, there are two kinds of grapes in Huailai, which were written in the fifty-first year of Emperor Kangxi of Qing Dynasty (1712), indicating that grapes were planted in Huailai 300 years ago and planting area was quite large.

In 1993, the sacrifices from the tomb owners of "Xiabali Liao Dynasty Mural Tombs", Zhang Shiqing, Zhang Shiben, Zhang Wenzao and Zhang Kuangzheng, excavated by Hebei Institute of Cultural Relics and Xuanhua District Cultural Protection Institute of Zhangjiakou City together. All contained dried grape seeds, which were sent to Institute of Botany, Chinese Academy of Sciences for identification and identified as Eurasian grapes. It shows that Xuanhua grapes have been enjoyed by the generations of "Zhang's Family" in Liao Dynasty. Zhang Shiqing was a senior official in Liao Dynasty, who checked Imperial Academy and supervised the censor. It was end in the sixth years (1117) in Yuan-qing period, which shows that the grape cultivation in this producing area enjoys a history of more than 900 years.

According to research, the earliest introduction and cultivation of Xuanhua grape might be in Tang Daizong period (AD 762-779), In Wuzhou City (Xuanhua City) of Tang Dynasty, the secretariat Liu Peng was stationed in Wuzhou. Because of no war, soldiers and civilians were organized to reclaim land, build gardens and plant chestnut fruits near Wuzhou. The officers and men of the army were recruited from Chang'an and Luoyang. They introduced grapes and fruits from the Central Plains area for trial, and planted in the military camps and temples, which has a cultivation history of more than 1,200 years.

After the founding of New China, the brewing of Huailai wine began in Shacheng Winery. In 1960, a wine workshop was built in Shacheng Winery with an annual output of 2000 tons, using longan grapes as the main raw material to produce red and white sweet wines, which sold well all over the country. In 1976, the first batch of dry white wines in New China were developed in Shacheng Winery. In 1978, "Research on New Dry White Wine Technique" was listed as a key scientific research project by the Ministry of Light Industry. In 1979, Shacheng Winery won the National Gold Award for Dry White Wine, and in 1983, it won the Silver Award at the 14th International Wine and Spirits Competition in London, England. It is the first time that Chinese wine products won awards abroad after New China's founding. "Research on New Technique of Dry White Wine" won the second prize of National Science and Technology Progress Award. Such an achievement has been fully popularized to the wine industry and is still in use today. The transformation of wine from sweet to dry in China began in that time.

After more than 40 years of development, Huailai County has an grape planting area of 120,000 mu (19768.43 acres), including 65,000 mu (10707.9 acres) of wine grapes and 55,000 mu (9060.53 acres) of fresh grapes with an annual output of 131,000 tons of grapes. Huailai County was named "National Grape Standardization Planting Demonstration County" by the Standardization Administration of the People's Republic of China, and "Shacheng Wine" was listed as a national geographical indication product by the State Administration of Quality Supervision. There are 41 wine processing enterprises in the county, including COFCO Great Wall Wine Co., Ltd., Great Wall Sungod Winery, Sino-French Manor, Rongchen Manor, Amethyst Manor and Noble Manor, producing 150,000 tons of wine every year. It has built more than 30 famous brands such as "Great Wall", "Domaine Franco-Chinois", "Amethyst" and "Kunjue", and won more than 800 famous wine awards at home and abroad.

1. China Great Wall Wine Co., Ltd.

China Great Wall Wine Co., Ltd., located in Shacheng Town, Huailai County, Hebei Province, is a wholly-owned subsidiary of COFCO, one of the world's top 500 companies.

The history of China Great Wall Wine Co., Ltd. (hereinafter referred to as company) is traced back to the "Yuchengming" tank room. In 1914, the "Boiled Red Wine" (Mulled wine) brewed by the "Yuchengming" tank room won the Panama Gold Award at the International Famous Wine Competition. In 1949, a local state-owned Sha Cheng Winery was established on the basis of six private wine-brewing tanks such as Yuchengming. In 1960, A wine-brewing workshop with an annual output of 2000 tons was built in Sha Cheng Winery. On August 1, 1983, China Great Wall Wine Co., Ltd. was jointly established by China National Cereals, Oils And Foodstuffs Import And Export Corporation (COFCO), Yuanda International Group Co., Limited, and Great Wall Brewing Company. As a Sino-foreign joint venture, Zhangjiakou Changcheng Brewery (Group) Co., Ltd. contributed all its wine industry assets (center, technology, equipment, plant, personnel, etc.), and those were injected into the new joint venture company. In 2003, China Great Wall Wine Co., Ltd. becomes a wholly-owned subsidiary of COFCO. Great Wall Wine has a history of 107 years since "Red Boiled Wine" brewed by "Yuchengming" tank room got an award in 1914.

By the end of 2020, the company has a registered capital of CNY 180 million (USD 27.77 million), floor area of 208,000 square meters, a building area of 88,000 square meters, total assets of CNY 976 million (USD 150.58 million) and fixed assets of CNY 749 million (USD 115.56 million). The company produces 88,000 tons of wine every year, stores 100,000 tons of wine and stores 1 million boxes of finished wine, with a daily output of 200,000 bottles per shift and a daily delivery capacity of 70,000 boxes. It has 6,526 oak barrels and more than 1,200 advanced production equipment of squeezing, fermentation, wine storage, filtration and packaging. Among 312 employees, 90 of them get a college degree or above, 10 members of National Liquor Judge Committee, 23 national qualified sommeliers and 11 national qualified winemakers.

The company has national, provincial, and ministerial R&D platforms such as the National Certified Enterprise Technology Center, the Key Laboratory of Wine Grape Processing of the Ministry of Agriculture and Rural Affairs and the Hebei Wine Technology R&D Center. It has successively completed two scientific research projects: "New Technology Research of Dry White Wine" of the former Ministry of Light Industry and "Development of Champagne Sparkling Wine Production Technology" of National "Seventh Five-Year Plan" project, and developed the first bottle of dry white wine and champagne wine in China, filling the domestic gap. In 1986, "Research on New Technique of Dry White Wine" won the first prize of scientific and technological progress of the Ministry of Light Industry, In 1987, "Research on New Technique of Dry White Wine" won the second prize of the National Scientific and Technological Progress. In 1990, "Development of Champagne Sparkling Wine Production Technology" won the third prize of Scientific and Technological Progress of the Ministry of Light Industry. In 2005, "Establishment of Great Wall Manor Model and Research and Application of Key Technologies of Manor Wine" won the second prize of National Scientific and Technological Progress.

Great Wall Wine is a pioneer following the international standards to brew and produce wine in China, and it is the first brand of Chinese wine. In 2004, the "Great Wall" is recognized by the State Administration for Industry and Commerce, as a well-known Chinese trademark. Great Wall's famous products covers Star Series, Great Wall Terroir Series, Great Wall Sungod Winery Series, etc. All of those have won the highest prizes at various international professional wine assessment such as Paris, Brussels and London for many times. Great Wall

Dry White wine won the National Gold Award in 1979, and won the Silver Award at the 14th International Liquor Show in London, England in 1983. People's Daily published "Chinese wine has got the highest honor of the world in recent 70 years", and successively won the Gold Award at Madrid, Spain and Paris, France in 1984 and 1986 respectively. In 2019, Five-Star Dry Red wine won the IWC London Special Gold Award again, which was the first product in China to win such an honor, and Five-Star Dry Red achieved the International Gold Award. Great Wall wine has won the international, national, ministerial and provincial gold, silver and bronze medals and the titles of high-quality products for more than 300 times. And its quality has reached the international advanced level. Its products are sold all over the country and exported to more than 20 countries and regions such as Britain, Germany, Italy, Japan and Hong Kong, and are praised as "the representative of oriental wines" by European and American experts.

The company's original star-rated product is one of the best series product in the wine industry, and Five-star Dry Red wine has become a star-level super single product, which is honored as banquet wine. With its outstanding quality, Great Wall wine has always been used by those important departments such as Diaoyutai State Guesthouse, Great Hall of the People, Chinese Embassies abroad and Air China. It is also the exclusive wine supplier for Beijing Olympic Games, the only designated wine for Boao Forum for Asia, the logo product of Beijing Asian Games, the designated wine for Shanghai World Expo and Guangzhou Asian Games, and frequently appears on the state banquet tables such as G20 China Summit, "the belt and road initiative" Summit Forum, BRICS Summit, Shanghe Summit and APEC Meeting. Over the past 40 years, it has appeared in more than 800 national level banquets. In 2004, Great Wall Wine was the only Chinese wine brand listed in Gallup's "Top List of Luxury Brands in the 21st Century". Nowadays, "State Banquet and Sharing the Great Wall" has been deeply rooted in people's hearts and become a well-known representative brand of Chinese wine.

The company is a key leading enterprise of agricultural industrialization, high-tech enterprise, technological innovation demonstration enterprise, leading wine enterprise, assured wine project demonstration enterprise, a national contract-abiding and trustworthy enterprise, and a national advanced unit of spiritual civilization construction. And it won the Quality Award of Hebei Provincial Government.

Events

In 2020, Great Wall Five-Star Red became the official cooperative wine of Chinese women's volleyball team.

From 2009 to 2019, Great Wall Wine has appeared in the Boao Forum for Asia for eleven years.

In 2019, Great Wall Five-Star Cabernet Sauvignon Dry Red wine won the first special prize of Chinese Red Wine in London International Wine Challenge (IWC), which is the only one in Asia and the pioneer in China.

In 2018, the Technology Center was appraised as the Key Laboratory of Wine Grape Processing of the Ministry of Agriculture.

In 2017, Great Wall Five-Star Dry Red Wine won the Gold Award in Asian Quality Competition, the Quality Award of Hebei Provincial Government, the official designated wine of "the belt and road initiative" International Cooperation Summit Forum and BRICS Meeting.

In 2016, Chateau Mingzhu Golden Star Red wine was successfully listed as a senior sponsor and designated product of G20 Hangzhou Summit.

In 2015, Great Wall Sungod Winery officially operated independently.

In 2014, as the official designated wine of the APEC meeting and the Asia Info Summit, it appeared in the Sochi Winter Olympics and was used to welcome the US First Lady Michelle as a banquet wine. It has been certified by ISO9001 \ FSSC22000 \ ISO14001 \ OHSAS18001 management system, and appeared in China House of Sochi Winter Olympics.

In 2013, the company started the new finished product warehouse project, covering an area of 72.44 mu (11.93 acres), it appeared as banquet wine to entertain Icelandic Prime Minister and Mexican President Niah at the G20 Summit in St. Petersburg, Russia.

In 2011, the Technology Center passed the National (CNAS) Accredited Laboratory Certification and the wine appeared in the welcome banquet of APEC Business Advisory Council.

In 2010, the only wine designated for the Shanghai World Expo and the Guangzhou Asian Games and the wine was also used for the banquet of the Forum on China-Africa Cooperation.

In 2009, the Great Wall Sungod Winery was established on the basis of Great Wall Manor, and the technology center was recognized as "Hebei Wine Engineering Technology Research Center". Great Wall wine was used for a banquet to welcome US President Barack Obama.

In 2008, traditional sparkling wine was used for celebrating that the Olympic flame reached the summit of Mount Everest successfully. Chateau SunGod Great-Wall 2008 Reserve Limited Release Red was permanently collected by Lausanne Museum in Switzerland, serving at the welcoming banquet for US President George W. Bush, IOC President Rogge and APEC Finance Ministers' Meeting.

In 2007, Great Wall Wine was selected as one of 1550 the top 500 Chinese brands in 2006 with a brand value of CNY 12.587 billion The Technology Center was designated as the "National Certified Enterprise Technology Center" by five national ministries and commissions, including the National Development and Reform Commission, the Ministry of Science and Technology, the Ministry of Finance, the General Administration of Customs and the State Taxation Bureau.

In 2006, Great Wall Wine was designated as the exclusive wine supplier for Beijing 2008 Olympic Games.

In 2005, "The Establishment of Great Wall Manor Model and the Research and Application of Key Technologies of Manor Wine" won the second prize of National Science and Technology Progress Award, and V·S·O·P Brandy won the great gold medal of London Wine and spirits International competition.

In 2004, the "Great Wall" was recognized as "China's well-known trademark" by the State Administration for Industry and Commerce, serving as banquet wine to welcome French President Chirac.

In 2003, China Great Wall Wine Co., Ltd. became a wholly-owned subsidiary of COFCO.

In 2002, it won the title of "China Famous Brand, National Inspection-Free Product" and passed the certification of "National Key Leading Enterprise of Agricultural Industrialization".

In 1999, the second phase of the national "Double Plus" project was completed, with a production capacity of 50,000 tons, and star-rated products were officially listed.

In 1997, China's first international standard brandy (V·S·O·P) was successfully developed, and the research center was recognized as "Hebei Wine Technology Development Center" by Hebei Light Industry Department.

In 1996, the first phase of the national "Double Plus Project" was completed, and the production capacity was expanded to 10,000 tons. The first one among the wine industry passed the ISO9002 quality system certification in China, and Great Wall Manor was established based on the technology center.

In 1995, the research center was recognized as the first "provincial enterprise technology centers" in Hebei Province by Hebei Economic and Trade Commission.

In 1994, the Scientific Research Center of China Great Wall Wine Co., Ltd. was established.

In 1992, Great Wall Champagne sparkling wine won the special gold medal in the first Bangkok International Wine Fair and the gold medal in International Food Fair in Hongkong.

In 1990, the champagne sparkling wine in China was successfully developed and became the "famous special product" of Beijing Asian Games.

In 1987, "Research on New Technique of Dry White Wine" won the second prize of National Science and Technology Progress Award, and champagne sparkling wine was used in the banquet for former US President Carter.

In 1986, Chinese wines won the gold medal at the 12th International Food Fair in Paris, France, and the wine was served for the Great Hall of the People and the banquet for Queen Elizabeth II.

In 1984, Great Wall Dry White wine won the gold medal in the third International Alcoholic Beverage Competition in Madrid, Spain.

In 1983, China Great Wall Wine Co., Ltd. was established. Great Wall Dry White wine won the Silver Award of the 14th London Wine and Spirits International Competition.

In 1979, Great Wall Dry White wine won the National Gold Award in China.

Contact Information

Address: Shacheng Town, Huailai County, Hebei Province

Tel: 86-313-6232216

2. COFCO Greatwall Huaxia Wine (Huailai) Co., Ltd.

COFCO Greatwall Huaxia Wine (Huailai) Co., Ltd. (hereinafter referred to as Greatwall Chateau Sungod) is located in the east of Dongshuiquan Village, Shacheng Town, Huailai County, Zhangjiakou City, Hebei Province, about 100 kilometers far away from the northwest of Beijing, located in Huaizhuo Basin formed by the Yanshan and Taihang Mountains, and on the left bank of the intersection of Sanggan River and Yanghe River. In 1978, led by the former Ministry of Light Industry and jointly inspected by five ministries and commissions of China, the first experimental field of Chinese wine was established in Huaizhuo Basin, where China's first bottle of dry wine was born, which opened a glorious road for GreatWall Chateau SunGod to be a well-known eastern winery in the world.

The vineyard of COFCO GreatWall Chateau SunGod covers an area of 1,122.5 mu (184.92 acres) and is planted with more than ten kinds of famous wine grapes, such as Riesling, Sauvignon Blanc, Semillon, Chardonnay, Chenin Blanc and other white grapes, with red grape varieties such as Cabernet Sauvignon, Syrah, Merlot, Pinot Noir and Zinfandel, with brandy grape varieties such as Ugni Blanc, Folle Blanche and Colombard, and with grape varieties for brewing sweet white wine such as Traminer. In recent years, new wine-brewing grape varieties have been introduced including Petit Manseng, Malbec and Petit Verdot and rootstock grape varieties. The grape plantation of Great Wall Sungod Winery is the earliest vineyard with large scale, old tree, complete varieties and high starting point in China.

GreatWall Chateau SunGod has a production workshop of 9,300 square meters and a wine cellar of 8,200 square meters, an annual fermentation capacity of 1,000 tons and a wine storage capacity of 4,000 tons. It is equipped with 3,000 bottles/hour automatic production line. It also has a scientific research building of 2,781 square meters, a modern nursery stock breeding center of 3,000 square meters and modern analytical equipment. GreatWall Chateau SunGod products have reached the domestic and international advanced level in terms of product research and development, composition research, quality control, quality assurance, ecological environment protection and tourism.

GreatWall Chateau SunGod has 112 workers, including 25 professional and technical personnel, 5 national judges, 6 national winemakers and 12 national sommeliers. The main products are high-end dry red wine such as Cabernet Sauvignon, Syrah, Merlot and so on; Riesling dry white wine and other high-end dry white products; Gewurztraminer sweet white wine, traditional sparkling wine, brandy and other wine products.

In 2005, "The Establishment of Great Wall Manor Model and the Research and Application of Key Technologies of Wine" won the second prize of national scientific and technological progress. In 2007, it passed the National Good Agricultural Practices (GAP) certification. In 2012, it was awarded the title of "Leading Forestry Enterprise in Hebei Province" by the Forestry Department of Hebei Province. In 2015, it was recognized by the Hebei Provincial Department of Agriculture as the "Top Ten Modern Leisure Agricultural Parks in Hebei Province" and became the "Pilot Project for the Integration of Rural Primary, Secondary and Tertiary Industries". In 2016, it was appraised as "Key Leading Enterprise of Agricultural Industrialization in Zhangjiakou City". In 2016, it was appraised as a five-star leisure agricultural park in Hebei Province. In addition, scientific research platforms such as National Accredited Enterprise Technology Center, National Accredited Laboratory, Key Laboratory of Wine Grape Processing of the Ministry of Agriculture and Rural Affairs, and Hebei Provincial Wine Engineering Technology Research Center have been set up in the winery.

GreatWall Chateau SunGod products won the gold medals in Concours Mondial de Bruxelles for five times, in China Alcoholic Drinks Association 'Qing-Zhuo' Awards twice, and in the Asian Quality Competition twice from 2010 to 2017.

Events

In 2019, the designated wine for the 8th China Listed Companies Summit Forum and 2019 Venture 50.

In 2018, the designated wine for Beijing Summit of the Forum on China-Africa Cooperation, and the Qingdao Summit for the Shanghai Cooperation Organization.

In 2017, the designated wine for Xiamen BRICS Meeting, and the "the belt and road initiative" Summit Forum.

In 2016, the designated wine for G20 Summit.

From 2009 to 2019, the designated wine for Boao Forum for Asia for eleven years.

In 2009, the Great Wall Chateau SunGod Dry Red in 2002 was a special wine for state banquets and the only designated wine for the 2010 Shanghai World Expo.

In 2008, Chateau SunGod GreatWall 2008 Reserve Limited Release Red was permanently collected by Lausanne Museum in Switzerland.

In 2006, it was the first exclusive supplier of Olympic Games among Chinese wine enterprises.

In 2005, "The Establishment of GreatWall Chateau SunGod Model and the

Research and Application of Key Technologies of its wine" won the second prize of National Science and Technology Progress Award.

Contact Information

Address: East of Dongshuiquan Village, Shacheng Town, Huailai County, Hebei Province

Tel: 86-313-6840294

3. Huailai County Nobility Chateau Winery Co., Ltd.

Huailai County Nobility Chateau Winery Co., Ltd. (hereinafter referred to as Chateau) is located outside the Tumubao Village on the side of Guanting Lake in Huaizhuo Basin, adjacent to the Great Wall Chateau SunGod. It is a winery integrating grape planting and wine brewing. In 2000, 1800 mu (296.53 acres) of a famous vineyard were established according to international standards, and special wine grape varieties such as Cabernet Sauvignon, Merlot, Syrah and Marselan are cultivated. At present, the age of vines is 20 years, and it is the period of brewing high-quality wines. In 2008, the winery has a building area of 6,500 square meters, according to the wine industry standards, including 3,800 square meters of production workshop and 1,000 square meters of wine cellar, with an annual production capacity of more than 300 tons. In 2009, with a registered capital of CNY 11 million, Huailai County Nobility Chateau Winery Co., Ltd. was established and Kunjue dry red wines were launched; Longan dry white wine with the characteristics of Shacheng production regions; Merlot semi-dry, semi-sweet, original ecological 5-degree sweet rose wines.

Events

In 2019, he won the Silver Award of China International Marselan Wine Challenge and the Excellence Award of the 5th China Fine Wine Challenge (DSW).

In 2018, Kunjue Longan Dry White Wine won the Quality Product Award.

In 2017, Kunjue Longan Dry White Wine won the Quality Award in China Rating System for Global Wine such as "Hexi Corridor Cup" and "Shangri-La

Cup" International Wine Competition.

In 2016, a postgraduate internship base was jointly established with Hebei Agricultural University; Kunjue Longan Dry White Wine won the Silver Award of "The Most Potential Chinese Wine of the Year" at the China Wine Summit; It was recognized as a high-level innovation team by Zhangjiakou Municipal Party Committee and People's Government.

In 2015, Kunjue Reserve Cabernet Sauvignon Dry Red Wine won the Quality Award in the international Leading Wine Quality Awards; it was also recognized as the international cooperation base of Hebei Province.

In 2014, Cabernet Sauvignon Dry Red Wine won the Quality Award in the international Leading Wine Quality Awards; The brand "Kunjue" was rated as a famous trademark in Hebei Province and won the Hebei Quality Product Award.

In 2013, Cabernet Sauvignon dry wine won a special award in the "international Leading Wine Quality Awards" and the Bronze Award of the Top 100 Wines.

In 2012, the research and development project of Merlot Rose Wine-Brewing Technology won the third prize of provincial scientific and technological progress; Quality Award of National Rose Wine Challenge; It was rated as Chinese Charming Winery of the "Wine in China".

In 2011, Kunjue wine products won the Silver Award of the first Beijing-Tianjin Food Industry Exhibition; the education and training base of Huailai Nobility Chateau Wine Co., Ltd. was established with Shaanxi University of Science and Technology.

In 2010, it passed ISO 9000: 2000 quality management system certification.

Contact Information

Address: Tumu Village, Tumu Town, Huailai County, Hebei Province

Tel: 86-313-6802256

4. Domaine Franco Chinois Wine Co., Ltd.

The predecessor of Domaine Franco Chinois Wine Co., Ltd. (hereinafter referred to as Domaine Franco Chinois) is a Grape Planting and Wine Brewing Demonstration Farm. Founded in 1999, it is a government agricultural cooperation project jointly organized and implemented by the Ministry of Agriculture of China, Hebei Provincial Government, French Ministry of Agriculture and French National Wine Industry Organization (ONIVINS).

Domaine Franco-Chinois witnesses the pursuit of quality by Chinese and French winemakers. In 1999, the agricultural ministers of China and France formally signed the Protocol on Establishing Sino-French Grape Planting and Wine Brewing Demonstration Farm in Paris. In 2000, "Sino-French Demonstration Farm" was officially built, and strived to make a demonstration for Chinese wine industry. In 2001, the "Sino-French Demonstration Farm" was officially completed with16 grape varieties including Marselan and Petit Manseng and a complete set of wine-making equipment introduced from France, and it started to brew wine in 2003. In 2005, "Sino-French Demonstration Farm" was officially renamed as "Domaine Franco-Chinois".

In 2010, Domaine Franco-Chinois was a winery owned by Canaan Investment Group and was a sister winery with its neighbor Canaan Winery. Domaine Franco-Chinois is located in Donghuayuan Town, Huailai County, with a registered capital of RMB 140 million. The winery covers 33 hectares, the vineyard planting area is 23 hectares, and the annual output of wine is 50,000-60,000 bottles.

Events

In 2021, Domaine Franco Chinois East Garden Dry Red wine 2015 won the gold medal of China Wine Summit.

In 2020, Domaine Franco Chinois Petit Manseng Sweet White wine 2015 won the gold medal in China Producing Areas of Bob Best of the Best and Decanter World Wine Awards.

In 2019, Domaine Franco Chinois Reserve Dry Red wine 2014 won the gold medal in the International Wine Challenge.

In 2015, Domaine Franco Chinois Reserve Marselan Dry Red wine 2012 won the gold medal in Berliner Wein Trophy (BWT).

Contact Information

Address: Donghuayuan Town, Huailai County, Hebei Province

Tel: 86-313-6849666

5. Huailai Rongchen Vineyard Co., Ltd.

Huailai Rongchen Vineyard Co., Ltd. (hereinafter referred to as Huailai Rongchen Vineyard), located in Huailai, Hebei Province, is a Sino-US joint venture integrating grape planting, brewing, marketing and sightseeing. It was founded in 1997 with a registered capital of RMB 64 million (USD 9.86 million) and an area of 3,000 mu (494.21 acres). In March 2001, the Vineyard was identified by UNESCO as the "Contact Center of International Rural Education Research and Training Center". The vineyard adopts controlled cultivation techniques (the yield per mu is controlled below 500kg) to stabilize the grape yield and improve the grape quality. The Rongchen Mannor includes three parts: vineyard, Rongchen Winery and Rongchen Vineyard Tourist Area.

Red grape varieties such as Cabernet Sauvignon and Merlot, and White grape varieties such as Chardonnay are planted in vineyards. All of those grapes are middle and late maturing varieties, and have achieved good performance under the natural climate conditions and soil water quality conditions in Huaizhuo Basin. 2000 is the first year of fruit hanging in vineyard grapes. After maturity, the sugar content of grapes reaches 195-226g/L, which is the best raw material for producing high-quality wines.

Rongchen Winery is located 1 km east of the neighbor vineyard, adjacent to it. The main building is European style, including a joint workshop, a filling workshop, a wine cellar, a sewage treatment station, an office building and a dormitory building, etc.

Rongchen Vineyard Tourist Area is located in the vineyard, near the vineyard lake, covering 4 hectares. The sparkling lake is surrounded by mountains. Its beautiful scenery is with four distinct seasons. The Vineyard has Central Plains

Resort and Yongding River Canyon rafting in the west, Woniu Mountain Summer Resort in the north, Tianmo Park, Kangxi Grassland and Longqing Gorge in the east, which is a totally fairyland on earth. Guo Moruo once praised "South China scenery crossing the Great Wall". In April 2004, Rongchen Vineyard was rated as a national agricultural eco-tourism demonstration site and a provincial AA-level tourist area.

Events

In 2005, Cabernet Sauvignon Dry Red Wine won the gold award and Chardonnay Dry White Wine won the silver medal at the London Wine International Competition (Beijing).

In 2003, at the wine tasting organized by China International Food Industry Association in Shihezi City, Xinjiang, Rongchen Vineyard dry red and dry white wines both won the highest honor and quality products Awards.

In 2002, the wine tasting competition is held in Yantai, and 60 domestic wine experts adopted blind tasting method. Among 45 kinds of wines from more than 40 wineries, Rongchen Vineyard dry red wine won the first prize.

In 2001, Rongchen Vineyard Dry White Wine won the first prize and Rongchen Vineyard Dry Red wine won the second prize in China at the 4th Annual Wine & Food Experience at Hilton Beijing.

In 2000, Rongchen Vineyard began to brew the first batch of wines with its own high-quality raw materials. In the production process, the new technology showed the characteristics of grapes totally in wines. On April 27, 2001, opening celebration of Rongchen Vineyard wine was held in Beijing Great Wall Hotel.

Contact Information

Address: Xiaoqiying Village, Xiaonan Xinbao Township, Huailai, Hebei

Tel: 86-313-6215336

6. Hebei Shacheng Jiahe Winery Co., Ltd.

Hebei Shacheng Jiahe Winery Co., ltd. (Jiahe Winery) is located in Jiahe

Village, Sangyuan Town, Huailai County. The company was established in 2004 with a production capacity of 6000 tons. Both enterprise managers and ordinary employees of Jiahe Winery adheres to their belief, "quality is the key of enterprise survival". The company has successively passed certification of QS, ISO9001 quality management system and HACCP system, safety production standardization, wine industry access conditions audit, etc. It also has won the title of high-quality enterprise in Hebei Province and in Zhangjiakou City for more than one time. In 2015, Jiahe Winery was listed on the incubator board of Shijiazhuang Stock Exchange.

In 2015, Jiahe Winery Co., ltd. is taken over by the daughter of the founder of the enterprise. She returned from Bordeaux Wine Business School in France in 2014. With the broad vision, she has a higher requirements and innovative ideas for the quality of Jiahe Winery and the design of products. Thus, she opened the road of Jiahe Winery culture. Relying on professional wine brewing and wine tasting experts, senior art designers and excellent wood art creative talents, the company has reached the intention of school-enterprise cooperation with many art colleges in Beijing. This injected young and fresh creative teams and design philosophy into the company, and provided customers with all-round, fashionable and personalized products and professional innovative services. In 2019, Jiahe Winery Merlot 2017, Cabernet Sauvignon 2017 and "Good time" dry white blend were recognized by the wine industry and witnessed by awards. In 2019, Jiahe Winery was recognized as a high-tech enterprise in Hebei Province.

Contact Information

Address: Jiahe Village, Sangyuan Town, Huailai County, Hebei Province

Tel: 86-313-6800119

7. Hebei Martin Wine Co., Ltd.

Hebei Martin Wine Co., Ltd. (Martin Winery) was established in 1997, covering 30 mu (4.94 acres) and a building area of more than 10000 square meters. The winery is located in Sangyuan Town, Huailai County, Zhangjiakou

City, Hebei Province. It has two wine production lines. The winery wine production line adopts advanced classifier equipment, producing 300 tons of high-end winery wine annually, and the other production line has an annual output of 5000 tons of wine. There are 1000 square meters of underground wine cellars.

Martin Winery has its own wine-brewing base of more than 500 mu (32.95 acres), planted with Cabernet Sauvignon, Cabernet Gernischet, Pinot Noir, Merlot, Marselan, Tempranillo, Chardonnay, Riesling, Petit Manseng and other wine grape varieties. The wines have won numerous awards in competitions at home and abroad, and have been exported to Britain and Austria many times. The company is open to industrial tourism, and can receive teams of 20-30 people to visit and taste wine.

Events

In 2021, it won three awards in IWSC International Wine and Spirits Competition.

In 2020, Marselan Dry Red wine won the Platinum Award in the International Leading Wine/Spirits Quality Awards.

In 2019, It became the executive vice president unit of the Working Committee of Fine Wine Union of China National Association for Liquor and Spirits Circulation. In the same year, Merlot Dry Red wine, Chateau Reserve Dry Red wine and Longan Dry White wine won gold medals in Hebei Wine Competition of China respectively. Marselan Dry Red wine and Petite Sirah Dry Red wine won the top 10 wines in China of the year, and the winery won the title "the most popular fine wine chateau in China of the year".

In 2018, It became a member of the Fine Wine Union of China National Association for Liquor and Spirits Circulation the Fine Wine. In the same year, Marselan Dry Red won the gold medal in Concours Mondial de Bruxelles (CMB). Chardonnay Dry White wine won the Bronze medal in the Decanter World Wine Awards (DWWA).

In 2017, it passed the certification trademark of Chinese winery wine, and was the first line of enterprises in China to legally use the certificated trademark of Chinese winery wine. At the same time, it became the council member of China Chateau Tour Union. In the same year, Petite Sirah Dry Red wine and Longan Dry White wine won the Silver Award in Decanter World Wine Awards, and Chardonnay Dry White wine won the Gold Award for Quality in China Fine Wine Challenge.

In 2016, Cabernet Sauvignon Dry Red wine was shortlisted for the Master Taste wine of Shanghai Wine Summit, and Petite Sirah Dry Red won the gold medal of Belt and Road Wine and Spirit Competition.

In 2014, Martin Winery wines passed the certification of "Shacheng Wine", a national geographical indication product.

In 2012, It became a member of China Alcoholic Drinks Association.

Contact Information

Address: Sanyuan Town, Huailai County, Hebei Province

Tel: 86-313-6870326

8. Hebei Shacheng Villa Wine Co., Ltd.

Founded in 1999, Hebei Shacheng Villa Wine Co., Ltd. is located in Shacheng grape producing area of China with the advanced fermentation, storage and filling equipment, wine cellar and excellent grape vineyard. The company passed ISO9001 international quality management system certification in 2006, HACCP system certification in 2011 and the national geographical indication products certification in 2014.

Product varieties: dry red wine, dry white wine, rose wine and sweet white wine.

Service items: grape planting, wine brewing, wine sales, wine customization, vineyard customization, vineyard tourism, wine tasting experience, etc.

Events

In 2020, Sung River Syrah Dry Red wine won the "Star Single Product Award" and "Consumer Favorite Product Award" from 2019 to 2020 in the 7th

China Wine Conference.

In 2019, it won three silver awards in the Belt and Road Initiative Gansu Ningxia International Wine Competition; Syrah Dry Red won the first gold medal in Hebei Wine Competition in China.

In 2018, Sung River Syrah Dry Red wine won the gold medal in the Shacheng Wine Competition.

In 2016, Sung River Marselan Dry Red wine won the RVF Bronze Award for China Fine Wine.

In 2014, it won the National Geographical Indication Protection Product.

In 2011, "Shazhuang" products won the gold medal at the Beijing-Tianjin Food Industry Exhibition. It has passed the certification of HACCP international food safety control system.

In 2010, the trademark "Sung River" was registered in the State Trademark Office.

In 2006, it passed the certification of ISO9001 international quality management system.

In 2003, it got the certification of the high-quality assured products of Chinese Quality Long March, and was praised as "National Food Industry Famous Wine Honest Products" by China Food Industry Association.

Contact Information

Address: Winery Road, South Tunnel Bridge, Shacheng Town, Huailai County, Hebei Province

Tel: 400 612 6055, 86-313-6829888

9. Hebei Chateau Nubes Co., Ltd.

Hebei Chateau Nubes Co., Ltd. (hereinafter referred to as Chateau Nubes), founded in 1998, covers 725 mu (119.43 acres), of which vineyards cover about 600 mu (98.84 acres). Hebei Chateau Nubes produces two single varieties, with an annual output of 60,000 bottles of Cabernet Sauvignon and Syrah wines. That the grape planting, harvesting, fermentation, finished product and labeling is all completed in the winery. In order to ensure the high quality of wine, Chateau Nubes only uses the grapes Cabernet Sauvignon and Syrah produced by itself as wine-brewing raw materials, and the harvesting and twice screening are all finished manually. All wines in Chateau Nubes are aged in oak barrels and stored in wine cellars. The wine is full and bright in color, outstanding in fruit flavor, balanced in sugar and acid, and high in tannin and phenols, which is suitable for long-term storage.

The winery has three multi-functional galleries, one large indoor cultural activity space, two museums, several exhibition halls, and an exquisite and natural winery restaurant and homestay. Chateau Nubes is open to industrial tourism, holding various art exhibitions, concerts, community art fellowship, pastoral sightseeing groups, artists' resident plans and other activities from time to time, and opening its doors to welcome people from all walks of life who come to visit and experience.

Contact Information

Address: Dongyulin Village, Donghuayuan Town, Huailai County, Hebei Province

Tel: 86-400-088-9118

10. Huailai Chateau Red Leaf Co., Ltd.

Huailai Chateau Red Leaf Co., Ltd. (hereinafter referred to as Chateau Red Leaf), located in Donghuayuan Town, Huailai County, Hebei Province, was established in 1998. It has a registered capital of CNY 1.98 million, covering an area of 60 mu (9.88 acres), a building area of more than 4,500 square meters and an annual comprehensive production capacity of more than 1,000 tons.

In April 1998, the company leased 1350mu (222.39 acres) of wasteland in Huoshaoying Village, Donghuayuan Town, and established the first vineyard in Donghuayuan Town, planting more than ten excellent wine grape varieties such as Cabernet Sauvignon, Merlot, Syrah, Marselan, Chardonnay and Gewurztraminer. It can produce 300-400 tons of high-quality wine grapes every year, providing fine raw materials for wine brewing.

Chateau Red Leaf has advanced wine production equipment, and the distilling wine fermentation and storage capacity of more than 3,000 tons. It has wine cellars with constant temperature and humidity and high-quality oak barrels. And it also has an advanced automatic beverage-packaging production line that can produce 3,000 bottles per hour, to keep the integration and automation of wine bottle cleaning, disinfection, filtration, packaging and cork pressing.

Since its establishment, Chateau Red Leaf has actively cooperated with professional colleges to improve its technical level and R&D capability. In 2006, the company cooperated with the Department of Food Science of Beijing Agricultural College as a training platform for production, education and research, and carried out scientific research and off-campus practice for students. In 2009, Beijing Agricultural College awarded Chateau Red Leaf "Excellent Off-campus Practical Education Platform", and in 2010, it was designated "Municipal Off-campus Talent Training Platform of Beijing Higher Education Institutions" by Beijing Municipal Education Commission.

Chateau Red Leaf has more than 20 products such as dry, semi-dry, semi-sweet and sweet wine. Brand series wine products such as "Sanggan Valley", "Romantic Lovers", "Garrus" and "Golden Leaf" gain high reputation in the market. Reserve Cabernet Sauvignon Collection Merlot dry red wine was rated as the best "Chinese wine" in the 2012 wine tasting of "Wine in China". Sanggan Valley Manor Special Chardonnay produced by Chateau Red Leaf won the gold medal in the 2018 Concours Mondial de Bruxelles.

Contact Information

Address: North Kangqi Highway, Donghuayuan Town, Huailai County, Hebei Province (formerly Donghuayuan Entrance Forest Farm)

Tel: 86-313-6849598

11. Huailai Yulong Winery Co., Ltd.

Huailai Yulong Winery Co., Ltd. (hereinafter referred to as Yulong Winery), established in 2010, is a wine chateau integrating grape planting, wine and brandy production and sales. Yulong Winery is located in Sangyuan Town, Huailai County, Hebei Province. It has a planting base of 1,500 mu (247 acres), two advanced pre-treatment production lines, 60 stainless steel temperature-controlled fermenters with a capacity of 60 tons, and a full-automatic packaging line with an annual output of 4 million bottles of wine and 400 tons of brandy. Yulong Winery has two national first-class winemakers, integrating with the international wine industry, creating the first music wine cellar in China, and cultivating the wine that grew up listening to music. The products are favored by consumers at home and abroad.

Yulong Winery has two main brands, Carlltiny and Yulongbao. "Carlltiny" is registered in France. At the same time, its subsidiary Carlltiny Wine Trading (Hong Kong) Co., Ltd. operates international trade. Yulong Winery wines are listed as national geographical indication protection products.

Events

In 2016, Ms. You Xiaofang, the owner of Yulong Winery, was awarded "Wine Princess" by China Agricultural Alliance.

In 2015, Yulong Winery was awarded as an international food safety model enterprise by the Global Food Safety Forum (GFSF).

In 2014, Yulong Winery products were designated as the National Geographical Indication Protection Products.

In 2012, Yu Long Winery was the main sponsor of the International Conference on Grapevine Breeding and Genetics.

In 2010, Yulong Winery was established.

Contact Information

Address: North Xinxiangling Village, Sangyuan Town, Huailai County, Zhangjiakou, Hebei Province

Tel: 86-313-6845572

12. Huailai Chixia Wine Co., Ltd.

Huailai Chixia Wine Co., Ltd., established in 1998, has a registered capital of CNY 1.3 million and covers an area of 6,667 square meters. It is located in Shacheng production area and has its own vineyard of 298.8 mu (49.22 acres) that mainly plants the grape Cabernet Sauvignon. The company has been taking grape planting as the starting point of the industrial chain, and its business covers the manufacture and sales of more than 20 kinds of products in wine, brandy, and beverage of fruit and vegetable. In 2017, the Company has got import and export business in prepackaged foods and about 20 kinds of imported original red wines from Australian.

Since its establishment, Chixia Wine adheres to taking quality management as the center, product innovation as the driving force and safe production as the guarantee. It establishes a production system suitable for the actual situation of the company, and continuously promotes technical transformation, and opened up a quality-benefit development path. Welcome friends.

Events

In 2019, Chixia Rose Wine and Chixia Dry White Wine won the Gold Award and Silver Award in the national white wine group in Hebei Wine Competition of China respectively.

In 2018, Chixia Sweet White Wine won the Special Award in the Jury of the International Leading Wine Quality Awards.

In 2016, Chixia Rose Wine won the gold medal in the Belt & Road Wine and Spirit Competition.

Contact Information

Address: North of West Street, Jingzhang Highway, Shacheng Town, Huailai County, Zhangjiakou City

Tel: 86-313-6801162

13. Huailai Dehou Manor Wine Co., Ltd.

Huailai Dehou Manor Wine Co., Ltd. (hereinafter referred to as Dehou Manor) was established in 2006 with a registered capital of 1 million euros. It is a Sino-foreign joint venture to brew wine (China and Belgium). The company is located in Donghuayuan Town, Huailai County, Hebei Province.

Dehou Manor has a grape planting base of more than 700 mu (115.32 acres), mainly planting wine grape varieties such as Cabernet Sauvignon, Merlot, Marselan and Chardonnay. The manor uses self-grown grapes as the main raw material, and mainly produces middle and high-grade winery wines. The annual fermented wine capacity is 200 tons, the total wine storage capacity is 450 tons and it produces more than a dozen wine products of different grades.

Contact Information

Address: XiYulin Village, Donghuayuan Town, Huailai County, Hebei Province

Tel: 86-313-6849699

14. Huailai Chateau Harvest Wine Co., Ltd.

Huailai Harvest Wine Co., Ltd. (hereinafter referred to as Harvest Chateau), founded in 2008, was invested and built by Beijing Harvest Wine Co., Ltd., with a registered capital of CNY12 million, a planned total investment of CNY 145 million and a building area of 65,000 square meters. The company is located in Dashankou Village, Ruiyunguan Township, Huailai County, Zhangjiakou City, Hebei Province, mainly producing dry red and dry white wines.

Beijing Harvest Wine Co., Ltd., formerly known as Beijing South Suburb Wine Factory, was founded in 1979. At present, it has developed into a parallelism operation mode with Beijing Harvest Wine Co., Ltd. as the main company, Beijing Shunxing Wine Co., Ltd. and Huailai Harvest Wine Co., Ltd.. It belongs to joint stock companies of the Beijing Enterprises Holdings Limited together with Yanjing Beer and Red Star Erguotou.

Huailai Harvest Chateau is a comprehensive region of integrating wine production and its culture. It's mainly responsible for the high-quality wine brewing, packaging, marketing and knowledge dissemination. It is estimated that after the completion of the project, the liquor storage capacity will reach 13,000 tons, and the annual output of wine will reach 6,000 tons, including 1,000 tons of fine winery wine.

Events

In 2018, it won the Beijing-Tianjin-Hebei Market Performance Award of China Wine Industry. And it is the first member unit of China Wine Brand Cluster.

In 2017, it won a special prize of the second Shangri-La Cup International Wine Competition.

In 2016, it won the special award of International Leading Wine (China) Quality Awards

In 2011, It won the silver prize of the Colombin Cup The Fifth Yantai International Wine Competition

In 2009, it became one of the ten China's top wine manufacturing enterprises.

In 2004, it won the gold medal in the first Decanter Asia Wine Awards.

Contact Information

Address: Ruiyunguan Township, Huailai County, Hebei Province

Tel: 86-313-6851000

15. Huailai Fresh Wine Co., Ltd.

Huailai Fresh Wine Co., Ltd. was established in 2008, located in 1,440m southwest of Xiyulin Village, Donghuayuan Town, Huailai County, covering an area of 2,677.29 square meters. Scope of business: production and sales of wine and fruit wine (raw wine, processing and packaging), grape planting, agricultural and sideline products planting and processing sales. The main products are rose wine, dry red wine and dry white wine, with a designed annual output of 100 tons. The main products are:

Fresh rose wine, Fresh dry red wine and Fresh dry white wine.

Contact Information

Address: Southwest of Xiyulin Village, Donghuayuan Town, Hebei Province

Tel: 86-313-6849690

16. Huailai JinTuMu Wine Co., Ltd.

Huailai JinTuMu Wine Co., Ltd. (hereinafter referred to as company) was founded in 2012 with a registered capital of CNY1 million, a total investment of CNY 10 million, fixed assets of CNY 4 million and an annual output value of CNY 10 million. The company covers an area of about 80,000 square meters and a building area of about 1,000 square meters. It is mainly responsible for the production and management of wine with an annual capacity of 100 tons per year.

The company owns 150 mu (24.7 acres) of vineyards, planting Cabernet Sauvignon, Marselan, Petit Manseng, Chardonnay and other wine grape varieties, which are now at the golden age of more than ten years. The winery has infrastructure and advanced production equipment, and is equipped with constant temperature and humidity wine cellar. The company has two national winemakers and sommeliers, and two senior engineer professors.

Contact Information

Address: Langshan Township, Huailai County, Hebei Province

Tel: 86-15831387892

17. Zhangjiakou Huaigu Manor Wine Co., Ltd.

Zhangjiakou Huaigu Manor Wine Co., Ltd. (hereinafter referred to as Huaigu Manor) was founded in 2013 and located in the north of Zhangguanying Village, Sangyuan Town, Huailai County. It covers an area of 12,500 square meters and has an annual wine production capacity of 1,800 tons.

The manor has made continuous breakthroughs in the inheritance and innovation of wine brewing technology, and has successively developed 11 unique small-variety wines. The unique technology of semi-carbonic maceration brewing has won 2 grand gold awards, 7 gold awards, 9 silver awards and 8 bronze awards in international competitions, especially the Grand Gold Medal in 2018 Concours Mondial de Bruxelles. It wins a total of 30 multiple awards, and is praised by wine experts and consumers at home and abroad.

Events

In 2021, Huaigu Syrah 2017 won the silver award in the 10th WINE 100 Challenge.

In 2020, Huaigu Marselan Reserve 2017 won the silver medal in Concours Mondial de Bruxelles. Four Huaigu Marselan Reserve Wines won the bronze award in Decanter World Wine Awards. Huaigu Vidal and Huaigu Marselan Reserve both won the silver awards and Huaigu Brandy won the bronze award in the 14th G100 International Wine & Spirits Awards.

In 2019, Huaigu Marselan Reserve 2017 won the annual Marseland Gold Award in WineLife World Wine Awards. Huaigu Marselan Reserve 2017 won the gold award in China International Marselan Wine Competition. Huaigu Marselan Reserve 2017 and Huaigu Cabernet Sauvignon 2016 both won the gold awards and Huaigu Cabernet Sauvignon 2017 won the silver award in World Desert International Wine Competition. Huaigu Merlot Reserve 2015 and Huaigu Marselan 2016 both won the silver awards and Huaigu Marselan Reserve 2015 and 2017 both won the bronze awards in Decanter Asia Wine Awards. Huaigu Cabernet Sauvignon won the silver award in the 10th Asian Wine Competition.

In 2018, Huaigu Marselan 2016 won the grand gold award and Huaigu Merlot Reserve 2015 won the gold award in Belt & Road Wine and Spirit Competition. Huaigu Merlot Reserve 2015 won the bronze award in Decanter Asia Wine Awards. Huaigu Cabernet Sauvignon Reserve 2015 won the grand gold award in Concours Mondial de Bruxelles.

Contact Information

Address: North of Zhangguanying Village, Sangyuan Town, Huailai County, Hebei Province

Tel: 86-313-6851919

18. Huailai Alan Chateau Co., Ltd.

Founded in 1998, Huailai Alan Chateau Co., Ltd. (hereinafter referred to as Alan Chateau) is an enterprise integrating grape planting, wine making, scientific research and science education, tourism and sightseeing. Alan Chateau is like a star with mysterious brilliance, which is inlaid in the beautiful Guanting Lake. To the south of the manor is the green Yanshan Mountain; to the north is the picturesque Guanting Lake. In this land endowed with abundance and great minds, Alan Vineyard and Chateau add radiance and beauty to each other.

Alan Vineyard is located in Shacheng production area which is the heart of grape planting in the world. It mainly plants various wine grapes such as Cabernet Sauvignon, Merlot, Chardonnay, and red, green, and black fresh varieties.

Alan Chateau is situated beside the vineyard. When entering the chateau, you will see the street lamps, iron chairs, architecture and decoration in European style. And you seem to be brought to the ancient and mysterious European castle by the lawns, flower pools, fountains and wine cellar. In the early morning, when you are in the chateau, you can see endless green grape waves of vineyards. In the evening, the afterglow of the setting sun reddens the sky, covering the whole chateau with wine red veil. The chateau is so quaint and quiet, as if it is escaped from the hustle and bustle, which makes people deeply intoxicated. Alan Chateau produces more than 1000 tons of manor wine per year. The underground wine cellar of 400 square meters can store 1000 tons of wine.

In April 2001, Alan Chateau Dry White Wine won the first place and Alan Chateau Dry Red Wine won the domestic second place at "the 4th Hilton International Wine and Food Experience" in Beijing. In 2002, Alan Chateau Dry Red Wine won the first prize at the wine tasting in which 45 kinds of wines of over 40 wineries were in competition in Yantai. In 2003, Alan Chateau Dry Red Wine and Alan Chateau Dry White Wine both won the highest honor at the wine tasting organized by China National Food Industry Association in Shihezi, Xinjiang. On January 20,2005, Cabernet Sauvignon Dry Red Wine won the Gold Medal, and Chardonnay Dry White Wine won the Silver Medal at the 2005 London Wine & Spirits International Competition (Beijing), the world's highest-level wine evaluation activity organized by the International Organization of Vine and Wine (OIV, 1978).

In 2004, Alan Chateau was approved as a demonstration base of national agricultural tourism and an AA national tourist attraction.

In 2001, Alan Chateau was designated as the "Contact Center of International Research and Training Center for Rural Education" by UNESCO.

Contact Information

Address: Xiaoqiying Village, Xiaonanxinbao Town, Huailai County, Hebei Province

Tel: 86-400-003-0059

19. Huailai Dragon Seal Wine Co., Ltd.

Huailai Dragon Seal Wine Co., Ltd. (hereinafter referred to as Dragon Seal), a wholly-owned subsidiary of Beijing Dragon Seal Wines Co., Ltd., was established in Dingzhouying Village, Xiaonanxinbao Town, Huailai County in 2007, with a registered capital of CNY 50 million. The business scope includes the production and sales of raw wine. Dragon Seal covers an area of 145 mu (23.8 acres) and has 127 tanks of ferment and storage. The wine storage capacity reaches up to 5900 tons and the wine fermentation capacity to 3000 tons.

In 2018, the head office moved a production line of Beijing company to Huailai Dragon Seal. In 2019, Huailai Dragon Seal obtained the license of filling production. The products represented by Huailai Reserve Dry Red Wine, Kuei Hua Chen Chiew, Gonggui Wine and Sparkling Wine won many awards in various competitions. In 2020, Huailai Dragon Seal had export qualification, and successfully completed the sales orders from the United States, Myanmar, Japan and other countries.

Events

In 2019, Dragon Seal Five-year Aged Gold Kuei Hua Chen Chiew won 2019 New Wine Product 'QingZhuo' Award.

In 2018, Five-year Aged Gold Kuei Hua Chen Chiew won the gold prize in the 2018 Belt & Road (Yinchuan, Ningxia) Wine and Spirit Competition. Dragon Seal Kuei Hua Lu Chiew won the silver medal of 2018 FISA French International Spirits Awards. Dragon Seal Chardonnay 2015 Dry White Wine won the silver award and Chinese Kuei Hua Lu Chiew (aged) 40% vol won the gold award at Concours Mondial de Bruxelles.

In 2017, Dragon Seal Sparkling Wine won Commended Award at Decanter Asia Wine Awards; Huailai Reserve Dry Red Wine won the silver medal at 2017 Concours Mondial de Bruxelles; Dragon Seal Huailai Reserve 2015 Dry Red Wine won the silver medal at Concours Mondial de Bruxelles.

In 2016, Five-year Aged Gold Kuei Hua Chen Chiew won the silver prize in the 2016 Belt & Road (Yinchuan, Ningxia) Wine and Spirit Competition.

In 2007, Dragon Seal Huailai Reserve Dry Red Wine was the only Chinese wine selected to Top 10 Asian Wines of Wine Report. It gained the reputation of the best "Chinese red wine".

In 2006, Dragon Seal Merlot Dry Red Wine won the silver award at Vinalies Internationales.

In 2005, Dragon Seal Cabernet Sauvignon Dry Red Wine won the gold medal at London Wine & Spirits International Competition. Dragon Seal Wine was the only Chinese wine selected to Top 10 Asian Wines of Wine Report. Dragon Seal Syrah Dry Red Wine won the first place in "the Most Exciting or Extraordinary Discovery in Asia".

In 2003, Dragon Seal Chardonnay Dry White Wine won the bronze medal in International Wine & Spirits Competition.

In 2002, Huailai Reserve Dry Red Wine won Gold Medal and the reputation of the Best China's Red Wine in China Wine and Spirits Competition.

In 2000, Dragon Seal Sparkling Wine won the silver medal in Montreal World Wine Competition. Dragon Seal Huailai Reserve 1997 Dry Red Wine won the bronze medal at Concours de Bordeaux Vins d'Aquitaine.

In 1999, Dragon Seal Cabernet Sauvignon 1997 Dry Red Wine won the reputation of the Best China's Red Wine in Hong Kong International Wine & Spirits Competition.

In 1996, Dragon Seal Chardonnay Dry White Wine won the silver medal in the World Chardonnay Wine Competition in Burgundy, France.

In 1994, Dragon Seal Dry White Wine won the gold medal in the international wine competition in Bordeaux, France.

Contact Information

Address: Xiaonanxinbao Town, Huailai County, Hebei Province

Tel: 86-313-6859952

20. Huailai Canaan Winery Co., Ltd.

Founded in 2003, Huailai Canaan Winery Co., Ltd. (hereinafter referred to as Canaan Winery) has a registered capital of 76.45 million US dollars, and the winery was completed in 2012. It covers a construction area of 15,000 square meters and has the designed production capacity of 1,500 tons. It has multiple sets of production equipment for dry white and dry red wine and more than 140 different fermenting tanks, and 3,000 oak barrels for aging, producing 500,000 to 600,000 bottles of high-quality wine annually.

In 2006, Canaan Winery hired a team of more than ten domestic and foreign experts. It took two years to select location in Huailai. In 2009, Canaan Winery introduced and planted the first seedling from the United States. Up to now, it has planted nearly 700,000 seedlings in 275 hectares of vineyards, with more than 40 varieties and 70 strains. Canaan Winery has three vineyards in the hills and valleys with an average altitude of 500 to 1000 meters, which are respectively located in Donghuayuan Town, Ruiyunguan Township and Wangjialou township, Huailai

County.

"Chapter and Verse", the brand name of Canaan Winery, is derived from *The Eight Immortals of the Wine Cup* written by poet Du Fu in the Tang Dynasty and the Chapter and Verse wines have won great awards for many years.

Events

In 2021, Chapter and Verse Cabernet Sauvignon Reserve 2015 won the gold award in China Wine Summit. Chapter and Verse Mastery Merlot 2015 won the gold medal in the 28th Concours Mondial de Bruxelles. Chapter and Verse Mastery Tempranillo 2014 won the gold award in WINE 100 Challenge. Chapter and Verse Mastery Chardonnay 2018 won the gold award in China Wine Summit.

In 2020, Chapter and Verse Syrah Reserve 2014 won the gold award in the 12th Golden Bottle Awards.

In 2016, Chapter and Verse Cabernet Sauvignon Reserve 2012 won the gold award in 2016 RVF China Fine Wine Competition.

In 2016, Canaan Winery won the title of the China Top 10 Wineries of the Year of Bettane + Desseauve.

Contact Information

Address: Donghuayuan Town, Huailai County, Hebei Province

Tel: 86-313-6849969

21. Yenong (Hebei) Winery Co., Ltd.

Huailaixian Classic Great Wall Winery Co., Ltd. was established in 2008 and renamed Yenong (Hebei) Winery Co., Ltd. in 2020.

Huailaixian Classic Great Wall Winery Co., Ltd. was formally established in 2008 in Xingshuwa Village, Guanting Town, Huailai County. It covers a total area of 40 mu (6.59 acres). The factory construction area accounts 12 mu (1.98 acres), and the raw wine fermentation and wine storage capacity reach more than 1,000 tons. The company has top winemakers and high-quality technical team. They adopt advanced brewing technology and equipment to produce "Shenmo" and "Moge" wine.

Events

In 2019, Yenong Manor Chardonnay Dry White Wine won the silver award of domestic group in Hebei 2019 Wine Competition.

In 2016, Yenong Manor Special Cabernet Sauvignon Dry Red Wine won the silver prize in 2016 Belt & Road Wine and Spirit Competition.

In 2014, Yenong Manor Cabernet Gernischt Dry Red Wine won the bronze award in the first Shacheng Wine Competition.

Contact Information

Address: Xingshuwa Village East, Guanting Town, Huailai County, Hebei Province

Tel: 86-400-0313-960   13831393888

22. Hebei Longquan Wine Co., Ltd.

Hebei Longquan Wine Co., Ltd. was founded in 1995 and was transformed from Huailai Longteng Winery Co., Ltd. by non-tradable shares reform in May 2016. The company is located in Sangyuan Town, Huailai County, with a registered capital of CNY 5 million, covering an area of 13,267 square meters. The raw wine production capacity reaches 3,000 tons and more than 30 employees are at work.

The company has grape bases of 734 mu (120.9 acres) for Cabernet Sauvignon, Merlot, Chardonnay and Syrah. It has four registered trademarks, namely "Golden Zone", "Longpan Zhuangyuan", "Xue Mo" and "Yiketeng". It mainly produces Aging series, Jing Xuan series and Zhuangyuan series wine.

Events

In 2021, the wine won bronze award in WINE 100 Challenge.

In 2020, the wine won the bronze medal in International Wine & Spirits Competition.

In 2019, the wines won the gold and silver awards of domestic group in Hebei 2019 Wine Competition.

In 2015, the wine won the gold award in Shacheng Wine Competition.

Contact Information

Address: Houhaoyao Village, Sangyuan Town, Huailai County, Hebei Province

Tel: 86-313-6878289

23. Huailai OPC'S Life Technology Development Co., Ltd.

Huailai OPC'S Life Technology Development Co., Ltd., founded in 2009, is the only domestic enterprise with grape seed deep processing. The annual grape seed processing capacity reaches 500 tons. The company introduces grape seed cold pressing technology and equipment and processes wine making by-product—grape skin residue into dozens of products such as cold-pressed grape seed oil and grape seed dietary fiber powder. Since its establishment, OPC'S Life has obtained the production license of cold pressed grape seed oil and ISO9001 quality system certification. The company creates China's own production standard of grape seed dietary fiber powder to establish an access mechanism for China's grape seed powder production industry.

It has established the first Grape Seed Antioxidant Center in Asia by integrating the grape plantations, wineries and Timan Hot Spring. The center has grape theme restaurant, grape theme SPA, grape culture and tourism leisure farm and health care courses about grape.

Grape Theme Restaurant

OPC'S Life deeply explores the history and culture of Huailai grapes and invites gourmets and nutritionists at home and abroad to give advice and exchange inspiration. OPC'S Life cold pressed grape seed oil and grape seed powder are used as ingredients to make various grape food relating to fresh grapes, wine, raisins, grape vinegar, grape leaves, grape wood, etc. The Grape Theme Restaurant is the first in Asia.

Creative Western Food

Every month, new grape combo meals are launched, and each contains 6 to 18 exquisite grape creative dishes paired with at least three local wines or homemade non-alcoholic grape drinks. For example, the traditional German New Year Combo Meal in January each year presents the traditional dishes and drinks in German New Year and Christmas with Huailai grape ingredients, such as German roast pork knuckles with grape seed oil, Christmas cakes decorated with grape seed powder, Glühwein, etc.

Huailai Grape Feast

The company explores 1,000 years of history and culture of Huailai grape to present a unique grape feast. They skillfully cook with various grape-related food materials which are accompanied by OPC'S Life cold pressed grape seed oil and grape seed powder. In 2019, the grape feast named "Grapes are Ripe" contained 18 dishes, each of which was cooked with grape seed oil or grape seed powder and other grape ingredients. And the dishes are named after poems describing harvest. It won the Best Popularity Award in Huailai Food Competition approved by national, provincial and municipal judges and public judges. The famous dishes include grape-like diced fish marinated in red wine and white wine (named as crape myrtle in the moonlight of the crescent moon), pork chops baked with grape wood (named as the trellis of roses spreading fragrance far and near), vegetable bags made up of grape leaves (named as green look lotus leaves and the pickers' thin silk skirts), frog-shaped bread sprinkled with grape seed powder (named as the ricefields' sweet smell promising a bumper year), etc.

Events

In 2021, the company was titled "International Science & Technology Cooperation Base" by Hebei Provincial Department of Science and Technology.

From 2019 to now, it has been titled "the Center Integrating Enterprises,

Universities and Research Institutes" by Beijing University of Agriculture.

In 2018, the founder won Outstanding Entrepreneur Woman awarded by China Association of Women Entrepreneurs (CAWE). The company was recognized as Talent and Intelligence Introduction Demonstration Center by Hebei Administration of Foreign Experts Affairs.

In 2017, the company was titled "One County, One Product" in the Eleventh Hebei Brand Festival. It was titled Poverty Alleviation through Handwork Demonstration Center by Hebei Provincial Women's Federation. It was titled "Hebei Four-star Leisure Agriculture Park".

In 2015, it was titled "One County, One Product" in the Ninth Hebei Brand Festival.

In 2014, it gained the support of Overseas Expertise Introduction Project of Hebei Administration of Foreign Experts Affairs. And it was awarded "Star Entrepreneur" by China Nutrition Association. It was recommended by Hebei Provincial Department of Commerce to participate in the Hi-Tech Fair held in Guangzhou.

In 2013, it gained support of Achievement Demonstration and Promotion Project of Foreign Technology Introduction and Talents Management of State Administration of Foreign Experts Affairs. And it was titled Hebei Province Science and Technology Oriented Small and Medium-sized Enterprise.

In 2012, it gained support of annual science and technology innovation fund of Ministry of Science and Technology of PRC.

Contact Information

Address: Sangyuan Town, Huailai County, Hebei Province

Tel: 86-313-6878250

24. Zhangjiakou Great Land Scape Winery Co., Ltd.

Located in Shacheng Town, Huailai County, Hebei Province, Zhangjiakou Great Land Scape Winery Co., Ltd. was established in 1997. The company covers an area of 9,789 square meters and has nearly 100 employees including over 20% various kinds of technical personnel. The company's production and filling workshops are equipped with advanced equipment. It is a winery integrating center construction, grape cultivation, scientific research, product development, and large-scale production.

"Great Land Scape" is the registered trademark of the company, taken from the four characters on the lintel of Zhangjiakou Dajing Gate. Zhangjiakou Dajing Gate is a historical landmark in Zhangjiakou. In order to organically integrate regional culture and product brand, the company promotes local culture on the basis of building brand, so that product brand and local culture can complement each other and promote each other.

The main products are Great Land Scape Dry Red and Dry White Wines and two high-quality liquor series—Jinyao Series and Shajiu Series.

Contact Information

Address: Gongye St., Shacheng Town, Huailai County, Hebei Province

Tel: 86-313-6251399

25. Zhangjiakou Great Wall Winery (Group) Co., Ltd.

Zhangjiakou Great Wall Winery (Group) Co., Ltd. is located in Shacheng Town, Huailai County, Zhangjiakou City, Hebei Province. It is formerly known as Shacheng Winery founded in 1949. Shacheng Winery was the birthplace of China's first bottle of dry white wine. The company covers an area of about 300,000 square meters, producing many kinds of products such as Shacheng Laojiao Liquor, Sha Cheng Wine, Sha Cheng Boiling Liquor, various fruit wines, beverages and so on. It is one of the biggest wine-making enterprises in North China.

Sha Cheng Laojiao Liquor has the history of 800 years. Known as imperial wine of the Yuan and Qing dynasties, it originated in the Yuan Dynasty, took shape in the Ming Dynasty, and flourished in the Qing Dynasty. In the 35th year of Kangxi Emperor during Qing Dynasty, the emperor granted it "Sha Cheng

Sha Wine". Shacheng Boiling Liquor won the international famous wine great awards of international famous wine competitions in Panama and Philadelphia for three times. In 1958, Shacheng Boiling Plum Liquor won the first place in China. The company's liquor features on strong aroma, with both light and sauce-flavored aroma. It has made great achievements in the practice and promotion of "Beidou technique" of strong aroma liquor and the research of ultra-low alcohol liquor. In 1994, Sha Cheng Laojiao Liquor was awarded as "China Wine King". It is a witness and live archive of liquor production in northern China.

Shacheng Wine originates from Yuhua Winery, China's third winery established in Shacheng in 1917. In response to the country's call, the company built the new workshops for producing fruit wines in 1959 (now the site of the birthplace of China's first bottle of dry white wine). In 1975, Shacheng Wine was included in the national wine development plan. In 1976, the first bottle of dry white wine in China was successfully developed by using Chinese unique longan grapes and independent technology. In 1978, the scientific research unit of the national key scientific research project "Research on the New Technique of Dry White Wine" was established in Shacheng Winery. A number of scientific research achievements promoted the transformation of Chinese wine to dry type. In 1979, Shacheng Dry White Wine won the honors of "National Famous Wine" and "National Quality Gold Award". Shacheng Dry White Wine was selected as the wine for the Supply Office of Diplomatic Missions Overseas of Ministry of Foreign Affairs. It took the lead in exporting dry wine, establishing the first mother garden of international famous dry wine varieties, and going abroad for investigation and exchange. All the achievements leave many national brand marks, and Shacheng Wine is known as the source of dry wine.

Events

In 2021, Shacheng Shuang Ling Liquor 409 won 2020 "QingZhuo" Award of China International Alcoholic Drinks. Shacheng Shuang Ling Liquor 409, Shacheng Laojiao Taocang Yuanjiang Liquor 20 and Shacheng Laojiao Tequ Liquor all won the double gold awards in San Francisco World Spirits Competition.

In 2020, the company was selected as the National Industrial Heritage and became the only National Industrial Heritage Project with dual categories of liquor and wine. Shacheng Laojiao Liquor Brewing Technique and New Technique of Shacheng Dry White Wine were listed as the core items of National Industrial Heritage.

In 2019, the enterprise was successfully restructured. The company produced liquor and wine, and implemented the revival strategy of Shacheng famous liquor. *The Birth of China's First Bottle of Dry White Wine* was published.

In 2010, it was recognized as the production enterprise of "China's First Bottle of Dry White Wine".

In 2009, "Shacheng Laojiao Liquor Brewing Technique" was listed in Intangible Cultural Heritage Project of Hebei Province.

In 2003, the company transferred the equity of China Great Wall Wine Co., Ltd. to COFCO. Then, based on the old Shacheng Winery which used to do research and development of the first bottle of dry white, the company expanded the wine workshops and resumed the production and sales of Shacheng Wine.

In 1999, it won the Science and Technology Progress Outstanding Project Award of China National Food Industry Association.

In 1998, Hebei Great Wall Wine Industry Group Co., Ltd. was founded.

In 1996, the company was renamed Zhangjiakou Great Wall Winery (Group) Co., Ltd., with seven branch factories such as liquor factory, fruit wine factory, beverage factory, packaging factory, thermoelectric plant, etc, and two joint ventures of Great Wall Wine and Great Wall Biological Feed.

In 1994, Shacheng Laojiao Liquor won the honorary title of "China Wine King" in China International Famous Wines Fair.

In 1993, Shacheng Laojiao Liquor was awarded the Golden Medal in 1993 International Famous Liquor (Hong Kong) Expo. The company had an annual comprehensive production capacity of 85,000 tons and of them were 30,000 tons of liquor. The comprehensive production capacity ranked sixth in China. The company was rated as one of the Top 100 Liquor Manufacturing Enterprises in the first China Sugar and Wine Industry Enterprise Evaluation. It ranked one of the China's Top 100 Industries according to major economic indicators of 1993 issued by National Bureau of Statistics.

In 1992, Shacheng Laojiao Liquor won International Famous Liquor Special Gold Prize at the first Bangkok International Famous Liquor Expo. The company was approved as a state owned second-grade enterprise.

In 1991, it obtained the National First-class Enterprise Archives Management Certificate.

In 1990, Shacheng Laojiao Liquor was rated as the high-quality product by Ministry of China Light Industry. Chinese Cocktail won the Science and Technology Progress Second Prize of Hebei Light Industry.

In 1989, the company was granted by the People's Government of Hebei Province as "Provincial Advanced Enterprise", "Advanced Enterprise in Energy Saving" and "Provincial Civilized Unit". The company was awarded "Golden Dragon Soaring Award for Promoting Enterprise Technology Progress" by the Ministry of China Light Industry.

In 1986, Suanzao Kele won the second prize of Hebei Outstanding New Products, and Suanzao series products won the third prize of Hebei Science and Technology Progress. In 1988,54 degrees Shacheng Laojiao Liquor and Laolongtan Boiling Plum Liquor won the gold medal at 1st China Food Fair. Xuexian Suanzao Kele and Longtan Chinese Suanzao Champagne won the silver medal. Longtan Geli Malt Beer won the bronze medal.

In 1983, with the approval of State Administration of Import and Export Commission, Zhangjiakou Great Wall Winery (Group) Co., Ltd., China National Cereals, Oils and Foodstuffs Import and Export Corporation (COFCO) and Hong Kong Yuanda Co., Ltd. jointly established China Great Wall Wine Co., Ltd. COFCO and Hong Kong Yuanda each held 25% shares. Zhangjiakou Great Wall Winery (Group) Co., Ltd. held 50% shares, and its investment covered the expanded workshops producing 10,000 tons of wine. China Great

Wall Wine Co., Ltd. produced and sold Great Wall Wine. In the same year, dry white wine won the silver medal at the 14th London Wine & Spirits International Competition. It was the first time that China won the award in the international famous wine competitions in 70 years.

In 1981, "Research on the New Technique of Dry White Wine" won the Third Prize of Scientific and Technological Achievements, awarded by the Ministry of China Light Industry.

In 1980, 54,000 seedlings of 13 varieties (white 8 and red 5) were introduced from West Germany and the United States and planted in the mother garden in Shacheng Winery. The plant survival rate is more than 90%. This was the first time that China introduced many varieties of international famous wine grapes.

In 1979, Shacheng Dry White Wine was rated as "National Famous Wine", and it won Gold Award of National Quality Award, together with Maotai and Wuliangye Liquor. Shacheng Semi Dry Wine won High Quality Product Award of the People's Republic of China. Shacheng Dry White Wine was listed as wine for Diplomatic Missions Overseas of Ministry of Foreign Affairs and exported to more than 10 countries such as the United States and Britain.

In 1978, the scientific research unit of the key scientific research project "Research on the New Technique of Dry White Wine" of Ministry of China Light Industry was established in Shacheng Winery. It consisted of a total of 16 scientific research projects. Guo Qichang, a leading authority of wine, was the project leader, and 22 personnel from the company formed a scientific research team. It took five years for scientific research achievements to be identified and promoted to the industry free of charge. Chinese wine transformed from sweet type to dry type.

In 1977, the company was rated as Daqing-type Enterprise. In the same year, it signed a contract with Coca Cola to export dry white wine to the United States. It independently designed and expanded the workshops producing 10,000 tons of wine.

In 1976, China's first bottle of dry white wine was produced in the company, filling the gap of China's dry wine.

In 1975, five national ministries and commissions visited Huailai for investigation and made the high-quality wine production in Shacheng Winery incorporated in the national development plan.

In 1959, it independently designed and built workshops for producing sweet Shacheng wine and Shacheng Boiling Plum Liquor. The wines sold well in over 10 provinces and cities in China.

In 1957, Shacheng Winery expanded its production and sold its products to 18 provinces and cities in China.

In 1949, Chahar provincial government took over six private Gangfang and established the 46th Public Winery in North China, which was renamed Shacheng Winery in 1950.

Contact Information

Address: Jiuchang Road, Shacheng Town, Huailai County, Hebei Province

Tel: 86-313-6256666

26. Huailai Amethyst Manor Co., Ltd.

Huailai Amethyst Manor (hereinafter referred to as manor) is a Sino-foreign joint venture established in 2008. Located in Huailai County, Hebei Province, the manor has 600 mu (98.84 acres) of vineyards and grows wine varieties such as Cabernet Sauvignon, Merlot, Chardonnay, Marselan and Petit Manseng. The manor has atmosphere pressers, fermentation and filling equipment, and high-quality oak barrels. The underground wine cellar with 4,000 square meters provides storage conditions of constant temperature and humidity for wine.

Amethyst wines won nearly 200 awards in major international and domestic competitions, such as Concours Mondial de Bruxelles, Decanter World Wine Awards and Berliner Wein Trophy, and the manor was awarded "Winery of the Year" by La Revue du Vin de France. In 2018, Amethyst wines entered the French markets for trial sale and were selected as customized wines for entertainment in the Israeli embassy.

Events

In 2019, the manor was selected as "Most Popular Chinese Quality Wine Producer" at 2019 China Wine Summit.

In 2018, Amethyst Manor wine was selected as "the Top Brand of Chinese Wine Market in 2018" in the Annual Top of Chinese Wine Market.

In 2017, the manor was titled "High Quality Product of Hebei Province" and launched new products "crystal series", including Brilliant (Jingcai), Fairy (Jingling), Classic (Jingdian), and Treasure (Jingcang). It was awarded "Winery of the Year" in the RVF Chinese Wine Awards 2017.

In 2016, it was titled Hebei Province Science and Technology Oriented Small and Medium-sized Enterprise and was rated as the Well-known Trademark of Hebei.

In 2014, it was rated as the Key Leading Enterprise of Agricultural Industrialization.

In 2008, Huailai Amethyst Manor was formally established and began to plant selected wine grapes in its own vineyards.

In 2007, Huailai Amethyst Manor began to make establishment plan.

Contact Information

Address: Ruiyunguan Township, Huailai County, Hebei Province

Tel: 86-313-6850519

27. G9 Lee World Chateau

G9 Lee World Chateau is an international winery cluster in the Great Capital Wine Region created by Lee World Group with high-quality resources at home and abroad. G9 is an exclusive international platform that connects the world through wine, wellness and tourism. G9 Lee World Chateau is located on the north bank of Guanting Lake in northwest Beijing, adjacent to the national wetland park and the Badaling Great Wall. It covers an area of about 5,000 mu (823.68 acres) and is surrounded by Yanshan Mountain. It has a temperate monsoon-influenced continental climate, featuring distinct four seasons and sufficient sunshine. Therefore, it is known as "Hometown of Chinese Grapes" and "Hometown of Chinese Wine". It is only 75 kilometers away from Beijing, about an hour and a half by car and 20 minutes by high-speed rail. G9 is in the center of Huailai Wine Region. Currently, there are 41 wineries surrounding the Guanting Lake, Such as Sungod GreatWall, Canaan and Sino-French Chateau, etc. Huailai Wine Region has a long history in the area.

G9 project is a new attempt to explore the integration of primary, secondary and tertiary industry, providing an answer to upgrade wine industry and winery economy. G9 creatively proposes a concept of "Great Capital Wine Region" (GCWR), to learn and become a leader in the world's wine industry. The GCWR shall provide services from primary, secondary and tertiary business sectors, to satisfy the high-end consumer needs of Beijing. G9's mission is to build a high-end global communications platform relying on Beijing, China's capital. As a platform, it needs to integrate world top luxury brands and IP at home and abroad, and cooperate with multiple parties to build a complete industrial chain integrating wine, wellness and tourism, and international exchanges. G9 will give support to the Olympic Winter Games with its outstanding characteristics and international advantages.

G9 project includes a thousand mu of vineyards and nine national top manors: featured hotels, exhibition centers, health care centers, high-end wedding, winery museums, wine cellar conference rooms, polo clubs, high-end British management service, a diamond chapel, other leisure and entertainment, activity space, etc.

G9's first chateau covers a total area of about 100 mu (16.47 acres), with a construction area of about 12,000 square meters. It is located in the southwest of Lee World G9 international estate, and is designed by Jean-Pierre Errath (Chief restoration architect for the palace of Versailles, France). The G9 project was formally launched in March 2018 and started operation in September 2020.

Contact Information

Address: North of Guanting Reservoir National Wetland Park, Huailai

County, Hebei Province

Tel: 86-19919911929

28. Huailai, China · Window of Global Wine Exhibition Hall

Huailai, China · Window of Global Wine exhibition hall is located in the east of Dongshuiquan village, Shacheng Town, Huailai County, north of Chateau SunGod GreatWall. The construction area is 7,877 square meters, and the exhibition area is 4,923 square meters. The exhibition is at first and second floor, and Hebei Wine Industry Technology Research Institute is at third floor.

Wine is the core of Window of Global Wine. The exhibition hall is designed with characteristic cultural symbols and is a large-scale comprehensive exhibition hall, integrating the functions of cultural expo, tasting and trading, large-scale commerce and trade, cultural and recreational activities, forum training, education and research, catering services, etc. There are common exhibition halls, temporary exhibition halls, multi-function halls, cultural and creative brand stores, catering areas and offices.

The common exhibition hall shows the dual layouts of the world and Huailai wine industry, including four main exhibition halls: Global Culture of Wine, Chinese Wine Culture, Huailai Wines and Wine Art. It builds an international exhibition and exchange platform for wine products, wine talents and technology, and wine culture and art. Through advanced modern multimedia technology, the viewers can fully mobilize various sensory functions such as sight, hearing, touch and smell, and is led to experience the immersive tour of the world wine manor in interesting interaction. It realizes the three-dimensional birth of wine culture and industry.

Functional exhibition area adheres to market-oriented operation, and multi-dimensional business forms are put forward simultaneously. Temporary activities such as theme exhibitions, tasting exchanges, commercial exhibitions, art exhibitions, forum trainings, etc. are regularly held and world-class wine professionals and wine lovers gather in these activities. Combined with the most innovative and interesting fashion trends nowadays, it will bring visitors a high-quality and economical consumption experience, and international and forward-looking aesthetic appreciation.

The construction of Huailai, China • Window of Global Wine will become a showcase of Huailai characteristic grape (wine) industry. Integrating the resources of Hengda Wine Exchange, G9 International Wine Culture Town, Ten Thousand Mu of Vineyards, Chateau SunGod and so on, it will become a platform for guiding and displaying the grape industry. It will better show Huailai wine culture and inherits Huailai wine history, thus accelerates the integrated development of Huailai grape industry that brings together the joint efforts of enterprises, universities, and research institutes. It also promotes the high efficiency, high quality brewing and high value-added development of grape industry, and speeds up the construction of the industrial system of integrated development of primary, secondary and tertiary industries. This will continuously enhance the popularity and influence of Huailai production area, and create an important window for famous wine production areas in China.

Contact Information

Address: East of Dongshuiquan Village, Shacheng Town, Huailai County

Tel: 86 + 152-9732-9578

29. COFCO Huaxia Greatwall Wine Co., Ltd.

COFCO Huaxia Greatwall Wine Co., Ltd. is located in Changli County, Hebei Province, with a registered capital of CNY 200 million. It covers an area of 800,000 square meters, with a construction area of 85,000 square meters. It has 1200 sets of equipment of juicing equipment, fermentation equipment, wine storage equipment, filtration equipment and filling equipment, and the original value of fixed assets is CNY 410 million. By the end of 2014, the company had 1,340 hectares wine-brewing center. The annual comprehensive production capacity of wine is 50,000 tons, and the wine storage capacity is 100,000 tons. The company has 234 employees, including 2 consultants of National Wine Technical Committee, 2 members of National Wine Technical Committee, 6 members of National Wine Evaluation Committee, 34 national wine tasters (including 16 national first-level wine tasters), 15 national winemakers (including 12 national first-level winemakers) and 86 with college degree or above.

COFCO Huaxia Greatwall Wine Co., Ltd. grows out of Changli Fruit Wine Factory in Tangshan (renamed as Hebei Changli Wine Factory after 1973), which was established in 1958. In 1955, in order to fill the production gap of fruit wine, Industry Department of Hebei Province decided to build the first fruit wine factory in Changli County. In 1956, Ren Guiyuan, a wine making technician from Hebei Province was sent back to his hometown Changli, and he established a fruit wine fermentation experimental station where he engaged in fruit wine trial production and training workers. Under his leadership, they quickly developed Rosé Wine, dimocarpus longan wine and other fruit wines. After the successful trial, he founded Hebei Changli Wine Factory in 1958. In 1964, the state took Changli Wine Factory as a scientific research pilot unit. Wine experts including Zhu Mei, Guo Qichang, Yang Zipei and Lin Wenbing successively completed the "Project of Hebei Fruit Wine Stability Test" together with the technical backbone of Changli Wine Factory, and solved many domestic problems in wine brewing. In 1966, the enterprise paid more than CNY 6 million of profits and taxes to the state. In 1973, the factory developed a red wine with local rose and other grapes. In order to open up the international market, Guo Qichang and Yan Shengjie, famous grape wine experts, were employed as project leaders to develop the internationally popular dry red wine. In January 1981, China National Research Institute of Food and Fermentation Industries of Ministry of China Light Industry reached a technical cooperation agreement with Changli Wine Factory. They signed three agreements including the "Research Tasks for Selection and Breeding of Excellent Grape Varieties for Wine Making Materials", "Research Contract for the Trial Production of Dry Red Wine Equipment with Intermittent Heat Treatment Pulp" and "Scientific Research Contract for New Technology or New Products". Guo Qichang was a senior engineer of China National Research Institute of Food and Fermentation Industries of Ministry of China Light Industry, and Yan Shengjie was a technical director of Heibei Changli Wine Factory. They signed the contract on behalf of both parties. In May 1983, China's first bottle of Beidaihe Dry Red Wine was developed in Changli Wine Factory. In December 1987, China National Cereals, Oils and Foodstuffs Import and Export Corporation (COFCO) and Changli Wine Factory formally established a "joint venture" mainly producing dry red wine, with a total investment of CNY 4 million and an annual production capacity of 500 tons. Yan Shengjie was appointed as the general manager and he set up a new workshop for high-end wine production in Changli Wine Factory. At first, eight employees in the workshop produced Great Wall Dry Red Wine.

On August 9, 1988, Huaxia Grape Winery Co., Ltd. was officially established. With a total investment of CNY 7 million, the company was jointly funded by COFCO, Changli Wine Factory and Penley Corp. Yan Shengjie, the former technical director of Changli Wine Factory, was appointed as the general manager and chief engineer. In December 2005, the company was renamed COFCO Huaxia Greatwall Wine Co., Ltd.

In June 2008, a fine workshop was completed with capacity of 1,000 tons and a total construction area of 6,272 square meters. The workshop consisted of grape cultivation, wine-making, research and development, and sightseeing tour. Also, an automatic filling production line was introduced, which could produce 3,000 bottles of wine per hour. The company had a 19,000-square meters wine cellar with Chinese traditional characteristics, which was the largest underground granite wine cellar in Asia. The cellar consisted of three parts: underground arch wine cellar, celebrity collection wine cellar and fine round wine cellar. There were more than 20,000 oak barrels in it.

The company has provincial scientific research platforms such as Hebei Wine Grape Engineering Technology Research Center, Hebei A-level R&D Institutions, Hebei Enterprise Technology Center. It has undertaken 7 national scientific research projects, 32 provincial and municipal scientific research projects, and won National Science and Technology Progress Award and Hebei Science and Technology Progress Award.

The company has developed "Huaxia Vineyard Parcel A" as the representative of domestic high-grade wine production area. It forms three wine series of 60 varieties, including 92, 94, 95 as the representative of the Year series, Asian Great Cellar series, as well as wines of personalized, high-quality winery with typical regional style.

Events

In 2020, Huaxia Greatwall Great Cellar Reserve Cabernet Sauvignon Dry Red Wine, Huaxia Greatwall Special Reserve 92 Cabernet Sauvignon Red Wine, and Huaxia Chateau Dry Red all won the gold medal in Concours Mondial de Bruxelles.

In 2019, the wines won one silver award and two commended awards in London International Wine Competition; the wines won one silver award and one commended award in Decanter World Wine Awards.

In 2018, the wines won one silver award, one bronze award and one commended award in Decanter World Wine Awards; the wines won two commended awards in London International Wine Competition; the wines won two silver medals in Concours Mondial de Bruxelles.

In 2017, the wines won two silver awards in Concours Mondial de Bruxelles, and one bronze award and one commended award in London International Wine Competition.

In 2016, "Key Technology Innovation and Application of China's Wine Industry Chain" in cooperation with College of Enology of Northwest A&F University won the second prize of National Science and Technology Progress Award.

In 2009, it independently innovated and developed a product traceability system of COFCO Liquor Industry.

In May 2008, technical renovation projects such as a filling workshop for 10,000 tons of high-grade wine and a fine workshop with the capacity of 1,000 tons of wine, wastewater comprehensive utilization and ecological park construction project were officially launched.

In 2006, COFCO Wines became the exclusive supplier for Beijing 2008

Olympic Games.

In 2005, Huaxia Grape Winery Co., Ltd. was renamed COFCO Huaxia Greatwall Wine Co., Ltd.

In 2003, GreatWall Huaxia Parcel A Red, Changli, China was successfully developed and put on the market.

In 2002, the company was titled "Science and Technology Innovation-Oriented Spark Leading Enterprise" by the Ministry of Science and Technology of PRC.

In 2001, Huaxia first developed the 3000 ml and 6000 ml super capacity "Dry Red Wine Carrier Pack" for group celebrations, changing the old single 750 ml in the wine industry. It was refreshing.

In March 2000, Huaxia Greatwall 92 Red Wine was officially put on the market.

In May 1999, Huaxia officially became a wholly-owned subsidiary of COFCO.

In 1997, the company was rated as "High-tech Advanced Enterprise" by Hebei Provincial Department of Science and Technology.

In 1996, the wine products of Huaxia Grape Winery Co., Ltd. got the certificate of using green food trademark issued by China Green Food Center.

In 1994, the Rose Wine produced by Huaxia Grape Winery Co., Ltd. was listed in the national "Eighth Five Year" Spark Achievement Promotion Plan.

In 1992, Greatwall Dry Red Wine won the gold prize at the first International Food Fair, Hongkong.

In 1991, Huaxia Greatwall High-end Dry Red Wine won the gold medal at the "Seventh Five Year Plan" National Spark Project Achievement Exposition.

In 1990, Huaxia Greatwall White Label Dry Red Wine won the gold medal at the 14th International Food Fair in France. The company undertook the key scientific research project of "High-end Dry Red Wine" in the "Seventh Five Year Plan" of State Scientific and Technological Commission of PRC.

In 1989, Huaxia Greatwall White Label Dry Red Wine won the special award of 29th French International Wine Appraisal.

In 1988, Huaxia Grape Winery Co., Ltd. was officially established.

In 1986, Yan Shengjie, deputy director of Changli Wine Factory, led a delegation to France for inspection and introduced Cabernet Sauvignon and Cabernet Franc.

Contact Information

Address: West of Chengguan Changfu Highway, Changli County, Qinhuangdao City, Hebei Province

Tel: 86-335-7169969

30. COFCO Greatwall Huaxia Wine (Qinhuangdao) Co., Ltd.

COFCO Greatwall Huaxia Wine (Qinghuangdao) Co., Ltd. hereinafter referred to as Huaxia winery is a new industrial and cultural tourist attraction established by relying on the fine wine industry tourism resources of COFCO Huaxia Greatwall Wine Co., Ltd. The winery is located in Changli County, Qinhuangdao City, Hebei Province. Changli County is a beautiful coastal town, 20 kilometers away from the Funing exit of Beijing— Shenyang Expressway. It is 30 kilometers east to Beidaihe, a summer resort, and only 10 kilometers south to the gold coast, one of the eight most beautiful coasts in China. Surrounded by mountains and sea, it has high sky and light clouds, beautiful scenery and pleasant climate. Visitors can enjoy unlimited scenery here.

Huaxia winery, at the foot of Jieshi Mountain, is located in the center of Jieshi Mountain production area of Qinhuangdao. The only production area is surrounded by mountains, seas and rivers in China. The winery has a temperate continental climate with abundant sunshine and high grape maturity. The three-layer volcanic sedimentary soil full of gravel and sand in the vineyard is rich in minerals and trace elements, which is conducive to the accumulation of more abundant aroma substances for grapes. The winery has been adhering to the spirit of Huaxia, with the mission of inheriting Chinese culture, and with the guidance of "pioneering China, innovative China, humanistic China, and technological China". It adopts advanced planting concept and excellent wine-making technology, and the employees work hard and respect the local conditions. Finally, they make Huaxia wines with unique characteristics of Jieshi Mountain production area.

In 2017, Johnson Finn Architects of the United States (the design team of the iconic building No. 1 in Napa Valley, the United States) was invited to design the winery, which integrates wine brewing, sales, exhibition, training and other functions. Huaxia winery sets up finance department, general management department, tourism management department, catering department and guest room department. All the departments mainly engage in tourism reception, catering accommodation, conference training, commodity sales and other business. The winery has a wine exhibition and sales center with a total construction area of 14,137 square meters, which is located in the vineyard and connected with Huaxia factory. Following the trend of mountains and slopes, the visitors can see the whole picture of the vineyard in the winding building. The center has three floors. The first floor covers an area of 4,765 square meters, and it has twelve parts such as wine museum, retail area, storage room, conference room, clinic, office area, wine tasting room, wine tasting hall, wine storage room, multi-function area, guest room, entertainment room, etc. The second floor covers an area of 6,670 square meters, including storage room, conference room, multi-function hall, guest room, banquet room, banquet hall, cigar bar, etc. The third floor covers an area of 2,702 square meters, mainly for logistics service space, guest room, cigar bar, classrooms, etc. The center is a winery complex integrating tourism, catering and accommodation, conference training, cultural exchange and commodity sales.

The winery has 125 mu (20.59 acres) of international famous grape varieties, strains and parent vineyards of grape seedlings over 30 years old, more than 800 mu (131.79 acres) of wine grape standardized production demonstration garden. It has a total of 39 tanks, including 22 wine storage tanks of 30 tons, 9 wine storage tanks of 10 tons and 8 wine storage tanks of 5 tons, and the wine storage capacity is over 700 tons. The automatic filling production lines can produce 3,000 bottles of wine per hour in the modern filling workshops. Relying on its unique natural conditions and geographical advantages, it has received more than 150,000 party and state leaders and domestic and foreign tourists in the past three years, with a main business income of nearly CNY 30 million (USD 194.4 million).

Contact Information

Address: West of Chengguan Changfu Highway, Changli County, Qinhuangdao City, Hebei Province

Tel: 86-335-7169888

31. Bodega Langes (Qinhuangdao) Co., Ltd.

Mr. Langes, the founder of Bodega Langes, is the heir of the famous Austrian entrepreneur Swarovski crystal family. His mother once said to him that with the wealth and luxury brought by the success of crystal business, it was more meaningful for him to do something beneficial to human health. Since then, Mr. Langes had forged a special bond with wine. He created Bodega Langes (Qinhuangdao) Co., Ltd. It becomes his persistent pursuit to make fine wine for the world.

After visiting world-famous production areas, Langes's team came to Changli, Hebei Province in 1998. Along the way, they saw a wealth of vineyards. When they walked to Jieshi Mountain, they appreciated the splendid landscape. The mountain was characterized by the rolling ranges, the top in shape of reverse-bell and the Jieshi-like appearance. Climbing to the peak and overlooking the golden coast, they deeply understood the meaning of the verse "I come to view the boundless ocean from Story Hill on eastern shore". They lingered over with admiration. They looked the information up in the Records of Changli County and found it surrounded by mountains and sea. It boasted superior natural ecological conditions of sufficient sunshine, distinct temperature differences between day and night, and long frost-free period. The potential of wine market was huge. People here were also enthusiastic, rustic and hardworking. Finally, Mr. Langes determined to spend hundreds of millions of euros to build the bodega at the foot of the Qiaofu hill of Jieshi Mountain branch, cutting hills and rocks and filling soil to open ways. The company was called Bodega Langes, named after his surname.

Bodega Langes (Qinhuangdao) Co., Ltd., was founded in 1999 and located in Jieshi Mountain production area, Changli County, Qinhuangdao City, Hebei Province. It was acquired by Qinhuangdao Hongxing Iron and Steel Co., Ltd. in May 2018, with a registered capital of CNY 248 million. The company covers a total area of more than 2,000 mu (329.47 acres), including more than 1,800 mu (296.53 acres) of self-operated irrigation-free planting and management wine grape base, with an annual output of 400 tons of high-quality wine grapes and a wine storage capacity of 1,000 tons. The company has 130 employees, including 8 national winemakers and 49 with college degree or above.

Adhering to the concept of "Great brewing, Natural taste", the bodega took the lead in adopting natural gravity brewing technology in China. With the beating notes and flowing crystals, it is the first winery in China that plays music to vineyards and wines. The winery is built close to the mountains. And its European garden architectural style is reflected in the blue sky and green fields. It is a high-grade comprehensive winery integrating grape planting, high-grade wine production, wine culture display, wine tasting, conference reception and tourism. It is known as "the first humanistic green winery in China".

Events

In 2020, Hebei Provincial Department of Science and Technology approved the establishment of Hebei Wine Industry Technology Research Institute, with Bodega Langes (Qinhuangdao) Co., Ltd. as the supporting unit. The company participated in the 21st International Wine Festival and was titled "Famous Winery in Jieshi Mountain production area". The Ministry of Science and Technology approved Bodega Langes (Qinhuangdao) Co., Ltd. as a "High-tech Enterprise". Glory 2018 Small Verdot Dry Red Wine won bronze award in the 23rd Interwine Grand Challenge (IGC). Marquis De Mont Noir-B258 Syrah Dry Red Wine and Marselan Special Dry Red Wine won the Quality Award, and Cabernet Sauvignon

Special Dry Red Wine won the Platinum Award in the International Leading Wine & Spirits Quality Award.

In 2019, the 20th International Wine Festival in Changli Qinhuangdao, that is the 20th Anniversary of Bodega Langes, was held in Bodega Langes. The anniversary commemorative wine was launched. Reserve Marselan Dry Red Wine won the grand gold medal and Small Verdot Dry Red Wine won the gold medal in China International Marselan Wine Contest.

In 2018, Bodega Langes was successfully acquired by Hongxing Iron and Steel Co., Ltd. Viognier Dry White Wine won the "New Wine Award" in 2018 China Fine Wine Challenge.

In 2015, it was named "Safe Wine Brand" by the Organizing Committee of China International Food Safety Technology & Innovations Expo.

In 2013, Bodega Langes was invited to attend the 2013 China Wine Conference and made a speech at the forum. It was rated as "China's Five-star Famous Winery".

In 2011, Bodega Langes launched the fifth edition-2009 Red Reserve Wine. Bodega Langes attended the Swiss Bad Ragaz International Wine Festival as the only winery in Asia to be invited, and 2009 Reserve Dry Red Wine was awarded the Special Honor Award by the organizing committee.

In 2010, "Research on Domestic Oak Barrels and Storage of High-grade Dry Red Wine" of Bodega Langes won the second prize of Hebei Science and Technology Progress Award.

In 2008, Bodega Langes launched the third edition, 2006 Blue Reserve Wine, and the fourth edition, the 10th Anniversary edition of 2006 Syrah Single 1.5L Package.

In 2007, Bodega Langes launched the second edition, 2005 Gold Reserve.

In 2005, Bodega Langes launched the first 2003 Silver Reserve of its reserve series. The preparatory meeting of China Chateau Union (CCU) was held in Bodega Langes. In December of the same year, CCU was officially established, and Bodega Langes became one of the first eight wineries of CCU.

In 2003, the first bottle of Dry Red Wine and the first bottle of Rose Red Wine were formally launched.

In the spring of 1999, the first grape plantation was established in Changli, Hebei.

In 1998, Mr. Langes and his experts team inspected the site in China.

Contact Information

Address: North to Duanjiadian Village, Liangshan Township, Changli County, Qinhuangdao City, Hebei Province

Tel: 86-4000901999

32. Hebei Xiadu Winery Co., Ltd.

Hebei Xiadu Winery Co., Ltd. is located in Changli County, Hebei Province. It covers an area of more than 80,000 square meters and has a registered capital of CNY 50 million. Its main product is rose wine. It integrates R&D, production and sales. It is the first enterprise specializing in the production of rose wines and the first Chinese Rose Wine Technology Research and Development Center. With the business philosophy of "committed to brewing the most suitable wine for the tasting of Chinese", "Enterprise Standards for Rose Wine" was drafted and formulated in 2007. Since then, it has become the only first professional enterprise standard in domestic wine industry, and set an example for the wine industry.

The company has two enterprise technology centers, "Hebei Engineering Technology Center" and "Qinhuangdao Characteristic Wine Engineering Technology Center". The company cooperates with University of Science and Technology of China, China Agricultural University, Hebei Agricultural University, Yanshan University, Hebei Normal University of Science & Technology and other colleges and universities and promotes joint efforts of enterprises, universities, and research institutes. They together develop new products such as Aronia dry red series wines, strawberry icewine, mulberry wine, sparkling rose wine and so on. It has independently developed core technologies such as low-temperature complex fermentation, carbonic maceration brewing, thermomaceration and flash steam technology. The technologies have won Hebei Science and Technology Progress Award and the products have been titled Consumer Trusted Products of Hebei Province and Famous Brand Products of Hebei Province for many times. The company was awarded "China Pastoral Complex and Beautiful Rural Characteristic Town Agricultural Demonstration Unit".

Events

In 2021, "Shengshi Xiadu Abloom" was rated as "Hebei Food Special Brand" by Industry and Information Technology Department of Hebei Province.

In 2015, General Administration of Quality Supervision, Inspection and Quarantine of PRC approved Hebei Xiadu Winery Co., Ltd. to use the "Changli Wine" special logo for products protected by Geographical Indication of P. R. China.

In 2014, Hebei Xiadu Winery Co., Ltd. was recognized as "Hebei Key Leading Enterprise of Agricultural Industrialization" by the People's Government of Hebei Province and was evaluated as "Credible Enterprise in Hebei Province".

In 2014, Hebei Xiadu Winery Co., Ltd. was rated as "Hebei Enterprise Technology Center" by Hebei Development and Reform Commission.

In 2013, Hebei Xiadu Winery Co., Ltd. was recognized as "Hebei Province Science and Technology Oriented Small and Medium-sized Enterprise" by Hebei Provincial Department of Science and Technology.

In 2011, Hebei Xiadu Winery Co., Ltd. was awarded the honor of "Hebei No. 1" Xiadu Abloom Rose Wine by Hebei Province Food Industry Association and Hebei Province Food Expert Committee.

In 2010, Shengshi Xiadu Abloom Five Diamond Rose Wine won the silver award in Colombin Cup The Fourth Yantai International Wine Competition.

In 2009, the company was awarded the title of "2009 Most Valuable Wine Enterprise for Investment".

In 2008, "Xiadu" brand won the "Prettech Cup" 2008 China's Most Competitive Potential Brand of Wine.

In 2007, "Enterprise Standards for Rose Wine" passed the expert appraisal by China Alcoholic Drinks Industry Association, filling the gap of China's rose wine standards and creating an example for China's wine industry.

Contact Information

Address: North of Changhuang Highway (Zhangguan Village), Changli County, Qinhuangdao City, Hebei Province

Tel: 86-335-2208999

Chapter 2
Dairy Processing Industry

Shijiazhuang Junlebao Dairy Co., Ltd.

Junlebao Dairy Group, founded in 1995, is now the biggest dairy processing company in Hebei Province, China. It is also awarded National Agricultural Industrialization Key Leading Enterprise, National New-and High-tech Enterprise, as well as National R&D Center for Milk Processing. The group has 14,000 employees, 20 factories, and 13 modern ranches in Hebei Province, Henan Province, Jiangsu Province, and Jilin Province, etc. Junlebao's business can be divided into 4 sections, namely infant milk powder, low-temperature yogurt, normal temperature liquid milk and husbandry. And it is also noted for its entire industrial chains operation to fully guarantee the quality from raw materials to final products, and to provide the consumers nutritious healthy, and safe products.

In order to produce top milk powder of the world, Junlebao pioneered two production modes. One is the entire industrial chains mode, which includes forage planting, cow breeding, production, and processing to ensure the safety of products; the other is the four world-class mode, which includes the world-class advanced ranches, world-class leading factories, world-class partners and world-class quality management system to ensure the quality of products.

Junlebao infant formula is the first one to pass the BRC Global Standard for Food Safety in the global milk powder industry and has become the first domestic milk powder sold in Hong Kong and Macao. Since 2017, Junlebao's Banner

Infant Formula has won the Special Gold Medal of the World Food Quality Evaluation Conference for 3 consecutive years and was awarded the International High-Quality Trophy. In November, 2018, Junlebao won the Nomination of the China Quality Award, which was the first time for milk enterprise to win such an honor.

Junlebao owns the National R&D Center for Milk Processing, the national-local joint engineering laboratory for functional lactic acid bacteria resources and application technology, and other scientific and technological platforms. It has undertaken more than 30 national and provincial scientific research projects, 6 national projects included. It received more than 20 scientific and technological awards, including 4 first prizes of Science and Technology Progress Award of Hebei Province. Junlebao also won some international innovation awards: the JunLebao Comfort-Grow Infant Milk Powder won the Innovation Award of the Global Food Industry Award at the World Congress of Food Science and Technology. In June 2019, Junlebao Dairy's LePlatinum K2 Growing-up Milk Formula and its Yuexianhuo milk won the World Dairy Innovation Awards.

With continuous efforts, Junlebao Dairy has kept the highest sales growth rate in recent years. Junlebao leads milk powder sales in China, with sales growth rate ten times higher than other domestic enterprises, ranking the first in the global market. Its sales of low-temperature drinking yogurt break the sluggish market, ranking the first in the industry.

Events

In 2020, the Pilot Dairy Project, the second stage of Junlebao Banner Dairy, was started in Chabei Management District, Zhangjiakou City, which produces 50,000 tons annually. Junlebao Dairy Group won the award of China Top 500 Private Manufacturing Enterprises.

In 2019, Junlebao Dairy Group won the award of China Top 500 Private Manufacturing Enterprises and won the first prize of Science and Technology Progress Award (Enterprise Technology Innovation Award).

In 2018, Wei Lihua, president of Junlebao Dairy Group, attended the First

Session of the 13th National People's Congress as a representative of the National People's Congress. Weilihua was entitled one of the 100 outstanding Chinese private entrepreneurs at the 40th anniversary of China's reform and opening-up by the United Front Work Department of CPC Central Committee and the All-China Federation of Industry and Commerce.

In 2016, the Junlebao platinum loading infant formula milk powder products started selling in Hong Kong.

In 2015, Junlebao won the first prize of the Science and Technology Progress Award of Hebei Province; Junlebao was approved to build the Postdoctoral Research Station.

In 2014, the Chinese Nutrition Society -Junlebao Infant Nutrition Cooperative R&D Center was established; Junlebao won Hebei Provincial Government Quality Award.

In 2013, Junlebao was approved to build as National-Local Joint Engineering Laboratory.

In 2012, Junlebao won Shijiazhuang Municipal Government Quality Award.

In 2011, Junlebao's probiotic yogurt obtained The Domestic Health Food Approval Certificate.

In 2010, Junlebao won the award of Influencing China: 2009-2010 New Leading Brand.

In 2009, Junlebao won the National R&D Center for Milk Processing.

In 2006, Junlebao won the Well-known Trademark of Hebei Province.

In 2004, Junlebao passed the double certifications of ISO9001 and ISO14001 and won the title of Hebei Top 100 Private Enterprises.

In 2003, the company was the first batch of enterprises to pass the market access examination of General Administration of Quality Supervision, Inspection and Quarantine (AQSIQ) and obtained the production license.

In 2001, the market share of Junlebao bagged activated milk products ranked first in the industry.

In 1995, Junlebao Dairy was established.

Contact Information

Address: Luquan, Shijiazhuang, Hebei

Tel: 86-311-67362665

Chapter 3
Food Processing Industry

1. Jinmailang Mianpin Co., Ltd.

Founded in 1994, Jinmailang Mianpin Co., Ltd. is a large-scale modern integrated food enterprise specializing in producing instant noodles, flour, snack food, fine dried noodles, and beverage. Jinmailang is recognized as National Agricultural Industrialization Key Leading Enterprise and is on the list of China's top 500 private firms. Jinmailang has 28 manufacturing bases across the country and more than 20,000 employees. Its annual processing capacity of wheat is 3 million tons, and the annual production capacity of instant noodles is 14 billion bags or buckets, ranking the top three in the world. The company can produce 20 million tons of drinks, and 500 million marinated eggs a year. It owns the world's largest instant noodle manufacturing base, the world's largest independent instant noodle workshop, and the fastest beverage production line. The annual sales of Jinmailang exceeds CNY 20 billion.

With about 250 thousand mu (41184.2 acres) of high-quality wheat production base and the entire industrial chains, Jinmailang forms a full-service mode including farming, processing, packaging, logistics, information technology, and sales. It is also noted for its provincial R&D platforms such as Hebei Enterprise Technology Center, Hebei SME Cluster Technology Service Center, Hebei Convenience Food Innovation Center, and Hebei Flour Products Industrial Technology Research Institute. The series products of one bucket and a half, one bag and a half, Spicy Lahuangshang instant noodles, and Fan's Kitchen Steam-Cooked Non-Fried Noodles enjoy great popularity in China. Jinmailang products have also been exported to more than 50 countries and regions such as the United States, Canada, Australia, South Korea, and Japan, etc.

Events

In 2020, the company officially started the construction of the Jinmailang Mianpin (Heyuan) project with a total investment of over CNY 1 billion; the construction opening ceremony of the world's first new-generation instant noodle project was held at the Longyao Headquarter with a total of CNY 1.02 billion; the dried noodle high-speed production line project of intelligent production of flour products was started in Yanzhou District, Jining City with a total investment of CNY 1.08 billion; the opening ceremony of the Anyang Hualong Farm Flour Co., Ltd was held; the sales of one bucket and a half and one bag and a half exceeded 5 billion; the sales of Jinmailang plain boiled water exceeded 2.4 billion bottles.

In 2019, the contracts for the constructions were signed for the Jinmailang Heyuan base in Guangdong Province and the Jinmailang Qujing base in Yunnan Province; Beijing Beverage Factory was selected as a National "Green Factory" by the Ministry of Industry and Information Technology; the Fan's Kitchen Instant Noodles won the awards of Best Innovative Product in China's Convenience Food Industry in 2018-2019 and Most Popular Convenience Food in 2019.

Contact Information

Address: No.1, Hualong Street, Xingtai High-tech Industrial Development Zone, Hebei Province.

Tel: 86-319-6598888

2. Hebei Jinshahe Flour Manufacturing Group Co., Ltd.

Jinshahe Group dates back to 1971, and it was originally a dried noodle shop of the Second Production Team of Qingjie People's Commune in Shannan Village of Shahe County. Over 50-year development, Jinshahe Group now employs more than 6,000 people, and has 100 fine dried noodle production lines, with 13,500 tons of wheat processing capacity, and produces 5,000 tons of fine dried noodles. Its production and sales of fine dried noodles and flour rank No. 1 and No. 5 in China respectively. Jinshahe Group has now become a private company engaging in the primary, secondary, and tertiary industries coordinately.

The companies related to the primary industry include Jinshahe Crop Planting Cooperative in Nanhe District, Xingtai City, Hebei Sweet Potato Ridge Agricultural Development Co., Ltd., and Shahe Fozhaoshan Barren Mountain Comprehensive Development Co., Ltd.

The companies related to the secondary industry include Hebei Jinshahe Flour Industry Group Co., Ltd., Xingtai Jinshahe Flour Industry Group Co., Ltd., Langfang Jinshahe Flour Industry Group Co., Ltd. Shanxi Jinshahe Flour Industry Group Co., Ltd., Anhui Jinshahe Flour Industry Group Co., Ltd., Shandong Jinshahe Flour Industry Group Co., Ltd., Xinjiang Alashankou Jinshahe Flour Manufacturing Co., Ltd. and Hebei Jinshahe Beverage Co., Ltd.

The companies related to the tertiary industry include Jinshahe Ecological Restaurant and Hebei Jinshahe Logistics Co., Ltd. The Group also develops industrial tourism. Visitors can watch the production process of flour and fine dried noodles, and enjoy rape flowers in the vast field and red leaves covering Fozhao Mountain.

Jinshahe has passed HACCP, ISO9001, and ISO14001 certifications, and was granted National Agricultural Industrialization Key Leading Enterprise by the Ministry of Agriculture and Rural Affairs in 2010. In 2019, Jinshahe Agricultural Cooperative was awarded National Demonstration Agricultural Cooperative.

The headquarter of Jinshahe Group is located in the bordering area of Hebei,

Shandong and Henan, with a superior geographical position and unique natural environment. This area is also a national high-quality wheat production base, providing company with grain sources and ensuring product quality.

Jinshahe always sticks to the principle of "raising the welfare for the employees, promoting the benefits for the cooperative partners, producing healthy food for the people, and creating a harmonious environment for the society." Over 50 years of efforts, Jinshahe has built constant relationships with more than 5,000 cooperative partners, and the products are popular all over the country, entering the supermarkets such as Wal-Mart, Carrefour, RT-Mart, CR Vanguard, and Tesco, and they are also exported to more than 60 countries and regions in Europe, North and South America, Oceania and Africa, etc.

Events

In 2020, Jinshahe Group won Top 100 Agricultural Industrialization Leading Enterprises and Top 10 Integrated Development Enterprises.

In 2019, Jinshahe was recognized as the National Demonstration Agricultural Cooperative, the National Assured Grain and Oil Demonstration Enterprise, and the Champion of Single Manufacturing Enterprise in Hebei Province.

In 2018, Jinshahe won Hebei Provincial Government Quality Award, Hebei Leading Food Brand, and the Provincial Agricultural Demonstration Cooperative.

In 2017, Jinshahe was awarded the National Demonstration Base for Food and Nutrition Education.

In 2016, Jinshahe won Xingtai Municipal Government Quality Award.

In 2015, Jinshahe was awarded National Staple Food Processing Demonstration Enterprise.

In 2014, Jinshahe won the CIFST Technology Innovation Award: Technology Progress Award.

In 2012, Jinshahe won Henan Science and Technology Progress Award.

In 2011, Jinshahe was awarded China Well-known Trademark.

In 2010, Jinshahe was awarded National Agricultural Industrialization Key Leading Enterprise.

In 2007, Jinshahe was awarded China Top Brand Product.

Contact Information

Address: Eastbound 200 meters along Shahe Crossing of Beijing-Shenzhen Expressway

Tel: 86-4000639222

3. Wudeli Flour Group

Wudeli Flour Group (hereinafter referred to as Wudeli Group) was founded in 1989. The company has grown from a small workshop with a daily wheat processing capacity of less than 15 tons to a large-scale flour milling company with 5,500 employees, 18 branch companies in 18 cities of 6 provinces. It can daily process wheat more than 55,000 tons which ranks No.1 in the world. In 2020, Wudeli's output value was CNY 33.28 billion. Wudeli Group has been ahead of China's flour processing industry in production and sales since 2003. Wudeli aims to be the leading company to provide consumers quality, healthy, and tasty products. And now its products sell well all over the country, with a national market share of 18%. In the next three years, it is estimated that the market share will reach 33%, ranking No.1 among similar products. The titles Wudeli has won are as follows: China Top 500 Enterprise, China Top 500 Manufacturing Enterprise, China Well-known Trademark, the most competitive brand, National Agricultural Industrialization Key Leading Enterprise, National Standardised Behaviour Enterprise, National Food Industry-Leading Enterprise, China's Top 50 Wheat Flour Processing Enterprise, China Top 100 Grain and Oils Enterprise and Top Enterprise in Flour Industries, etc.

Wudeli Group has made a huge investment in scientific and technological innovation to improve flour processing degree and flour yield and to produce different types of flour to conform with Chinese dietary habits. At present, Wudeli can produce more than 140 types of flour. These high-quality flours are white and delicate, with a strong wheat flavor, and suitable for cooking and baking. They can be widely used for making bread, dumplings, noodles, buns, steamed twisted rolls, pancakes, and other flour products. As good raw materials for making various kinds of flour foods, it can keep the delicate shapes of food, and is an ideal choice for families, canteens, hotels, and factories, and is quite popular with consumers.

Events

In 2019, Tianmairan Flour Industry Co., Ltd was established; Handan Flour Co., Ltd. of Wudeli Group, with a daily wheat processing capacity of 3,000 tons, was put into operation; all workshops of Wudeli Group with a production capacity of 45,000 tons passed ISO9001, ISO22000, FSSC22000 and HACCP quality and food safety management system certifications.

In 2016, Wudeli Group ranked 487 in China Top 500 Enterprises and 253 in China Top 500 Manufacturing Enterprises.

In 2015, the AB line of the first workshop of Wudeli Shangqiu Company was put into operation, and the daily processing capacity of the Group reached 40,000 tons for the first time.

In 2013, the fourth workshop of Wudeli Xinxiang Company, processing 600 tons of wheat per day, was put into operation.

In 2012, the third workshop of Wudeli Shenzhou Company was put into operation, and the daily wheat processing capacity of the Group reached 20,000 tons for the first time.

In 2010, the first workshop of Wudeli Xiongxian County Company was put into operation.

In 2009, the first workshop of Wudeli Suqian Company was put into operation.

In 2008, the first workshop of Wudeli Xianyang Company was put into operation, and the daily production capacity of the Group reached 10,000 tons for the first time.

In 2006, the workshop with a daily processing capacity of 80 tons of fine dried noodle was put into operation.

In 2005, Wudeli Group ranked 485 in China Top 500 Manufacturing Enterprises.

In 2004, the Group was awarded National Agricultural Industrialization Key Leading Enterprise by eight Ministries and Commissions.

In 2003, Wudeli Flour Group was established.

In 2000, the fifth factory with a daily processing capacity of 500 tons of wheat was put into operation. The first workshop of Shenzhou Company with a daily wheat processing capacity of 500 tons was put into operation.

In 1999, the fourth factory with a daily wheat processing capacity of 200 tons was put into operation.

In 1997, the third factory with a daily wheat processing capacity of 200 tons was put into operation.

In 1996, the second factory with a daily wheat processing capacity of 200 tons was put into operation.

In 1989, Wudeli's predecessor, New Market Flour Mill, with a daily wheat processing capacity of 15 tons was established in Daming, Hebei Province, and put into operation.

Contact Information

Address: Daming County, Handan City, Hebei Province

Tel: 86-310-6592569

Chapter 4
Beverage Industry

1. Hebei Yangyuan Zhihui Beverage Co., Ltd.

Hebei Yangyuan Zhihui Beverage Co., Ltd., founded in 1997, has been focusing on research, development, production, and sales of walnut milk, a vegetable protein beverage. Since its establishment, the company has been committed to research and market development of walnut milk beverage and aims to change it from a minor flavored beverage with a small market share to a popular mainstream beverage in China. In February, 2018, Yangyuan Beverage was listed on the Shanghai stock exchange and successfully landed on the A-share market.

Yangyuan Company is located in Hengshui Economic Development Zone, Hebei Province and the registered capital is CNY 1.2 billion. The company has 3 wholly-owned subsidiaries, with 1,842 staff and 812 professionals for research and development, 5 manufacturing bases, and 40 walnut milk production lines at an internationally advanced level. Yangyuan walnut milk beverage occupies nearly 10% of the vegetable protein beverage market share in China and 80% market share in the walnut milk market. The annual production capacity has reached 2 million tons, making it the largest walnut milk company in China.

Yangyuan Beverage is known for its strong technical strength and continuously breaks through technical barriers. This company led and participated in the drafting of the industry standard and the national standard of walnut milk beverage; it created the productive technology, which solved the problem of bitter, astringent, and greasy taste of walnut milk; it independently developed full walnut CET cold extraction process, keeping over 97% of the nutrients; it developed the five-fold refinement grinding process, and with the cell lysis technique, the minimum diameter of walnut milk particles can be 80 nanometers, so nutrition is more easily absorbed.

To ensure food safety and product quality, Yangyuan Beverage has introduced advanced inspection and testing equipment. The company's inspection center has testing equipment such as high-performance liquid chromatograph, gas chromatograph-mass spectrometer (GC-MS), Perkin Elmer Atomic Absorption Spectrometer, FOSS dairy analyzer, Malvern Panalytical particle size analyzer, flow cytometer, Kjeldahl analyzer, etc. This center has obtained CNAS lab accreditation qualification and the international mutual recognition qualification. The company is awarded Hebei Enterprise Technology Center, Hebei Walnut Beverage Technology Innovation Center, Hebei Walnut Nutrients Processing Technique Key Laboratory, Key Laboratory of Walnut Beverage in China Light Industry, and Hebei Plant Derived Fermented Beverage Engineering Laboratory. At the end of 2018, the Academician Workstation and the Postdoctoral Research Station for the Six Walnut Milk went into operation.

The company's honors are as follows: National Agricultural Industrialization Key Leading Enterprise, National Agricultural Product Processing Industry Demonstration Enterprise, Annual National Leading Enterprise of Food Industry, Benchmark Brand of Chinese Food Industry (Vegetable Protein Beverage Industry), China Well-known Trademark, China's Top 20 Beverage Industries, Hebei Provincial Government Quality Award, Hebei Top Brand Product, Hebei Quality & Benefit Enterprise, Hebei Leading Light Industry Enterprise and Hebei Key Leading Enterprise.

Events

In 2020, the company won three awards: Food Safety Units (2019-2020), 30 Excellent Cases of the Food Safety Management and Innovation (2019-2020), and the Leading Responsible Enterprise in the 18th China Food Safety Conference.

In 2019, Yangyuan Company co-built Hebei Walnut Nutrients Processing Technique Key Laboratory with Beijing Technology and Business University and Hebei Medical University, and it was approved by Hebei Provincial Department of Science and Technology.

In 2018, Yangyuan Company established the Hebei Academician Workstation jointly approved by Hebei Provincial Department of Science and Technology, Organization Department of Hebei Province, and Hebei Association for Science and Technology; Yangyuan Company established the Postdoctoral Research Station approved by the National Postdoctoral Administrative Committee of Human Resources and Social Security Department.

In 2017, Six Walnuts, a brand of Yangyuan Company, was rated as the Top 10 Most Trusted Beverage Brands by the China Foundation of Consumer Protection and China Food Newspaper.

In 2016, Yangyuan Company won the National May Day Labor Certificate awarded by the All-China Federation of Trade Unions, and the Contribution Medal by China Red Cross Society; the company has passed the European Union's Class A certification of BRC.

In 2015, Yangyuan was awarded the Nutrition Promotion Contribution Award by Chinese Nutrition Society; the company was rated as Top 20 Beverage Industries by China Beverage Industry Association; Six Walnuts was recognized as a Well-known Trademark by the State Administration for Industry and Commerce; Jiangxi Yingtan Yangyuan Zhihui Beverage Co., Ltd. was established.

In 2014, the inspection center of Yangyuan Company obtained the qualification of "CNAS National Laboratory"; the project of Hebei Plant Derived Fermented Beverage Engineering Laboratory was approved by Hebei Development and Reform Commission.

In 2013, Yangyuan Company won Hebei Provincial Government Quality Award; The Nanchang project, covering an area of over 100,000 square meters, was completed and put into operation.

In 2012, Yangyuan Company was awarded Hebei Leading Light Industry Enterprise; Anhui Chuzhou Yangyuan Zhihui Beverage Co. , Ltd. was completed and put into operation.

In 2011, Yangyuan Company was awarded the Annual National Leading Enterprise of Food Industry.

In 2010, Yangyuan Company invested in the promotion of their brands through China Central Television (CCTV) and other famous media; the company's technology center was awarded Enterprise Technology Center of Hebei Province; YANGYUAN and the icon have been recognized as the Well-known Trademark by the Trademark Office of the State Administration for Industry and Commerce.

In 2009, Yangyuan Company passed ISO22000 certification; based on the analysis of customers' needs, the company fixed the slogan "If Using Your Brains Frequently, Drink More Six Walnuts."

In 2008, Yangyuan Company completely moved to the new factory in the North District of the Hengshui Economic and Technological Development Zone.

In 2007, Yangyuan was awarded the Most Potential Enterprise in China's Food Industry.

In 2005, Six Walnuts, a new walnut milk beverage brand was created.

In 2004, Yangyuan Company obtained the certification of ISO9001.

In 2002, Yangyuan Beverage Marketing Company was established.

In 1999, Yangyuan walnut milk won the first prize of Science and Technology Progress Award in Hebei Light Industry and the first prize of Outstanding New Product Award.

In 1997, Hebei Yangyuan Health Beverage Co. , Ltd. , the predecessor of Hebei Yangyuan Zhihui Beverage Co. , Ltd. was established; Yangyuan Company played a leading part in drafting walnut milk beverage industry standards.

Contact Information

Address: North District, Hengshui Economic and Technological Development Zone, Hebei province.

Tel: 86-318-2215883

2. Beijing Huiyuan Beverage & Food Group Co., Ltd.

Beijing Huiyuan Beverage & Food Group Co., Ltd. (hereinafter referred to as "Beijing Huiyuan Group"), established in 1992, is a large-scale joint-stock modernized enterprise group specializing in fruit juice and fruit juice drinks. China Huiyuan Juice Group Co., Ltd., separated from Beijing Huiyuan Group, was listed on the main board of the Stock Exchange of Hong Kong Limited in February 2007. Beijing Huiyuan Group has built 50 modern factories in 22 provinces across the country, which links more than 10 million mu (1.65million acres) of excellent and standardized fruit production base. The networks for sales and service nationwide are built and the national fruit juice industrialized operation system is constructed.

Beijing Huiyuan Group has nearly 200 advanced fruit and vegetable processing and beverage filling production lines. The group has optimized the quality, safety, and environmental management systems and implemented the ISO9001, ISO22000, OHSAS18000, ISO14001 certification systems. It has introduced internationally advanced techniques of fruit puree cold break, juice concentrates ultrafiltration, high-temperature short-time pasteurization fpr beverage filling, cold-aseptic filling, Combi Predis^{TM} Fma, gas containing fruit juice beverage carbonation with aseptic conditions, and gas containing fruit juice sterilization. In addition, it independently developed centrifugal-adsorption coupling technology for debittering and deacidification, which is the most advanced technology in China.

Beijing Huiyuan Group manages to cooperate with other companies, universities, and research institutes. The group cooperates with large companies both at home and abroad and introduces equipment, technology, and functional ingredients, which opens the door for the group to get to know the development of international juice technology. The group has built a cooperative relationship with China Agricultural University, Jinan Fruit Research Institute, Hebei Agricultural University, and the Research Institute of Pomology of CAAS to carry out specific research projects and build a communication platform for product development and innovation. It participated in 3 national scientific and technological support plan projects, one of "Tenth Five-Year Plan", one of "Eleventh Five-Year Plan" and one of "Twelfth Five-Year Plan", two national key research and development plan projects of "Thirteenth Five-Year Plan" and 1 project of the "intergovernmental international scientific and technological innovation cooperation" and undertook 1 project of the National High-tech R&D Program (863 Program). The project Key Technologies and Industrialization of High-quality Preservation and Processing of Special Berries won the second prize of National Science and Technology Progress Award in 2020.

Events

In 2018, Beijing Huiyuan further accelerated the channel optimization and started a new phase in the development of China's top juice brand.

In 2015, it completed the share acquisition of 100% interest of the Shanghai Sandeli Food Company, and established a joint venture, and started to produce tea and coffee drinks, realizing the diversification of products.

In 2013, the listed company acquired the fruit industry subsidiary of the group, merged the fruit processing and fruit pulp manufacturing business into the listed company, which successfully integrated the entire industrial chains and further improved the efficiency.

In 2010, after the internal structural adjustment, the company formed a management system which composed of Huiyuan Juice, Huiyuan Fruit, Huiyuan Agriculture, and Huiyuan Investment, also the company set specific development goals for the whole company.

In 2006, cooperating with strategy and fund investors from Danone of France and Pincus of America, the company completed the overseas restructuring of Huiyuan Juice, and the company successfully listed on the main board of the Stock Exchange of Hong Kong Limited in February 2007.

In 2003, it passed the Safe Beverage Certification of the Chinese beverage industry.

In 2001, Huiyuan introduced the PET cold-aseptic filling production line, which was the first time in Asia, and started to produce True Orange, a new juice beverage packed with PET. Huiyuan obtained many honors such as China Well-known Trademark, China Top Brand Product and National Agricultural Industrialization Key Leading Enterprise, etc.

In 1999, it became one of the Top 10 Juice Beverage Industries in China.

In 1995, Huiyuan produced the first batch of 100% Fruit Juice.

In 1994, Huiyuan moved its headquarter to Beijing.

In 1993, Huiyuan introduced the concentration equipment from abroad and equipped the first cold-aseptic filling production line in China.

In 1992, Huiyuan Group was established.

Contact Information

Address: Beixiaoying Town, Shunyi District, Beijing

Tel: 86-010-60483388

Chapter 5
Potato Processing Industry

1. SnowValley Agriculture Development Co., Ltd.

Located in Chabei Management District, Zhangjiakou City, Hebei Province, the SnowValley Agriculture Development Co., Ltd. (hereinafter referred to as SnowValley Agriculture) was established in 2007 with a registered capital of CNY 85.6487 million. SnowValley Agriculture is a whole industry chain group with potato seed industry as its core, food processing as the main business, modern agricultural service as the extension. The business covers seed breeding, reproduction, promotion, storage, processing and sales. It is an agricultural high-tech industry platform which combines seed selection and breeding of new potato variety, commercialization of varieties and IP (Intellectual Property), agricultural data management, agricultural financial services, development of potato foods and comprehensive deep processing.

SnowValley Agriculture won the titles of National Agricultural Industrialization Key Leading Enterprise, New-and High-tech Enterprise, the Construction and Demonstration Unit of Potato Stock Breeding Base of the Ministry of Agriculture and Rural Affairs, the First Batch of Seed Quality Certification Experiment Units of the Ministry of Agriculture and Rural Affairs, the Key Breakthrough Enterprises of National and Provincial Potato Variety, the Key Credit Enterprises of Chinese Seed Industry, the Vice-President Unit of China Seed Association, the Presidency unit of Potato Branch, and the Experiment Units for

Improving the Protection Ability of New Plant Varieties of the Ministry of Agriculture and Rural Affairs.

SnowValley Agriculture owns 5 seed industry subsidiaries, 2 planting industry subsidiaries, 11 large-scale mechanized farm, 1 potato frozen food processing subsidiary, 1 potato industrial technology research institute and provincial enterprise technology center, 1 postdoctoral innovation and practice base, 1 agricultural machinery service subsidiary, 1 trade service subsidiary and 2 scientific and technical service subsidiary.

Core Seed Industry—Potato "Core Chip"

SnowValley Agriculture has 5,400 m^2 potato tissue culture room, 47,800 m^2 intelligent mini-potato net house, 17,000 m^2 potato industrial technology research institute, 25,000 m^2 processing workshop and 51,500 m^2 intelligent constant temperature storage warehouse. It has a large scale modernized and mechanized large-scale virus-free seed potato breeding base of 160,000 mu (26357.9 acres), which produces 150,000 tons of seed potatoes of different varieties and grades every year and sells them all over the country.

In 2011, SnowValley Agriculture was awarded Provincial Enterprise Technology Centre, and in 2017, it was appraised as Hebei (Zhangjiakou) Potato Industrial Technology Research Institute, now it has 84 R&D personnel. SnowValley Agriculture began to breed new potato varieties in 2008. It introduced, and collected from home and abroad, and independently developed more than 400 potato varieties. With modern breeding techniques, it carried out breeding new varieties through variation in the field and hybridization. SnowValley Agriculture can create 100-150 hybrids every year, and get 300,000-500,000 seeds. The progeny selection nursery area has reached more than 200 mu (32.95 acres). Among its 32 experimental sites in different ecological areas in China, SnowValley can select 3-4 strains with developing trend every year. It has selected and bred more than 40 new varieties and strains of "Snow Peak" and "Snow Valley" series, of which 10 varieties obtained the certificate of plant variety rights (PVR) and 7 have been registered. Many potato varieties of SnowValley Agriculture are suitable for production in different ecological fields in China, which are highly valued by the market. Now SnowValley Agriculture potatoes have been planted in an area of more than 2.8 million mu (461263.38 acres). In 2020, SnowValley participated in the experimental spacecraft project of manned spacecraft and its potato seeds were sent into the space for experiments. The seeds returned from the space have been planted for experiments, which means that SnowValley has made a solid step in breeding innovation and research.

SnowValley Agriculture—the Potato Food Leading Enterprise

In 2012, SnowValley Food was established, targeting at the unbalanced domestic potato varieties, low added value of potato sales and low returns. In 2017, SnowValley Agriculture invested CNY 1 billion to build Phase II Project of the SnowValley Food Potato Processing Project. The project introduced the world's advanced potato frozen fries and snack production line, and built a modern biomass energy supply center, zero emissions environmental protection center, automatic stereo cold storage and related equipment. The annual processing capacity was 400,000 tons of potato raw materials, 150,000 tons of frozen fries, and 10,000 tons of potato powder. SnowValley Food covers a series of products such as crispy fries, canteen special fries, straight cut (1/4″), straight cut (3/8″), potato specialities, potato flakes, etc. At present, it has several product brands such as Cazzi, Snow Peak and Potato Crisp Time. SnowValley Food has developed into one of the leading suppliers of frozen potato processing industry in China, and is a high-quality fries supplier for domestic large-scale chain catering enterprises, large supermarkets, hotels and restaurants, as well as a high-quality potato powder supplier for domestic brands of potato chips and snack foods. SnowValley Food has been exported to more than 10 countries in Southeast Asia, West Asia and Africa.

In 2020, SnowValley Food was certified as the National High-Tech Enterprise and the National "Green Factory". Its processing workshop passed the BRC-A+ and BRC-AA certification, which is characterized by high standards, strict requirements and low pass rate in the industry. The workshop also passed the Halal food certification, ISO9001-2015, GB/T19001 and HACCP food safety system certification. SnowValley Food truly achieves "from the seeds to the table, take care of every step."

Collaborations Among the Company, Universities and Research Institutes

SnowValley Research Institute has undertaken five provincial and ministerial projects for Pilot Project to Improve the Protection Ability of New Varieties of Agricultural Plants of Development Center of Science and Technology of Ministry of Agriculture and Rural Affairs. Also, the institute obtained 1 patent for invention, 19 utility model patents, and 10 appearance patents. SnowValley Research Institute has built close cooperative relationships with high level potato research units at home and abroad, including Institute of vegetables and Flowers of Chinese Academy of Agricultural Science, Heilongjiang Academy of Agricultural Sciences, Institute of Environment and Sustainable Development in Agriculture of Chinese Academy of Agricultural Sciences, South China Agricultural University, Shenyang Agricultural University and Wageningen University & Research. Also, SnowValley Research Institute has established a potato scientific research platform to promote market operation and achievement sharing. In 2018, the Project of Research on High Yield Potato Varieties and Cultivation Mode in Heilongjiang Province was completed. Measured by experts from the Heilongjiang Academy of Agricultural Sciences and Heilongjiang Bayi Agricultural University, the yield of "Snow Peak" new potato varieties reached 5.74 tons per mu, setting a new record in Heilongjiang Province.

Quality Assurance

SnowValley Agriculture started the construction of product quality traceability system from its establishment. In 2008, it took the lead in passing China G. A. P. certification, and in 2009, it passed the Global G. A. P. certification, ISO9001 Quality Management System Certification, ISO22000 Food Safety Management System Certification, and passed the supplier qualification audit of multinational supermarket chains and the third party audit of SGS and Starfarm. It has also obtained organic food certification, and the production, planting system of fresh potato and product quality management system have reached the standards required by the European Retail Alliance.

In 2011, SnowValley Agriculture was recognized as the agricultural product traceability system construction unit by Ministry of Agriculture and Rural Affairs. At present, SnowValley Agriculture is the only domestic potato company that has passed the certifications of China G. A. P, Global G. A. P., ISO9001, ISO22000 and Green Food. SnowValley Agriculture has the largest planting area among all the companies with single corp and is the only one passing the Global G. A. P.

SnowValley Agriculture is committed to achieving the ecological empowerment agriculture, benefiting all the participants in the entire industrial chains, realizing the integrated development of agricultural modernization and informationization, and creating a new model that features comprehensive and win-win effects. Through these actions, SnowValley Agriculture promotes China's potato industrialization and helps ensure food security in China. Above all, SnowValley lights the way to China's potato industry development with science and technology.

Events

In 2020, the first domestic Postdoctoral Innovation Practice Base of potato enterprises was settled in SnowValley Agriculture; SnowValley Agriculture Group participated in the national space breeding research project, sending potato seeds into the space and began a new stage in breeding; SnowValley Food was appraised as the Excellent Private Enterprises in Hebei Province.

In 2019, SnowValley Agriculture obtained the license of national integration of planting, reproduction and promotion of crop seed production and management.

In 2018, Hebei (Zhangjiakou) Potato Industrial Technology Research Institute was approved and listed in Hebei Industrial Technology Research Institute.

In 2017, Hebei (Zhangjiakou) Potato Industrial Technology Research Institute was established.

In 2016, the construction of the potato technology research and development center was started, and the expansion project of the potato processing production line was completed.

In 2015, SnowValley Agriculture Development Co., Ltd. held the founding meeting & the first shareholders' meeting.

In 2014, SnowValley Agriculture Group successfully introduced a new round of investment, and its registered capital increased to CNY 65.7 million.

In 2013, the First Phase of Potato Fries Processing Project was tested and debugged; SnowValley Food passed QS certification; SnowValley potato was recognized as the Grade A Green Food Products; SnowValley Agriculture has been recognized as the National Agricultural Industrialization Key Leading Enterprise; the construction of State-owned Chabei ranch base for virus-free processing type potato stock breeding was started.

In 2012, Zhangjiakou SnowValley Food Co., Ltd was registered; the construction of the production line of the First Phase of Potato Fries Processing Project launched.

In 2011, the company invested in the construction of SnowValley Xar Moron farm in Balin Youqi, Chifeng city, Inner Mongolia; Hexigten SnowValley Farming and Animal Husbandry Science and Technology Co., Ltd was registered; the company's technology center was recognized as the Provincial Enterprise Technology Center.

In 2010, Zhangjiakou SnowValley Agriculture Machinery Service Co., Ltd. was registered; the branch company of Beijing Science and Technology of Zhangjiakou SnowValley Agriculture Development Co., Ltd. was registered; SnowValley 100% acquired Inner Mongolia Xueyuan Potato Seed Industry Co., Ltd; SnowValley was rated as the Provincial Key Leading Enterprise in Agriculture Industrialization by Hebei provincial government; Snow Valley's seed potato was awarded the Hebei Top Brand.

In 2009, Xilinhot Snow Valley Agriculture Development Co., Ltd. was registered.

In 2008, the registered capital of Zhangjiakou Snow Valley Agriculture Development Co., Ltd. increased to CNY 50 million.

In 2007, Zhangjiakou Snow Valley Agriculture Development Co., Ltd. was established with a registered capital of CNY 10 million; the demonstration project of potato industrialization in Zhangjiakou city was established with a planned total investment of CNY 850 million; the company formally signed a cooperation agreement with HZPC company from the Netherlands, the largest potato breeding company in the world, to jointly carry out the breeding project of new potato varieties in China.

Contact Information

Address: Snow Valley Industrial Park, Chabei Management District, Zhangjiakou City, Hebei Province

Tel: 86-400-851-6000

2. Zhangjiakou Hongji Agriculture Science and Technology Development Co., Ltd.

Established in 2008, Zhangjiakou Hongji Agriculture Science and Technology Development Co., Ltd. is the National Agricultural Industrialization Key Leading Enterprise and the National Agricultural Product Processing Industry Demonstration Enterprise, which is engaged in potato seedling, breeding, planting, storing and potato powder processing. It has more than 300 employees and the annual business revenue is nearly CNY 200 million. The company is located 260 kilometers away from Beijing, adjacent to Inner Mongolia, Shanxi, Beijing and Tianjin, and enjoys convenient transportation. The company has potato powder processing production lines and seed potato breeding systems. Also, it has the leading potato powder processing capacity and market share in China. The company's main products are potato flake, potato cake premixed powder, oat and quinoa.

The company has a planting base of 30,000 mu (4942 acres), 15,000 mu (2471 acres) for potatoes and 15,000 mu for oat, quinoa and buckwheat. This company annually produces 10,000 tons of potato flakes, 50 million virus-free potato seedlings, 100 million mini-potatoes, and 40,000 tons of virus-free seed potatoes; it has a constant temperature and humidity gas-adjusted storehouse with a total storage capacity of 90,000 tons, a potato powder processing workshop with an area of 6,000 square meters, a tissue culture center with an area of 3,800 square meters, a solar greenhouse with an area of 10,000 square meters and 400 greenhouses. The company drafted and participated in developing national industrial standard for potato flakes (SB/T10752-2012) and national industrial standard for circulation of seed potatoes. Hongji potato flake has won the Well-known Trademark of Hebei Province. In 2017, it won the gold medal for the 15th International Agricultural Exposition and was selected as the franchised supplier of Zhang Jiakou the Belt and Road Initiative international skiing events.

The company has established close scientific research cooperation with the Chinese Academy of Agricultural Sciences, Hebei Agricultural University, Zhangjiakou Academy of Agricultural Sciences, etc. Besides, it established Hebei Potato Processing Technology Innovation Center with Hebei Agricultural University and Hebei North University.

Events

In 2012, Hongji Potato Breeding Center was put into operation.

In 2011, the potato powder production line with an annual output of 10,000 tons was put into operation. The company was recognized as the fifth batch of National Agricultural Industrialization Key Leading Enterprise.

In 2010, Zhangjiakou Hongji Potato Breeding Center Co., Ltd was established.

In 2008, Zhangjiakou Hongji Agriculture Science and Technology Development Co., Ltd. was established.

Contact Information

Address：Yushugou，Saibei Management District，Zhangjiakou City，Hebei Province

Tel：86-313-5755901、5755000

Chapter 6
Liquor Brewing Industry

1. Hebei Hengshui Laobaigan Liquor Co., Ltd.

Hebei Hengshui Laobaigan Liquor Co., Ltd., is a holding subsidiary of Hebei Hengshui Laobaigan Liquor-making (group) Co. Ltd. In 1946, the 18 traditional private brewage workshops in Hengshui were nationalized and built the State-owned Hengshui Brewery of South Hebei Administrative Office, the predecessor of the company. Hebei Hengshui Laobaigan Liquor Co., Ltd. is the first liquor production company built after the founding of the New China. In 2002, the company was listed on Shanghai Stock Exchange. It has been recognized as the backbone enterprise of Chinese liquor and the national standard drafting unit of Laobaigan, one of the liquor flavor types. In 2018, with the approval of the China Securities Regulatory Commission, the company annexed Fenglian Liquor Industry and became a listed company with five enterprises, which was the first to produce liquor of three flavor types (laobaigan flavor, strong-flavor, sauce-flavor) in China. The company covers an area of more than 4,000 mu (659 acres), with more than 5,000 employees and an annual production capacity of 120,000 tons quality liquor.

Hengshui Laobaigan liquor, the leading product of the company, has a long history of more than 2,000 years. According to written records, it emerged in Han Dynasty, flourished in Tang Dynasty, and was officially named in Ming Dynasty. In 1915, it won the highest award, Grand Prize in Panama Pacific International Exposition, and became well-known all over the world. Hengshui Laobaigan liquor adopts the technique of medium-temperature Daqu, fermentation in underground vats, and Laowuzeng mixed-steaming and mixed-heating multiple feedings solid fermentation technology. It features elegant and fragrant, mellow and thick, refreshing, harmonious, and long aftertaste. In recent years, Hengshui Laobaigan and its products have won honors of China Well-known Trademark, Chinese Time-honored Brand, representative liquor of laobaigan flavor, national intangible cultural heritage, etc. In 2018, Hengshui Laobaigan liquor won the Double Gold, the highest prize in Las Vegas Global Spirit Awards Competition, and was appraised as the Best In Show. In 2019, the company won the National Quality Award, a very important prize in China. In 2020, the liquor, Hengshui Laobaigan 1915, won the Grand Gold Quality Award, the highest award in the Monde Selection, and the liquor Shibajiufang (15 years) won the Gold Award.

Events

In 2015, the 100th anniversary of Hengshui Laobaigan liquor winning the Grand Prize in 1915 Panama Pacific International Exposition.

In 2013, Hengshui Laobaigan liquor won Hebei Provincial Government Quality Award.

In 2010, at the Shanghai World Expo, Laobaigan liquor was recognized as the only designated liquor to be exhibited in the Hebei pavilion and won the Millennium Gold Award from related organizations of the United Nations.

In 2008, the traditional brewing technique of Hengshui Laobaigan liquor was selected as national intangible cultural heritage, and its brand Shibajiufang won China Well-known Trademark. So the company has two China Well-known Trademarks.

In 2006, Hengshui Laobaigan was recognized as a Chinese Time-honored Brand by the Ministry of Commerce.

In 2005, the company was approved by China National Tourism Administration as the first batch of national model sites for industrial tourism.

In 2004, the registered trademark Hengshui and the icon of Hengshui Laobaigan liquor were recognized as China Well-known Trademark by the State Administration for Industry and Commerce, and became the first liquor brand to receive this honor in Hebei Province; initiated by Hengshui Laobaigan, the evaluation work of Laobaigan flavor was successfully conducted, and Laobaigan became one more liquor flavor in China.

In 2002, Hebei Yufeng Industry Co., Ltd, mainly invested by Hengshui Laobaigan, got listed on Shanghai Stock Exchange and became the only listed company in the liquor industry in Hebei Province at that time.

In 1996, Hebei Hengshui Laobaigan Liquor-making (group) Co. Ltd. was formally established.

In 1994, Hengshui Laobaigan took the lead in passing ISO9001 certification and quality management system certification in Hebei Province and obtained the pass for export trade.

In 1993, it was renamed Hebei Hengshui Laobaigan Brewery; the press conference of Hengshui Laobaigan winning double gold medals was held in the Great Hall of the People, Beijing.

In 1992, Hengshui Laobaigan won the gold medal of International Food Expo (Hong Kong); Hengshui Laobaigan won the gold medal of China High-end Wine and Spirits Expo, which was the only gold medal in Hebei Province.

In 1991, Hengshui Laobaigan was awarded the medal and certificate of excellent new products prize at the China Food Industry New Achievement Exhibition.

In 1989, the registered trademark Laoqiao was appraised as the Hebei Famous Trademark by the Hebei Administration of Industry and Commerce.

In 1988, Hengshui Laobaigan liquor won the gold medal at the first China Food Industry Exhibition.

In 1946, the State-owned Hengshui Brewery of South Hebei Administrative

Office was established.

In 1915, Hengshui Laobaigan won Grand Prize in the Panama Pacific International Exposition.

Contact Information

Address: Hengshui City, Hebei Province

Tel: 86-318-2992385

2. Hebei Xiongan Baofu Winery Co., Ltd.

Hebei Xiongan Baofu Winery Co., Ltd has a long history, and "Wanquanyong", its predecessor, was founded in Guangxu period of Qing Dynasty. The ruins of Shaoguo, the ancient producing liquor workshop, Were in Rongcheng County, Xiong'an New Area, Hebei Province. Li Junshan, a scholar of Dongsizhuang Village, Rongcheng County, lived in the Guangxu period of Qing Dynasty. He once taught in a private school, and later assisted in collecting salt and liquor production tax. He founded Wanquanyong and managed the business very well. At its peak, Wanquanyong had 9 fermentation ponds, 1 liquor producing workshop, and more than 20 employees. Every day, the workshop could produce 400 kg of wine with 2,000 kg of grain. It had branch workshops in the town of Rongcheng County and Baoding City. The liquor was sold well and distributed to Yixian County to the west, Anguo County to the south, Tianjin City to the east, and Beiping City to the north. On July 7th, 1937, the Chinese People's War of Resistance against Japanese Aggression broke out. The Chinese people were living in poverty, and the liquor business failed to survive. The relics of fermenting tank, liquor workshop, and the well were partially preserved.

In 1996, Li Hongtao, the great-grandson of Li Junshan, visited folk winemakers and collected ancient wine-making recipes. In 2009, he founded Hebei Baoding Fu Wine Co., Ltd. at the original site of Wanquanyong, and in 2018, he renamed it Hebei Xiongan Baofu Winery Co., Ltd with the approval of Xiong'an New Area Management Committee.

Hebei Xiongan Baofu Winery Co., Ltd is located in Rongcheng Town, Rongcheng County, Xiong'an New Area, with a registered capital of CNY 168 million, an area of more than 200 mu (33 acres), and a building area of 58,000 square meters. It has a series of modern equipment such as grain crushing, fermentation and distillation, liquor cellar storage, blending, and filling. The company has total assets of CNY 229 million and an annual output of 1,000 tons of original liquor.

After 20 years of development, the company has become a collectivized company with liquor brewing and marketing as its core, consisting of six major sections, including cultural tourism, hotel catering, financial guarantee, series commerce, and central kitchen. The company has original brands of liquor products such as Baoding Hundred Years and Millennium Plan and has been rated as Famous Trademark Enterprise of Hebei Province, Hebei Quality and Integrity AAAAA Brand Enterprise, Hebei Assured Wine Production and Marketing Demonstration Base, and National Standard Assured Wine Project Demonstration Enterprise. Its core product Baoding Hundred Years was rated as Hebei's High-quality Products and Hebei's Time-honored Brand and was awarded Most Popular Hometown Brand at the First Industry Exhibition in Baoding in 2006, which became a model of local liquor. The popular liquor has been sold in more than 10 provinces for 15 years and is the best-selling local liquor in Baoding.

The company manages to seek innovative development, and jointly establishes Liquor Innovation Center with Jiangnan University, which is at the forefront of microbial fermentation research in China. In August 2018, the company employed Mr. Lai Dengmin, the former chief engineer of Sichuan Swellfun Co., Ltd., and national brewery master, as its chief engineer, to improve the Laowuzeng brewing technology and improve the product research and development level, and realize the great-leap-forward development. The company has been rated as the High-tech SMEs and the National New-and High-tech Enterprise.

Based on exploring the long history and cultural allusions of Xiong'an New Area, the company invested in the construction of Xiong'an Liquor Culture Museum, which vividly demonstrated the long history and cultural heritage of Xiong'an and the unique charm of Laowuzeng liquor making technology. At the same time, it built the theme park of Baoding's classic story "Top 10 Liquor Legends", Wanquanyong Site, Yujing Ganquan Site, cafe, lotus ponds, covered bridges, Emperor Yao Square, which realized the perfect combination of modern liquor enterprise and elegant garden scenic spots and was awarded China AAA Scenic Areas.

Events

In 2019, Hebei Millennium Plan Liquor Co., Ltd was established.

In 2018, Hebei Baoding Fu Wine Co., Ltd. was renamed Hebei Xiongan Baofu Winery Co., Ltd.

In 2016, Hebei Jinyuankang Food Co., Ltd. was established.

From 2010 to 2012, the group company was built whose business covered finance, hotel, tourism development, landscaping, and commerce.

In 1998, Baoding Hundred Years Brewery Co., Ltd. was established.

In 1996, Hebei Baoding Fu Wine Co., Ltd. was established.

Contact Information

Address: Rongcheng Town, Rongcheng County, Xiong'an New Area, Hebei Province

Tel: 86-312-5608222

Chapter 7
Other Food Industries

1. Baoding Huaimao Food Technology Co., Ltd.

The history of Huaimao can be traced back to 1671, when Zhao's couple from Shaoxing, Zhejiang Province started their business in Baoding and established Huaimao. With the continuous accumulation of wealth, they became one of the leaders in the northern sauce industry and were called one of the Four Sauce Brands in North China together with Beijing Liubiju sauce, Linqing Jimei sweet sauce, and Jining Yutang sauce. In 1956, the State-owned Baoding Pickles Factory was established based on the original Huaimao and other 26 sauce shops in Baoding. In 1983, to keep it developing well, the Joint State-owned Baoding Pickles Factory was renamed Baoding Huaimao Pickles Factory and registered the trademark of Huaimao. Later in 1999, it was reorganized as a joint-stock enterprise, namely Hebei Baoding Huaimao Co., Ltd. In 2006, Huaimao was first recognized as a Chinese Time-honored Brand by the Ministry of Commerce. In 2007, the production technique of Huaimao pickles was recognized as provincial intangible cultural heritage by the People's Government of Hebei and Hebei Provincial Department of Culture. Over the years, Hebei Baoding Huaimao Co., Ltd. has won many honors, including the Most Popular Chinese Time-honored Brand Award, the Ministry of Commerce of the People's Republic of China Quality Product Award, Hebei Famous Brand, Hebei Best-Selling Brand, the Famous Commercial Enterprises in Hebei Province, etc., and the products have entered the International wholesale center for quality products. In 2013, in order to break the bottleneck of development, Hebei Baoding Huaimao Co., Ltd. decided to move to a new site and registered a wholly-owned subsidiary namely Baoding Huaimao Food Technology Co., Ltd. Huaimao has a history as long as 350 years since its establishment in 1671.

Baoding Huaimao Food Technology Co., Ltd. is located in Jintai Economic and Technological Development Zone, Dingxing County, Hebei Province. It has a registered capital of CNY 150 million, covers an area of 300 mu (49.4 acres), and has a building area of 64,000 square meters. It is a comprehensive seasoning production enterprise. Its main products are Huaimao sweet flour paste, Huaimao sauce, Huaimao pickles, and Huaimao vinegar. It has 500 feeding hoisting equipment, continuous cooking equipment, fermentation equipment, pressing equipment, storage facilities, cleaning equipment, pickling facilities, and filling equipment, etc., and the total value of assets reaches CNY 520 million. The annual design capacity: 30,000 tons of sweet flour paste, 20,000 tons of sauce, 20,000 tons of vinegar, 5,000 tons of pickles, 30,000 tons of seasoning, and 20,000 tons of storage capacity. The company has 160 employees, including 1 national condiment industry specialist, 2 senior engineers, and 36 people with college education or above.

The company has specialized scientific research and quality inspection institutions. In 2000, it set up an Edible Condiments Technology R & D Center. In 2019, the Hebei Provincial Department of Science and Technology approved the construction of the Hebei Sweet Sauce and Pickled Vegetables Technology Innovation Center. In 2018, the Key Technology Research Project on Golden Silk Jujube Vinegar Brewing, which was jointly completed by the company and Hebei Agricultural University, reached the international leading level and won the second prize of Science and Technology Progress Award of Hebei Province.

With the standardized operation, the company has obtained the double certification of GB/T19001-2016/ISO9001-2015 Quality Management System and HACCP. In 2021, it was recognized as High-tech SMEs by the Hebei Provincial Department of Science and Technology and an Education Demonstration Base of

Food Safety Management by the Administration for Market Regulation, leading the industry in quality management and technological innovation.

Events

In 2018, Baoding Huaimao Food Technology Co., Ltd. was put into operation.

In 2013, Baoding Huaimao Food Technology Co., Ltd. was established.

In 2007, the production technique of Huaimao pickles was recognized as provincial intangible cultural heritage by the People's Government of Hebei Province and Hebei Provincial Department of Culture.

In 2006, Huaimao was recognized as the first batch of Chinese Time-honored Brand by the Ministry of Commerce.

In 1999, Hebei Baoding Huaimao Co., Ltd. was established.

In 1995, Huaimao was recognized as a Well-known Trademark of Hebei by Hebei Provincial Administration for Industry and Commerce.

In 1983, the State-owned Baoding Pickles Factory was renamed Baoding Huaimao Pickles Factory and the trademark Huaimao was registered.

Contact Information

Address: No. 6 Huaimao Road, Dingxing County, Hebei Province

Tel: 86-312-5875606

2. Baoding Way Chein Food Industrial Co., Ltd.

Baoding Way Chein Food Industrial Co., Ltd. is located in Baoding City, Hebei Province, and was founded in 1991, with a total area of 120,000 square meters. It has been engaged in the production and sales of condiments, solid drinks and convenience foods for nearly 30 years. The company is headquartered in Baoding National High-tech Industrial Development Zone and has two production bases. It has more than 600 employees, a registered capital of CNY 81.5 million and an annual comprehensive output value of CNY 360 million.

The first branch of Baoding Way Chein Food Industrial Co., Ltd. is located at No. 1630 Lianchi South Street, Lianchi District, Baoding City. It covers an area of 30 mu (4.9 acres) and is the main production base of solid drinks and convenience foods. It produces more than 250 kinds of products in 12 series, including fruit drinks, tea drinks, ice drinks, hot drinks, desserts, western-style thick soup, baking premixed powder, and blended tea products. The factory has three independent production lines for solid beverage, convenience food, and tea, with an average annual production capacity of 13,000 tons, mainly supplying Chinese and Western food factories, casual dining restaurants, and water bars.

The second branch of Baoding Way Chein Food Industrial Co., Ltd. is located at No. 167 Xinhua East Road, Qingyuan District, Baoding City. It covers an area of 130 mu (21.4 acres) and is the main condiment production base of the company. It mainly produces fermented soy sauce powder, hydrolyzed vegetable protein powder, compound condiment powder, etc. It has equipped with several production lines such as spray drying, hydrolysis, mixing, and packaging. The annual production capacity could reach 42,000 tons. The raw materials it used are non-transgenic soybean meal and corn protein produced in Northeast China. The annual consumption is equivalent to 3,500 tons of soybean and 40,000 tons of corn.

Way Chein Food has established a quality assurance system from the raw material acceptance, product inspection, to transportation and distribution. In 1998, 1999, and 2003, the company took the lead in passing the certifications of ISO9001, ISO14001, and HACCP food safety management system in the industry, and was included in the One Hundred First of China's Food Industry in the past five decades since the founding of the People's Republic of China.

Way Chein Food has its own R&D center and its laboratory has passed CNAS accreditation (CNAS L1597). The laboratory has the same testing effectiveness as national level laboratory, which ensures stable product quality and effective product output. With its independent research and development technology, more than 100 kinds of products of the nine series, such as fermented soy sauce powder, hydrolyzed protein powder, and compound seasoning powder have met the needs of domestic and international markets and fill the gaps in the domestic market. At present, Way Chein Food's sales network has covered more than 30 provinces, cities, and autonomous regions in China. The products are exported to 32 countries and regions such as Southeast Asia, the United States, Canada, Australia, etc. The company enjoys a steady growth in sales and holds a leading position in the industry both at home and abroad. Way Chein Food has become the most important condiment supplier for the Top 500 Companies in the international food industry.

In 2014, Way Chein Food was officially listed in the National Equities Exchange And Quotations Co., Ltd., and was the first Taiwan-invested company in Hebei. In 2015, it was appraised as a New & High-tech Enterprise and Little Giant of Technology Enterprise by the Science and Technology Department of Hebei Province. Way Chein Food has been rated as the National Top Tax Payer, Advanced Technology-based Enterprise, and AA+-Level Credit Company by provincial and municipal government units and R&D institutions. Due to its good credit, it was awarded the designated enterprise for business tendency survey by the People's Bank of China in 2018.

Events

In 2015, it was appraised as a high-tech enterprise by Hebei Science and Technology Department.

In 2014, it was officially listed in the National Equities Exchange And Quotations Co., Ltd. (stock name: Way Chein Food, stock code: 830915); it passed the ISO22000 system certification.

In 2010, it passed the IDCP Standard Attestation of the Philippines.

In 2006, Baoding Way Chein Food Industrial Co., Ltd. was established and two branches were set up at the same time.

In 2005, it passed the certifications of British BRC and Indonesian MUI.

In 2004, its laboratory passed CNAS accreditation.

In 2003, it passed the certifications of HACCP food safety management system and HALAL certification.

In 2002, Qingyuan Hongsheng Way Chein Food Industry Co., Ltd. was established, and Way Chein passed the certification of the KOSHER system.

In 1999, it passed ISO14001 environmental management system certification.

In 1998, it passed ISO9001 quality management system certification.

In 1992, Baoding Way Chein Food Industry Co., Ltd was established.

Contact Information

Address: No. 178 Tiane Middle Road, Baoding City, Hebei Province

Tel: 86-0312-2124937, 2132158

3. Chenguang Biotech Group Co., Ltd. (CCGB)

Chenguang Biotech Group Co., Ltd. (CCGB) is a high-tech listed company focusing on extracting effective ingredients from plants and has more than 30 subsidiaries in China, India, and Zambia, etc. The products cover more than one hundred varieties of six series, including natural colors, spice extracts and essential oils, nutritional and pharmaceutical extracts, functional food, natural sweeteners, oils, and protein. Nowadays, Chenguang Biotech has become a leading company in China's plant extracts industry, and also an important supplier of plant extracts worldwide.

Chenguang Biotech has obtained many honorary titles, such as National Agricultural Industrialization Key Leading Enterprise, National New-and High-tech Enterprise, National Contract-honoring and Credit-worthy Enterprise, and National Champion of Single Manufacturing Enterprise. It has established scientific research platforms such as National Enterprise Technology Center, Academician Workstation, Postdoctoral Research Station, and National-Local Joint Engineering Laboratory. Chenguang Biotech has more than 200 national authorized patented technologies and won 59 provincial and ministerial level scientific and technological awards. In 2013, it won the Hebei Provincial Government Quality

Award. In 2014 and 2017, it won two—second prizes of National Science and Technology Progress Award.

The company has more than 800 employees, with bachelor degree members accounting for more than 50%. Chenguang Biotech features a pioneering, innovative, and learning team with doctors and masters as the core, bachelors as the backbone, and professionals as the main body. It is also known for its advanced processing equipment and scientific and efficient technological innovation management system. Now Chenguang Biotech's technology and product quality occupy a leading position in the world. In the past 21 years, with its own strength, Chenguang has promoted China's paprika oleoresin production in the world, making China a world leader in the production of paprika oleoresin and added a world-leading industry to China. Today, Chenguang Biotech has become the world leader in the natural pigment industry and an important international supplier of plant extracts, which has promoted the re-upgrading of China's plant extracts industry and further enhanced the influence of "Made in China."

Events

In 2020, Chenguang Biotech won the Recognition Award of China Industrial Award.

In 2019, Chenguang Biotech (America) LLC was established.

In 2018, Chenguang Biotech won the title of China Intellegent Manufacturing Pilot Demonstration Enterprise.

In 2017, Chenguang Biotech won the title of Champion of Single Manufacturing Enterprise and obtained the second prize of the National Science and Technology Progress Award.

In 2016, the production and sales of lutein became the first in the world.

In 2014, the production and sales of capsicum oleoresin ranked first in the world; the company won the second prize of the National Science and Technology Progress Award.

In 2012, Chenguang Bio-Tech (India) Pvt. Ltd., the first overseas subsidiary, was successfully put into trial production.

In 2010, Chenguang Biotech was listed on the Second-board Market of the Shenzhen Stock Exchange. Stock code: 300138.

In 2008, the production and sales volume of paprika oleoresin became the first in the world.

In 2006, its first subsidiary was established in Xinjiang—Xinjiang Chenguang Natural Pigment Co., Ltd.

In 2002, the company signed the first export order of US$ 3,500.

In 2000, the company raised CNY 380,000, and built a joint-stock company, Quzhou Chenguang Natural Pigment Co., Ltd., and realized sales income of CNY 1.878 million.

Contact Information

Address: Quzhou County, Handan City, Hebei Province

Tel: 86-310-8859030

4. Qinhuangdao Haidongqing Food Co., Ltd.

Established in 2000, Qinhuangdao Haidongqing Food Co., Ltd., is a modern technology-based private company integrating aquaculture, processing, refrigeration, cold chain logistics and storage, aquatic products import and export trade and leisure fishery. The company is the Agricultural Industrialization Key Leading Enterprise in Hebei Province. The main business is to export vacuum-packed cooked clam.

The company has more than 500 employees and has set the professional R&D institution, the technology R&D management center and the R&D laboratory. The laboratory covers an area of more than 300 square meters and are equipped with advanced inspection and testing R&D equipment and facilities.

Events

In 2020, it was awarded the Special Food Brand in Hebei Province.

In 2017, it was approved to build the Vacuum Food R&D Center in Hebei Province.

In 2016, it was approved as the Demonstration Enterprise for Introducing Talents and Intelligence in Hebei Province.

In 2015, it won the first prize of Science and Technology Progress Award in Hebei Province.

In 2014, it was approved as the Agricultural Industrialization Key Leading Enterprise in Hebei Province.

In 2010, it was approved as the Technological Growth Enterprise.

In 2008, it won the title of Advanced Enterprise in Food Safety and Reassuring Project.

Contact Information

Address: Haigang District, Qinhuangdao City, Hebei Province

Tel: 86-335-3352212, 13513365850

5. Chengde Ruitai Food Co., Ltd.

Chengde Ruitai Food Co., Ltd. has been focusing on hawthorn series food. It produces more than 70 kinds of products including candied hawthorn, canned hawthorn drinks, hygienic hawthorn red wine, hawthorn dietary fiber, proanthocyanidins, etc. Ruitai is the first brand of hawthorn health foods in China.

Since its establishment in 2015, the company was awarded the Hebei Key Leading Enterprise in Agricultural Industrialization and Hebei Leading Enterprise of Poverty Alleviation and built four provincial R&D platforms including Academician Workstation, Hebei Hawthorn Industry Technology Research Institute, and Hebei Agricultural Innovation Center, etc. The company has deeply explored the potential of hawthorn's "homology of medicine and food", initiated 21 research projects with 10 universities including the Chinese Academy of Agricultural Sciences, the Chinese Academy of Sciences, and Hebei Agricultural University, etc. Now it has 14 patents and 13 independently developed brands. The company's hawthorn dietary fiber extraction technology has filled four international gaps which were authenticated by the Chinese Academy of Agricultural Sciences.

The company has more than 120 employees, with bachelor degree accounting for more than 50%. The company is developing rapidly with the joining of master's degree gradiates and advanced equipment and scientific and efficient technological innovation management system. The supply of Ruitai Hawthorn always falls short of demand. The industrial chain of three parks and one platform integrates hawthorn planting, processing, research, and development, sales and tourism. This project has been benefiting 1,600 poor households and more than 4,000 farmers in the county.

Events

In 2020, it was rated as the Hebei Key Leading Enterprise in Agricultural Industrialization.

In 2019, it was appraised as the Hebei Leading Enterprise of Poverty Alleviation.

In 2018, Hebei Hawthorn Industry Technology Research Institute was established; the company was rated as Hebei Leading Brand Enterprise of the Industry.

In 2017, the academician workstation was established.

Contact Information

Address: North District of Xinglong Town, Xinglong County, Chengde City, Hebei Province

Tel: 86-314--5606222

Part II

Local Customs and Places of Interest

1. Nihewan Civilization

Nihewan site, located in Nihewan villiage, Huashaoying Town, in the east of Yangyuan county, Hebei Province, is in Yangquan basin on the north bank of upper reaches of Sanggan river. About 1.77 million years ago, archaic humans lived on this land. Nihewan Standard Stratum records the history of earth evolution, biological and human evolution from the late Tertiary Period to Quaternary Period, which attracts a great attention from experts in geology, paleontology, paleoanthropology and prehistoric archaeology at home and abroad. Nihewan basin is more than 60 kilometers long from east to west and more than ten kilometers wide from north to south. More than two million years ago, Nihewan basin was once a large lake, providing a habitat for archaic animals. At that time Mountains around the basin were covered with dense forests. With warm and humid climate, it became an ideal living place for both wildlife and archaic humans. In the 1920s and 1930s, Chinese and foreign scientists discovered many bivalve fossils and mammal fossils in this place. After the founding of the People's Republic of China, Chinese geologists and paleontologists visited it many times and found various and hundreds of animal fossils and many Paleolithic cultural sites. Cultural sites date back 10,000 years to one million years covering every stage of the early, middle and late Paleolithic age, and various remains were excavated. Among them, 18 cultural sites date back over one million years. It is rarely seen in the world.

Nihewan site is well-known for its abundant discoveries for mammal fossils human relics. The researchers made a great breakthrough to identify the age of Nihewan site through excavation work and research of Majuangou site in Nihewan basin, which provided an evidence that the origin of Asian civilization can be traced back to 2 million years ago. Thus, Nihewan site becomes the second relics of ancient human activity 2 million years ago on the earth after Olduvai Gorge in East Africa, challenging the theory that Africa was the sole origin of mankind. Meanwhile, re-creatable traces indicating what early humans 2 million years ago had eaten there were found, which was extremely rare in paleolithic archaeology in the world. Therefore, Nihewan site has directly rewritten the world's history about the origin of mankind and the development of human civilization, and has become a holy place for people to find who they are and where they are from.

In September 1924, Pierre Teilhard de Chardin and Emile Licent came to Zhangjiakou on their way back from their investigation of Salawusu, and conducted a short geological investigation in Nihewan site with American geologist George Barbour. In their scientific report, Barbour named river and lake sediments in the basin as Nihewan Layer. Thereafter, the scientific research in the Nihewan basin started.

Since then, it has been more than 90 years for more than 500 experts and scholars from more than 20 countries and regions to excavate and research in the area of Sanggan river, 82 kilometers long from east to west and 27 kilometers wide from north to south. They have discovered more than 80 sites containing cultural relics of archaic humans, with tens of thousands of unearthed archaic human fossils, animal fossils and various stone tools which record the whole process of development and evolution from Paleolithic age to Neolithic age. There are totally 25 cultural relics of archaic humans over one million years found in China. 21 of them are located in Nihewan.

The density and age of early cultural relics are unique not only in China but also in the world. Traces indicating what early humans had eaten there about 2 million years ago were found for the first time in the excavation work of Majuangou site in 2001, which becomes the earliest place of human origin found in China so far. Nihewan site proves a possibility that human beings originate from the Olduvai Gorge in East Africa or Nihewan in China. Nihewan is a unique paleolithic archaeological research site in China and even in the world. Quaternary standard stratum discovered in Nihewan basin is recognized by international geologists and archaeologists. Nihewan basin, Nihewan geological section, Nihewan flora and fauna and Nihewan cultural sites have become treasure house of multi-disciplinary research of ancient human culture in the world. In 1978, Chinese archaeologists discovered a large number of paleolithic stone tools and mammal fossils in Xiaochangliang site near Nihewan basin, including a large number of stone cores, stone flakes, stone tools, and discarded stones in tools making.

Nihewan Nihewan site was listed as the first provincial-level geological relics protection zone in Hebei Province in 1997 and it was declared one of the ten major archaeological discoveries in China and listed as the fifth batch of major historical and cultural sites protected at the national level in 1998.

In 1994, Jia Lanpo, a famous geologist and paleontologist in China and one of the discoverers of Peking man, and his colleagues discovered a large number of the world's earliest microliths at the Xiaochangliang site. Most of these stone tools weigh between 5 and 10 grams, and the smallest is less than 1 gram. There are about 2000 pieces including sharpeners, scrapers, carvers and cones. Paleomagnetism experts determined that these stone tools can be traced back about 1.6 million years ago. Jia Lanpo said that the dating of Xiaochangliang site is "the most detailed and reliable". It is not hard to understand that these microliths found at Xiaochangliang site in Nihewan basin "are in a large number with a long history, and the processing technology is advanced", and there is no record of similar microliths in other parts of the world. In 1957, Jia Lanpo observed that "Peking man" had made great progress in making stone tools, and they could use and control fire. Therefore, he inferred that "Peking man" five or six hundred thousand years ago were neither the earliest humans nor the first generation of humans. These microliths discovered prove that "the stratum during Nihewan period was the place where the earliest human originated". Jia Lanpo believed that such advanced stone tools made 1.6 million years ago proved that the origin of human beings was much earlier than we thought in the past. Therefore, it is no exaggeration to say that there were humans four million years ago.

From August 1995 to September 1998, on the basis of previous excavations, Hebei Institute of Cultural Relics and the Department of Archaeology of Peking University cooperated to excavate and discovered the extremely rare stratigraphic sections and cultural sections from the end of Pleistocene to the middle of Holocene in North China at Yujiagou site (located in the Nihewan basin in Yangyuan county, Hebei Province, China). This excavation was declared as one of "Ten Major Archaeological Discoveries in China in 1998". From June to August in 1996, a Sino-US joint archaeological team, composed of Indiana University and

Hebei Institute of Cultural Relics, excavated and researched at Nihewan site for two months. They discovered a large number of precious animal fossils, stone tools and other materials, which further confirmed that Nihewan basin is the cradle of early humans in China and one of the birthplaces of archaic humans. Nihewan basin is a huge treasure with scientific value and world cultural heritage to be further studied, developed and utilized. In October 2001, there was a site with the lowest horizon and the earliest age discovered at Majuangou site in Nihewan basin. Hundreds of unearthed stone products and animal bones proved that the Paleolithic age in Nihewan basin could be traced back about 2 million years ago. In view of its importance and value of in prehistoric culture, Nihewan site was declared as one of "100 Archaeological Discoveries in China in the 20th Century" in March 2001 and was announced by the State Council as a major historical and cultural site protected at the national level. In early 2002, Nihewan geological relics were promoted to a national nature reserve.

Nihewan sites include Majuangou Site, Xiaochangliang site, Houjiayao site and Hutouliang site

Majuangou Site Majuangou site, 1000-meter away from Cenjiawan village, lies in the northern margin of Datianwa platform on the south bank of Sanggan River, in the east of Nihewan basin. This is the concentrated distribution area of early Paleolithic cultural sites. Several giant gullies in the north-south direction have formed in Nihewan layer due to water flow, and Majuangou site is one of them. There is a bedrock normal fault in NE-SW direction here, and Majuangou site is located on the hanging wall of the fault, which is very close to the fault plane. Small-scale excavations have been carried out in Majuangou since 1993, and consecutively from 2001 to 2005. The animal skeleton fossils found at Majuangou site include elephants, rhinoceros, deer, horses and rodents. Stone tools, including cores, flakes, stone hammers and scrapers, had been excavated. In the third cultural layer of Majuangou site, extremely rare traces indicating that early humans had eaten elephants were found. Archaic humans ate large animals for survival, which becomes the only case in Paleolithic archaeological excavations in the world. Those findings at the Majuangou site prove that Paleolithic site in the Nihewan basin can be traced back 1.8-2 million years ago as the earliest human activity site with exact strata discovered in East Asia so far. More importantly, they challenge the theory that Ethiopia in Africa was the sole origin of humans. In July 2014, Hebei Institute of Cultural Relics discovered two new cultural layers at Majuangou site in Nihewan basin. Experts named them Majuangou IA and IB cultural layers. It can be confirmed that these two cultural layers were from 1.32 to 1.55 million years ago by comparing with strata. On July 20, 2015, the Nihewan Archaeological Research Institute of Hebei Normal University made new progress and discovered traces indicating what early humans had eaten at the Shigou site (about 1.5-1.6 million years ago), which is another such discovery after the discovery at Majuangou site.

Xiaochangliang Site Xiaochangliang site lies in Guanting Village on the south bank of Sanggan River. On August 21, 1978, institute of vertebrate paleontology and paleoanthropology of Chinese Academy of Sciences found stone artifacts and mammal fossils in the early Pleistocene strata at Xiaochangliang, north of Guanting Village, when researchers conducted Quaternary geological survey in Datianwa platform. At the same time, they found the Houshishan site in the same strata on the east side of Xiaochangliang site. It is the first time that Paleolithic relics 1 million years ago have been discovered in the early Pleistocene strata in the Nihewan basin. This discovery is of epoch-making significance for Paleolithic archaeological research in the Nihewan basin. After several excavations there, a large number of mammal fossils have been discovered. The species that can be identified include mink, Palaeoloxodon, Hipparion, Equus sanmeniensis, Coelodonta antiquitatis, deer, antelope and cattle. Hipparion is a typical animal of Tertiary and can also be found in the early Quaternary. This archaic animal fossil has only been found at Xiaochangliang site in Nihewan basin. The stone tools unearthed at the Xiaochangliang site are mainly microliths, including more than 1,000 pieces of stone cores, stone tools, and bone tools. Xiaochangliang site was formed in the layer of lacustrine sediment, and its relics were protected well. It is an autochthonous burial site. Xiaochangliang site offers evidence that early humans once lived at this place. Xiaochangliang site is engraved on the bronze corridor of the China Millennium Monument in Beijing as the northernmost witness of human activities.

Houjiayao Site Houjiayao site is located in the northwest of Nihewan basin and it was discovered in 1974. Houjiayao site dates back 104,000 to 125,000 years ago and it is a typical middle Paleolithic site. Thousands of stone balls unearthed are representative artifacts at this site. Human fossils are one of the important discoveries at the site, with 18 human fossils, 2 occipital bones and 11 parietal bones. There are obvious cutting marks on some skull specimens, and scholars speculate that this may be due to cannibalism. In one case, there was a hole with a diameter of 9.5 mm in the posterior part of the parietal bone of the skull, and the edge of the hole had healed for at least two weeks. This may be the earliest surgical trephine operation discovered.

Hutouliang Site Hutouliang site is located 25 kilometers east of Yangyuan county. In 1965, scientists from Chinese Academy of Sciences first found this site. From 1972 to 1974, Chinese Academy of Sciences conducted an investigation and excavation in the area of Hutouliang. A large number of animal fossils were found here. Animal fossils that can be identified include frogs, ostriches, brandt's vole, brandt, Chinese zokor, cricetulus varians zdansky, wolves, przewalski's horse, Asiatic wild ass, deer, cattle, przewalski's gazelle, goitered gazelle, topi, and wild boar. Fossils of wooly rhinoceros and Asian straight-tusked elephant were also found near the ruins. There are 5 stone hammers and 2 stone anvils; 16 pieces of disk-shaped and tortoise-back-shaped stone cores; 236 pieces of wedge-shaped stone cores; 17 pieces of columnar stone cores; 10 pieces of bipolar stone pieces; 221 pieces of round-headed scrapers and 13 pieces of flat bead decorations unearthed. The geological age of Hutouliang site is in the end of the late Pleistocene and the cultural age is in the late stage of the late Paleolithic. The discovery of sandy yellow-brown pottery pieces and mammal fossils at Yujiagou site in Hutouliang is of great significance to the research of transition from Paleolithic to Neolithic, as well as the origin of agriculture and pottery making. It fills a gap in the Paleolithic cultural series in North China and is rated as one of the top ten new archaeological discoveries in China in 1998.

Archaeological value of Nihewan Sites

There are two Nihewan strata in the world: Nihewan and Villafranca d'Asti. The former is regarded as the standard stratum of the early Pleistocene in China. Compared with Villafranca d'Asti, Nihewan site in China is the most well preserved and internationally recognized Quaternary standard strata with the greatest number of profiles. The stratigraphic age of Nihewan sites is continuous. There are 2 million-year-old Majuangou site; 1.36 million-year-old Xiaochangliang site; 1.36 million-year-old Putaoyuan site and Guangliang site; 1 million-year-old Shanzumiaozui site, Madigou site, Donggutuo site, Feiliang site, Huojiadi site, Xujiapo site, Dongliang site, Zhaopo site, Houtushan site and Cenjiawan site; 780,000-year-old Maliang ruins and Que ruins and Ergou ruins; 120,000-year-old Shandui site and Xixianzi site; 100,000-year-old Houjiayao site and Manliubao site; 78,000-year-old Banjingzi site; 28,000-year-old Shangshazui site and Xinmiaozhuang site; 11,600-year-old Hutouliang site, Youfang site, Xigou site and Xibaimaying site; 4000-year-old Zhoujiashan site, Jiumafang site and Yutiaogou site; 3000-year-old Dingjiabaoleiniquan site. More than 130 sites are found in total. There are 124 graves of Warring States Period, Han Dynasty and Liao Dynasty in the Nihewan basin, so it has become the "World Natural Museum". The Nihewan Basin has long been famous for researching paleo-stratigraphy, paleontology, paleogeography and neotectonics. It becomes an aspiration for every archaeologist to discover and excavate early human fossils in the Nihewan basin. In 1988, Nihewan basin was opened to the public. Invited by Chinese Academy of Sciences, scholars from University of California came here for investigation, which further opened Nihewan basin to world. In 1990, the Sino-US Cooperative Nihewan Archaeological Project approved by State Council became the first Sino-foreign cooperative archaeological project since the founding of the People's Republic of China. So far, more than 500 scholars and experts from more than 30 countries and regions have participated in this project and published more than 700 papers about Nihewan basin. Nihewan basin has great value for history, science, culture, tourism and economy.

Nihewan sites are a unique Paleolithic archaeological research center at home and abroad. In 1924, western scholar George Barbour discovered abundant paleontological fossils here and named this place Nihewan Formation. Since then, more than 500 archaeological experts from more than 20 countries and a group of well-known Chinese experts have come here for investigation and research. Those experts believe that "it is unique to discover so many sites in such a small area", and that "Nihewan basin is an ideal place for both geology and Paleolithic archaeology". It fully proves that "Nihewan basin is the origin of human civilization in East Asia" and "the center of the origin of human beings and their culture in the world". Therefore, it is of great value to protect and develop Nihewan sites. Therefore, it is significant to protect and develop Nihewan sites for archaeological research and local economic growth.

2. Yellow Emperor City Ruins (Huangdi Cheng)

Yellow Emperor City Ruins (a relics and cultural sight in Zhangjiakou city, Hebei Province, China) is located 2 kilometers west of Fanshan town, Zhuolu county in Hebei Province. The ruins are irregular squares 500 meters long and 500 meters wide, and the city walls are made of rammed earth. The remaining city wall in the south, west and north are 3 to 5 meters high, and the east city wall is immersed in Xuanyuan Lake. There are a large number of pottery fragments in the Yellow Yellow Emperor City Ruins, most of which are argillaceous grey and black pottery and a small amount of coarse red pottery mixed with sand and clay. Remnants can be found everywhere, such as legs of pottery tripod, legs of a pot named Ge, thick-handled bean containers, undamaged stone pestles, stone axes, stone chisels, stone spinning wheels, and stone rings. Yellow Emperor City Ruins with 5000 years history is the origin of the Great Chinese nation and Chinese civilization.

Yellow Emperor Spring, also called as Banquan, is located 0.5 kilometers east of Yellow Emperor City Ruins. It is said that the Yellow Emperor (also known as Huangdi) used to bathe in this spring. So, it is also called "Zhuo Long Chi". Yellow Emperor Spring is artesian water, with water gushing out from the ground and forming a pool. This pool is 97.2 meters around and 31 meters in diameter. The spring water flows to the natural river formed over a thousand years from an outlet in the north of the pool, which provides water for more than 10,000 people in more than 10 villages in Fanshan Town. According to the experts from the National Water Conservancy Department, the Yellow Emperor Spring is a deep-water of 1700 meters to 5000 meters underground. Therefore, the spring water is clear and it does not freeze in winter. The running water is never stale in summer, and never dries up. Water is the source of life and civilization. Scientists of water conservancy said that the Yellow Emperor's unification war in Zhuolu began with the search for water sources. When scooping up sweet water in the Yellow Emperor Spring, we will question that whether it is because the abundant water resources here that makes Zhuolu the birthplace of ancestors' culture and the birthplace of Chinese nation.

Yellow Emperor Temple (which does not exist now and was converted into the "Three Ancestral Hall of China") was located on the east of Xuanyuan Lake and 200 meters north of Yellow Emperor Spring. It is said that it was built in the Yellow Emperor era together with the Yellow Emperor City. The Yellow Emperor Temple is a palace where emperors and generals of all dynasties in China offer sacrifice to ancestors and take look back at the bygone times. Famous emperors in the history, including Emperor Qin Shi Huang, Sima Dezong of the Eastern Jin Dynasty, and Qianlong Emperor in Qing Dynasty, traveled a long way here to pay their respects. Wen Tianxiang, a famous patriotic general in the Southern Song Dynasty, once wrote, "I visit Zhuolu to worship Yellow Emperor who once defeated Chiyou at this place. His superiority made tributaries with peace". Yellow Emperor City is a spiritual homeland for the Chinese nation. When you travel here, you will understand why the great spirit of the Chinese nation last for thousands of years. Yellow Emperor City is a good place with great authenticity, unique characteristics and profound meaning to reveal the cultural origin of the Chinese nation.

3. Jiming Mountain

Jiming Mountain is located in Xiahuayuan district in Zhangjiakou city, Hebei Province, China. It covers an area of 17.5 square kilometers and is 1128.9 meters above sea level. It is the highest solitary mountain outside the Great Wall in the plain and enjoys the reputation of "the peak that flew hither". Poet Hao Jing in the Yuan Dynasty once described Jiming Mountain with the poem "the mountain towered up towards the sky". This mountain is splendid, like towering giants and natural barriers. In summer and autumn, landscape is beautiful and amazing with white clouds embracing the hillside like sea waves.

There are 112 temples there, covering more than 1,300 square meters and with more than 200 statues. It is a historical and cultural resort where monks expound Buddhist sutras and pray for good luck in the country. The highest point is Pingshi Terrace next to Yuhuang Pavilion on its peak.

Jiming Mountain has been a famous mountain since ancient times. Many emperors, including Emperor Wencheng of Northern Wei, Emperor Taizong of Tang, Emperor Shengzong of Liao, Empress Dowager Chengtian, Toghon Temür (the last Khagan of the Mongol Empire) and Emperor Yingzong of Ming, climbed this mountain to enjoy the northern scenery. There is an ancient monument on the top of Jiming Mountain in the 46th year of reign of Qianlong Emperor in the Qing Dynasty (1781 A.D.). The inscription reads, "Emperor Taizong of the Tang Dynasty once rested there, and heard a pheasant crowing, so he named this place Jiming (literally a pheasant crowing in Chinese)". Therefore, Jiming Mountain was named by Emperor Taizong. From the 35th year to the 45th year of the reign of the Kangxi Emperor (1696-1706 A.D.), Kangxi Emperor visited Xiahuayuan district (a modern-day district of the city of Zhangjiakou, Hebei Province, China) four times and climbed Jiming Mountain twice. The Wolong Stone, where the emperor had rested, is still lying quietly beside the trail, which arouses visitors' imagination.

From the mountain gate, along the zigzag path paved with gravel, dozens of scenic spots can be seen, such as four-pillar memorial arch on the third floor, Mountain Temple, Pavilion of Empress Dowager Chengtian, Mingji Rock, Guanyin Courtyard, Longgu Rock, Yongning Temple, Wuzhi Peak, Luotuo Rock, Shougui Peak, Zhusha Cave, Suolu Gate, Shelter Bridge, Nantianmen, Yuhuang Pavilion, Bixia Yuanjun (the goddess of Mount Tai) Temple (commonly known as Grandma Temple, Nainai Temple in Chinese) on the west top and sun viewing platform on the east top can be seen in turn. Among them, Yongning Temple was built in the 4th year of the reign of Emperor Shengzong of Liao (1024 A. D.). This temple consists of the Hall of Four Heavenly Kings, the Mahavira Hall and the Hall of Three Buddhas. It is an open temple approved by the religious Department of Hebei Province. It is a place where lay Buddhist and pilgrims hold various Buddhist activities there and monks live monastic life. In recent years, lots of lay Buddhist from Beijing, Tianjin and other places come to Jiming Mountain.

The highest point is Pingshi Terrace next to Yuhuang Pavilion on its peak. From the mountain, you can enjoy a bird view of the beautiful surrounding scenery. It is interesting to watch these intermittently visible exotic rocks submerged in clouds and mists. Standing on the Shelter Bridge between the peak and the cliff and looking around against the rail, you are surrounded by clouds and mist, like standing in a fairy land. There is a huge rock on the bridge deck, commonly known as a shelter stone which can block strong wind. The scenes are unique in the Jiming Mountain and applauded by visiting tourists

4. Xuanhua Ancient City

From Warring States Period to Qin and Han Dynasties, ancient China was divided into 36 commanderies. Xuanhua belonged to Shanggu Commandery. Under the Tang Dynasty, it was the seat of both Wuzhou prefecture and Wende county. Under the Ming Dynasty, it was Xuanfu Town. In the Qing Dynasty, it continued to serve as the seat of Xuanhua Prefecture of Zhili Province. After the founding of the People's Republic of China, it belonged to Chahar Province as Xuanhua City, and then was parted to Hebei Province. It was changed from a city to a district in 1963 and belongs to Zhangjiakou City until now.

Xuanhua was once the political center of the area west of Beijing. Emperors of all dynasties often visited it. In Xuanhua, Kangxi Emperor of the Qing Dynasty reorganized the army and prepared for the war before his seven northern tours and western expeditions. In February of the 36th year of the reign of Kangxi Emperor (1697), Kangxi Emperor personally commanded troops to go on an expedition to Galdan for the second time. In December, he was stationed in the Xuanhua Town. He awarded a poem to administrator of Koubeidao, a plaque to Xuanhua General Commander (in charge of Xuanda, Shanxi and other military affairs, and managing grain and rates) with words "Pi Xun Lian" in Chinese and a plaque to Xuanhua Town with words "Qin Min" in Chinese.

Xuanhua is a provincial-level famous historical and cultural city. There are 3 major historical and cultural sites protected at the national level in Xuanhua Ancient City: Qingyuan Tower, Louzhenshuo and Mural Tombs of the Liao Dynasty; 6 major historical and cultural sites protected at the provincial level: Lou Gong Ji, former site of Chahar Democratic Government, Five Dragon Wall, remains of city wall, Shien Temple and Mural Tombs of the Liao Dynasty. In addition, there are a number of cultural tourism resources with great value, such as Lihua Temple Tower, Ma Zhai in Dabei Street and Nanzhai Quadrangle in Dabei Street, the "Wu Temple" Hall, the former residence of General Zhang Zizhong (anti-Japanese war general and national hero) in Yinyuan Street, and the palace of Empress Dowager Cixi in the late Qing Dynasty.

5. Grass Skyline (Zhangbei Grassland Highway)

Grass Skyline is located at the junction of Chongli county and Zhangbei county in Zhangjiakou, Hebei Province, China. From Daqing Mountain (National Forest Park) on the south side of Shangyi County in the west to Huapi ridge in Chongli county in the east, it is an important passage connecting Chongli grassland, Chicheng Hot Spring, Zhangbei grassland, Bailongdong Scenic Area and Daqing Mountain, and is considered as one of the top 10 beautiful highways in mainland China. With a total length of 132.7 kilometers (145 miles), Grass Skyline looks like a dragon winding on the gentle mountain slopes covered by endless grass. This highway blends with blue sky at the end, covered with white clouds, and therefore, it earns its nickname "Tian Lu" in Chinese (means a road to the sky). It is renowned for its intoxicating scenery with rivers, mountains, ravines, cattle and sheep eating grass on both sides. There are the ruins of the ancient Great Wall, Huapi ridge, Yehu ridge, Zhang Bei grassland, and many other cultural, ecological and geological tourism resources.

There are a lot of cultural, ecological and geological tourism resources along this road, such as the Great Wall, the martyrs' cemetery of the Soviet-Mongolia Army, Huapi Ridge, Yianpian Mountain, the Stone Pillars of Zhangbei Daye Pagoda and so on. Grass Skyline is just a plain highway on Zhangbei Bashang Plateau, with about 1,000 meters above sea level. Nevertheless, dark road contrasted by yellow line on it is itself a beautiful scenery. The road is winding and stretching for miles.

Huapi Ridge Huapi Ridge is dotted with wild flowers in summer and all leaves turn red in autumn. The average annual temperature is 4℃ at Huapi Ridge. The main peak of head base at an altitude of 2128 meters is covered by thousands of acres of birch forest, which gives its name "Huapi (birch bark) Ridge". The north ridge is covered by wild birches and one-meter-high wild grasses and flowers. In summer, it is covered with blooming wild flowers under the azure sky. In autumn, all leaves turn into different colors. So beautiful it is! Huapi Ridge has a pleasant climate. The oxygen content here reaches 27% and contains high negative ions. It is known as the "natural oxygen bar" and an ideal summer resort. In winter, it becomes more magnificent, with more than 120 days snowy days and 700 mm annual snowfall, making it an ideal place for skiing and skating.

Yanpian Mountain Yanpian Mountain is located 15 kilometers away from the entrance of Huapi Ridge and stands abruptly in hills on the side of Grass Skyline. Yanpian Mountain is located on the south of Dahulun Town, which is in the junction of Chongli grassland and Zhangbei grassland and you can also enjoy the scenery of hills. There are some villages surrounded by mountains, with beautiful and well-protected environment. It is truly an "oxygen bar" with high content of negative ions. In addition, its well-preserved village, (simple and unsophisticated) folk customs, and unique geographical environment lay a good foundation for rural tourism there.

Terrace Field　　Terraced fields are rarely seen in the north of China. But Grass Skyline makes it easy for northerners to enjoy this beautiful scenery without going south. In summer, terraced fields turn into green with distinct layers. In autumn, travelers can enjoy scenery of colorful and crisscrossing lines and various crops stacked in piles and rows after harvest. Terraced fields in the north of China are a place with a long history, as real and unsophisticated as its people are. They are a part of the nature, breathing the purest air, bathing in the brightest sunshine and enjoying peace.

Wind Turbine　　Wind turbines, also known as windmills, are built along the Grass Skyline, attracting tourists' attention. White windmills, blue sky, white clouds and green grasslands complement with each other. This is the typical Grass Skyline scene.

Wild Flowers　　The Grass Skyline are dotted with various wild flowers, including wild poppies, alfalfa, potato flowers, sunflowers and rape flowers. They are swaying in the wind, like in a fairy tale.

Prairie in the Air　　Nannihe Prairie in the Air is located in Xiaoertai Town, Zhangbei County. It is one of the representative landscapes of Grass Skyline with an altitude of over 1600 meters. It is cool in summer and autumn, with beautiful flowers and dancing butterflies.

The Luanhe River in Guyuan County　　Luanhe River flows 20 kilometers on the northeast of Guyuan county. Lightning River, the source of Luanhe River, crosses through mountains and lakes and flows on the vast wetland and grassland, with twists and turns. Luanhe River is another landmark landscape in Guyuan county.

6. Taizicheng Relic

Taizicheng Relic is in a village of Sitaizui, Chongli district of Zhangjiakou city in the northwest of Hebei Province, China. Its name means "City of the Crown Prince". The relic is surrounded by mountains, with a river in the south and a river in the north circling the relic from east to west and then merging in the west.

In a rectangle city, building materials unearthed included dragon and phoenix roof ornaments. Artifacts excavated included pottery fragments. The 15 white glazed porcelain bowls with impressed Capricorn patterns were marked with the characters "Shangshiju" in Chinese, meaning "Bureau of Imperial Cuisine", which further proves Taizicheng relic must be the remains of an imperial palace of the Jin Dynasty.

In preparation for developing the Taizicheng relic as a skiing venue for the 2022 Winter Olympic Games, archaeological excavations carried out between May and November 2017 uncovered the remains of an imperial palace of the Jin Dynasty (1115-1234). Based on the unearthed artifacts, Taizicheng resort was confirmed as a royal palace dated to the late middle period of the Jin Dynasty. It is thought that this was the summer palace for Emperor Zhangzong of Jin Dynasty, which is named Tai He Palace in the History of the Jin Dynasty.

On February 26, 2018, Taizicheng Relic was on the list of the final evaluation project of the top ten new archaeological discoveries in China in 2017. The relic was a rectangular walled settlement, about 400 meters in length (from north to south) and about 350 meters in width (from east to west), covering 140,000 square meters. There are underground bases under the east, west and south walls. The base of the north wall has been destroyed by rivers, and there are trenches outside the other three remaining walls. There are two west walls with a distance of 50 meters from east to west. The relic included a network of roads centered on a T-shaped main thoroughfare, with a south gate and a west gate, and barbican entrance outside. 28 base sites were found through drilling, of which there are 3 groups base sites on the north-south central axis: No. 9 base site facing the south gate in the south; the central base site group composed of No. 1, No. 2 and No. 3 base sites in the middle; No. 25 base site in the north. A large number of base sites on the north and south sides of the east-west street. Based on the size of the site and an analysis of the various artifacts found there, the archaeologists determined that this must be the remains of an imperial palace of Jin Dynasty.

7. Yu Dao Kou Grassland and Forest Scenic Spot

Yu Dao Kou Grassland and Forest Scenic Spot is located in the inner Mongolian plateau-Bashang plateau in Chengde city, in the autonomous county of Manchu and Mongolia minorities, the most north region of Hebei Province. In 1982, Bashang plateau was designated as a national park of China by the State Council; In 1998, Yu Dao Kou Grassland and Forest Scenic Spot was established; In 1999, it was designated as a Demonstration Area of Eco-Tourism in Hebei Province; In 2005, it was rated as a China 5A Scenic Areas; In 2006, it was rated as the best tourist scenic spot in China. Famous attractions include Shenxian Cave, Moon Lake, Gui Mountain, Taoshan Lake, Hongquan Valley and Turgen grassland.

Yu Dao Kou Grassland and Forest Scenic Spot has a semi-moist semi-arid continental monsoon climate and the annual average temperature is 3℃. It covers 1,000 square kilometers at an altitude of 1230-1820 meters. There are 700,000 mu (46666 hectares) of virgin grassland, 200,000 mu (13333 hectares) of wetland, 21 natural fresh water lakes, 47 springs (mostly mineral springs) and 13 rivers which is one of the origins of Luanhe River. There are 659 species of plants belonging to 50 families, more than 100 kinds of wild animals and dozens of treasures, demonstrating typical biodiversity. It is truly known as "the source of rivers, the world of clouds, flowers, forests, and the paradise of rare birds and animals". It is a good place for eco-tourism, including grassland sightseeing, bird watching, horse riding, fishing, boating, enjoying bonfire, driving, scientific research and exploration, having vacation, holding conferences, skating and skiing, and hunting. Yu Dao Kou Grassland and Forest Scenic Spot lies 400 kilometers away from Beijing, 220 kilometers away from Chengde city and 100 kilometers away from Mulan Paddock. The main highway there leads directly to the scenic spot.

Yu Dao Kou Grassland and Forest Scenic Spot together with Chengde Mountain Resort, the largest royal garden, become an important part of Beijing-Chengde Tourism. It used to be a part of Mulan Paddock, a royal hunting place and a summer retreat in Qing Dynasty (1644-1912). There are famous historical sites and scenic spots, including Shenxian Cave, Taoshan Lake, Sun Lake, Moon Lake, Baihua Hills, Grand Canyon, Gui Mountain.

Yu Dao Kou Grassland and Forest Scenic Spot is located at the starting point of famous self-driving route-First Scenic Boulevard, connecting to Saihanba Forest Park in the east and north and lying close to Duolun county in Inner Mongolia in the west. It has a wide field of vision and rich vegetation. It has been a natural hunting park for riding horses and bending bows since ancient times. It was once a royal summer resort and hunting resort during the Kangxi and Qianlong years of Qing Dynasty.

8. First Scenic Boulevard

First Scenic Boulevard starts at Saihanba National Forest Park, China's largest man-made woodland, and ends at Datan town in Fengning Manchu autonomous county of Hebei Province. Dotted with forests, grasslands, lakes, wetlands and hills, the road is a beautiful and well-traveled place. It is renowned for famous scenic spots such as Saihanba National Forest Park, Yu Dao Kou Grassland and Forest Scenic Spot, Wudao Valley, Luanhe River and Bashang Grassland along this boulevard. Along the way, there are green grass and fragrant wild flowers. This is the hometown of clouds, the source of water, the world of flowers and the ocean of forests.

9. Chengde Mountain Resort

Chengde Mountain Resort, also called Ligong or Rehe Temporary Palace, is situated north of Chengde city of Hebei Province, China. It was originally built for the royal families to spend the hot summer months, listed as China 5A Scenic Areas and one of the Four Best Gardens in China (the other three are Summer Palace in Beijing, Humble Administrator's Garden and Lingering Garden in Suzhou). The Palace is located in the narrow valley along the west bank of Wulie river in the north of Chengde city center, Hebei Province. It is a place where emperors of Qing Dynasty took summer vacation and handled government affairs in summer.

Chengde Mountain Resort is divided into four parts: the Palace Area, Lake Area, Plain Area and Mountain Area. It was built in the Qing Dynasty and took about 90 years to complete. The construction of the Mountain Resort was divided into two stages. The first stage was from the 4th year of the reign of Kangxi Emperor (1703) to the 5th year of the reign of Kangxi Emperor (1713).

The main job in this period was to expand the lake area, build artificial islets and embankments, then construct palaces, gardens and walls. The mountain resort began to take shape. The second stage started from the 6th year (1741) to the 19th year (1754) of the reign of Qianlong Emperor. Kangxi Emperor named each of 36 scenic spots with four Chinese characters. The second stage started from the 6th year (1741) to the 19th year (1754) of the reign of Qianlong Emperor. Large-scale of expansion of the resort happened during this time period. More palaces and a majority of large gardens were built. To emulate his grandfather Kangxi Emperor, Qianlong Emperor named each of another 36 scenic spots with three Chinese characters. Hitherto, the Mountain Resort is most famous for the 72 scenic spots named by the Kangxi Emperor and Qianlong Emperor.

Chengde Mountain Resort and its outlying temples was added to the first batch of major historical and cultural sites protected at the national level in 1961. From 1976 to 2006, the State Council successively approved and implemented three Ten-Year Renovation Plans for the Eight Temples outside Chengde Mountain Resort, which clearly defined protection principle of "rescue and renovation". The central government and local governments invested hundreds of millions of special funds for the maintenance of ancient buildings and garden renovation, and invested a large amount of funds for comprehensive renovation of surrounding environment of relics.

72 Scenic Spots in Chengde Mountain Resort

It is one of the China's three largest ancient building groups. More than 120 groups of buildings make a magnificent landscape that integrates gardens and mountains. 36 scenic spots named by Kangxi Emperor and 36 scenic spots named by Qianlong Emperor are well known as the 72 scenic spots.

Yanbo Zhishuang (hall of refreshing mists and waves), ZhiJing YunDi (a long and winding dike), Wushu Qingliang (hall of coolness), Yanxun Shanguan (the mountain hall of coolness brings breeze), Shuifang Yanxiu (limpid water and charming rockery), Wanhe Songfeng (surrounded with pines and gracious forests), Songhe Qingyue (dotted with lush ancient pines and watching cranes flying), Yunshan Shengdi (viewing-misty-mountain tower), Simian Yunshan (pavilion among clouds and mountains), Beizhen Shuangfeng (pavilion locates between twin peaks), Xiling Chenxia (tower enjoying morning glow), Chuifeg Luozhao (hammer-like peak in the sunset), Nanshan Jixue (pavilion with perpetual snow on the peak of the mountain in the south), Lihua Banyue (pear flowers and moon match well each other), Qushui Hexiang (pavilion of winding stream and lotus fragrance), Fengquan Qingting (sound of spring water coming with the wind sounds clear and pleasant), Haopu Jianxiang (transcendence and self-enjoyment), Tianyu Xianchang (tall pavilion seemed to be connected with the sky), Nuanliu Xuanbo (vapor above Wulie river likes cloud and splashing beads likes pearls), Quanyuan Shibi (the spring gushes out of the cliff), Qingfeng Lüyu (dense maples like green island), Yingzhuan Qiaomu (yellow warbler sings melodiously like playing music), Xiangyuan Yiqing (waterside hall full of appreciating lotus), Jinlian Yingri (the hall of the golden lotus silhouetted the sun), Yuanjin Quansheng (sound of spring water from far and near), Yunfan Yuefang (tower floating on the clouds and bright moon), Fangzhu Linliu (pavilion near the sandbar and the lake), Yunrong Shuitai (ever-changing clouds is integrated with sparkling water), Chengquan Raoshi (the spring water flows in twists and turns along the mountain), Chengbo Diecui (clear lake is rippling with continuous purple ripples), Shiji Guanyu (stone to watch fish), Jingshui Yuncen (glittering water waves and floating fog are constantly changing), Shuanghu Jiajing (mirror-like rivers), Changhong Yinlian (rainbow in the lake likes drinking water), Putian Congyue (plain likes a palm, with lush vegetation), Shuiliu Yunzai (running water and floating clouds matches funny each other).

Lizheng Gate (the main entrance of the resort), Qinzheng Hall (a place for emperor to handle official business), Songhe Hall (Qianlong Emperor's mother and his concubines lived here), Ruyi Lake, Qingque Boat, QiWang Building (a building to overlook beautiful scenery), Wanglu Pavilion (used for rest and deer appreciation), Shuixin Pavilion (a pavilion built in the center of the water), Yizhi Hall (a hall to remind keep aspiration), Changyuan Building (tower for overlooking), Jinghao Hall (tranquil hall), Lengxiang Pavilion (a pavilion to enjoy chilly fragrance), Cailing Pavilion (picking lotus and water chestnuts in boats), Guanlian Pavilion (Kangxi Emperor liked to watch the lotus flowers here), Qinghui Pavilion (refers to the brilliance of the sun and the moon), Ban Ruo Xiang Temple (the appearance of the Dharma shown by the wisdom of the Buddha), Canglang Pavilion (islet in rippling wave), A Cloud Pavilion (emperors and concubines watched play, viewed clouds and enjoyed the rain), Pinxiang Pan (lakeside hall of enjoying cooling fragrance), The Plain Area (to receive the ethnic group leaders and foreign envoys), Shima Dai (dam of grass for testing the horse), Jiashu Hall (to express gratitude for the love and care received from childhood), Lecheng Pavilion (a pavilion that can enjoy the joy of harvest with farmers), Suyun Building (a place where scholars compiled books), Chengguan Hall (a study), Cuiyun Rock (green and white clouds rise in the valley forest), Yan Hua Window (there are beautiful scenery outside the window), Ling Tai Xu (a pavilion for soaring high in the sky), Qian Chi Xue Falls (the splashing waterfall likes snow), Ningjing Hall (used to express the will of the ancestors and remind the future generations to have great aspirations), Yuqini Hall (the flow of water sounds like music), Linfang Hall (dotted with various wild flowers), Zhiyu Rock (the rock to watch fish), Yongcui Rock (creek-pouring emerald - crags temple), Su Shang Hall, Yongtian Hall (a hall for eternal peace of mind).

10. Eight Outer Temples

Eight Outer Temples are located on the northeast of Chengde Mountain Resort. Eight Outer Temples is a collective name given to eight Lamaism temples. The construction began in the 52nd year of the reign of Kangxi Emperor

(1713) and completed in the 45th year of the reign of Qianlong Emperor (1780) in Qing Dynasty. There were 40 temples, administered by Lifan Yuan, including 32 in Beijing and 8 in Chengde. As Chengde is located outside Beijing and beyond the Great Wall, they are called Eight Outer Temples. They are Puren Temple, Pushan Temple (now defunct), Puning Temple, Anyuan Temple, Putuo Zongcheng Temple, Shuxiang Temple, Xumi Fushou Temple, Guangyuan Temple. Eight Outer Temples incorporate the essence of Han, Tibetan and other ethnic architectural arts and culture. The architectures are magnificent.

The Eight Outer Temples as part of Chengde Summer Resort was listed in the first batch of National-level Scenic Spots by the State Council in 1982. UNESCO listed Chengde Mountain Resort and Eight Outer Temples as a World Cultural Heritage Site in December 1994.

11. Qingchuifeng National Forest Park

Qingchuifeng National Forest Park, next to Chengde Mountain Resort and Eight Outer Temples, is located in the suburbs of Chengde city. The total area is 10,600 hectares, about 2.5 kilometers away from Chengde city. It is renowned for natural scenery of exotic mountains and rocks and lush jungle, especially Danxia landform. It has a temperate continental monsoon climate. Qingchuifeng cable way is the longest suspended chair cable way in China. A stone pillar stands 59.42 meters tall and straight into the sky with a thick top and a thin bottom. It is like a wooden club, so it is commonly called Bangchui (wooden club) Mountain and Kangxi Emperor in Qing Dynasty named it Qingchuifeng. There is a mulberry tree growing at the halfway up of the cliff, which is more than 300 years old. Today this mulberry tree still bears mulberries every year, white and sweet.

12. Jinshanling Great Wall

Jinshanling is a section of the Great Wall of China located in Luanping county, Chengde city, Hebei Province, adjacent to Miyun of Beijing, 125 kilometers northeast of Beijing. It was built in 1368 during the Ming Dynasty. General Xu Da led the construction. In 1567, Qi Jiguang, a famous anti-Japanese general, and governor Tan Lun continued to expand the Great Wall. It is the best-preserved part of the Wall with many original features. "Jinshanling Great Wall has its unique charm compared with other parts of the Wall." The main scenic spots are barrier walls, horse barrier wall and bricks inscribed with Chinese characters. It is known as "the paradise of photographers". It is also recognized as National Scenic Spots, China 5A Scenic Areas and was listed as site.

With a total length of 10.5 kilometers, Jinshanling Great Wall stretches from the famous historic Gubeikou Pass in the west. Along the Great Wall, there are 5 passes, 67 watchtowers, and 3 beacon towers. This well-preserved section is famous for its wide vision, dense watchtowers, peculiar landscape and complete military defense system. Specially, the watchtowers are quite different from each other in materials, number of layers and roofs. The structure has been deemed a great representative of the military defense systems used on the Great Wall. It symbolizes the peak of Great Wall architecture and is well-known in the world.

Jinshanling Great Wall is 700 meters above sea level. Travelers can see Simatai reservoir like a mirror in the east and Miyun reservoir with waves in the south. The magnificent wall sets up defense along the mountain and builds up the fortresses to defend the enemy along the water. It becomes more splendid than Badaling Great Wall, Shanhaiguan and Jiayuguan with its dense towers in complex construction and various forms. It is one of the tourist attractions being developed in the Great Wall.

Jinshanling Great Wall was listed as a world cultural heritage site in 1987. It was listed in the third batch of major historical and cultural sites protected at the national level in 1988. It is also recognized as National Scenic Spots, China 5A Scenic Areas. Jinshanling-Simatai Great Wall ranks the seventh among China's top ten autumn scenery by the eleventh issue of *Chinese National Geography* in 2010. The magazine article wrote: the Great Wall is the most luxurious Mountain boundary in the world, the most beautiful observation deck and the historical ruins with time-honored history. There are many ways to appreciate its beauty which is hard to describe with words.

Jinshanling Great Wall is the best-preserved section of Ming Great Wall, which is known as "the essence of Ming Great Wall" by experts. Setting up defense along the mountain and building up the fortresses to defend the enemy along the water, the wall appears to be made by iron and steel. There are dense defense towers, as if soldiers stood here. "One man can hold out against ten thousand". It is famous for its wide vision, dense watchtowers, peculiar landscape and complete military defense system in the world.

Its construction is complex. There is a 5-8-meter-high defense tower every 50-100 meters, built with giant rocks as its base and architecturally different from each other. The wall is in various forms, such as brick and wood structures, brick and stone structures, single-story and double-story, flats, domes, and canopy-styles. "Each building has its own style." Each building has its own style and sets up barrier wall, pilaster, battle platform, artillery battery, watchtower, rock-throwing hole, perforation, horse barrier wall, bracing wall and siege wall, which are impregnable. It symbolizes the peak of Great Wall architecture and demonstrates the spirit of greatness and boldness of Chinese nation.

It is dotted with flowers in spring; cool in summer; all turns into red in autumn; while in winter it is covered with snow. All these create an intoxicating ambiance of scent and color.

Part III

Food Education

1. Hebei Agricultural University

Hebei Agricultural University is a key provincial university jointly established by the People's Government of Hebei Province, the Ministry of Education, the Ministry of Agriculture and Rural Affairs, and the State Forestry and Grassland Administration. It is a national demonstration base for mass entrepreneurship innovation, a national demonstration university for deepening innovation and entrepreneurship education reform, and the Ministry of Education. The Excellent Engineer Education and Training Program is implemented by colleges and universities, and the State Forestry and Grassland Administration are among the first batch of colleges and universities that implement the Excellent Agricultural and Forestry Talent Education and Training Program and the "Double-First Class" university in Hebei Province.

Founded in 1902, the school was one of the earliest institutions of higher agricultural education in China, and the earliest institution of higher learning in Hebei Province. It has successively experienced Zhili Agricultural School, Zhili Higher Agricultural School, Zhili Public Agricultural College, Hebei Provincial Agricultural College, Hebei Agricultural College, Hebei Agricultural University, etc. In the historical period, during the adjustment of colleges and universities in the 1950s, the forestry department of the school was adjusted to Beijing, participated in the establishment of the Beijing Forestry College (now Beijing Forestry University), the animal husbandry and veterinary department was adjusted to Inner Mongolia, and participated in the establishment of Inner Mongolia Agriculture and Animal Husbandry (the college now Inner Mongolia Agricultural University) and the Department of Farmland Water Conservancy were reorganized to Wuhan, and participated in the establishment of the Wuhan Institute of Water Conservancy and Hydro power (now merged with Wuhan University). In 1995, it merged with the former Hebei Forestry College to form the new Hebei Agricultural University. In 2000, the original Hebei Fisheries School and Hebei Animal Husbandry Technology School were merged into Hebei Agricultural University.

With a century of accumulation, Hebei Agricultural University has formed a distinctive school-running characteristic. The school adheres to the school-running philosophy- "In agricultural education, truth could not be obtained without practice; the subtleness of matters could not be approached without experiments; and neither practice nor experiments should be neglected in favor of the other." It has cultivated the "Taihang Mountain Spirit" of "hard-working, dedication, truth-seeking and pragmatic engagement, patriotism and serving the people". It has been affirmed and commended by the Party and the State many times, and a group of rooted grassroots and services represented by Professor Li Baoguo have emerged. The well-known experts and professors of "agriculture, rural areas and farmers" have become a banner of higher education.

The disciplines make a good respond to biological applications, information technology, intelligent equipment design and manufacturing for agricultural modernization. "Agriculture, industry, management, science, economics, literature, law, art" and other disciplines realize cross-integration and coordinated development with training system of bachelor's degree, master's degree and doctor's degree. The school has 8 post-doctoral research stations; 11 first-level discipline doctoral programs, 1 professional degree doctoral program; 24 first-level discipline master programs, and 12 professional degree master programs. 1 discipline is listed in the world-class discipline construction sequence of Hebei Province, 3 disciplines are listed in the Hebei Province national first-class discipline construction sequence; 1 national key (cultivation) discipline, 3 ministerial-level key disciplines, 4 strong characteristic disciplines in Hebei Province, 16 key disciplines of Hebei Province; 2 disciplines of agricultural science, plant and animal science have entered the top 1% of ESI global rankings. There are 93 undergraduate majors, including 15 national-level first-class undergraduate major construction sites and 26 provincial-level first-class undergraduate major construction sites. More than 400,000 graduates have been trained, and a number of industrial elites, academic backbones, and management talents have emerged, such as Dong Yuchen, Liu Xu, Yang Zhifeng, Zhao Chunjiang, Guo Zijian, etc. 11 academicians, and Saihanba outstanding graduate group and many outstanding representatives of entrepreneurship.

The school closely focuses on the major national agricultural needs to carry out scientific research, and has consistently ranked among the top universities in the province in terms of the number of scientific and technological innovation projects undertaken, the total amount of funds, and the level of awards. It has established 68 national, provincial and ministerial key laboratories (engineering centers, bases, test stations, collaborative innovation centers, Industrial Technology Research Institute), 20 national-level modern agricultural industrial technology system experts and 62 provincial-level experts. The school always takes serving the country's major strategies and regional economic development as its own responsibility, and continuously deepens and expands the "Taihang Mountain Road", which fully serves the rural revitalization and modernization of agricultural and rural areas in Hebei Province. It has built the "Taihang Mountain Agricultural Innovation Station" strategic brand which has aroused widespread concern in the society and was fully affirmed by relevant provincial leaders. and it was selected as the national typical case of industrial poverty alleviation, the best case of "global poverty reduction case collection activities", and to be promoted in Hebei Province. It has established 347 teaching, scientific research, and production "three-combination" bases in the six major ecological regions of the province, and 50 agricultural innovation stations in Taihang Mountain, with regional integration There are 9 experimental stations, 41 modern agricultural education technology innovation demonstration bases, and Since the "13th Five-Year Plan", more than 1,000 new achievements, new varieties and new technologies have been promoted, which has effectively promoted the local economic and social development.

Hebei Agricultural University set Food Science and Engineering in 1931. The Department of Food Science was established in 1987, and the College of Food Science and Technology was established in 2000. It has a first-class doctoral degree authorization program and a post-doctoral research station. It is one of the first batch of national-level first-class undergraduate major construction sites in China and a first-class discipline in Hebei Province. This discipline began to recruit undergraduate students in 1985 and graduate students in 1998. It was selected as the key discipline of Hebei Province in 2002; secondary disciplines have been authorized to confer doctor's degree in 2005; first disciplines have been authorized to confer doctor's degree in 2017; postdoctoral scientific research station has been established in 2019; it was listed in the first batch of national-level first-class undergraduate major construction sites in 2019. It is the cradle of Food Science and Engineering talent in Hebei Province.

2. Hebei University of Science and Technology

Hebei University of Science and Technology (HEBUST) is one of the first batch of key multi-disciplinary backbone universities in Hebei Province. Since its founding, HEBUST has always adhered to the mission of "committing to the all-round development of people, serving the regional economic construction and social progress". It adheres to the characteristics of "regional, applied, international" and seizes opportunities to accelerate development. In 2007, it has passed the evaluation of undergraduate teaching level of the Ministry of Education with excellent results; it was selected to the "Excellent Engineer Education Training Program" university of the Ministry of Education in 2011; In 2016, it was supported by Hebei Province as national first-class university.

Hebei University of Science and Technology (HEBUST) is located in Shijiazhuang, Hebei Province, covering an area of 2,760 mu with building area covers more than 800000 square meters. The total value of fixed assets is 3.25 billion yuan. HEBUST currently has more than 23,000 full-time undergraduate, postgraduate, and international students. It also has more than 2,400 faculty members, 1 double employed academician, 2 foreign members of HEBUST, 2 national-level candidates for the New Century Talent Project. There are over 140 talents enjoy various types of experts from the State Council and provincial high-end, 2 national outstanding teachers, and 45 provincial-level teaching teachers.

The university has 16 teaching schools (departments), 79 undergraduate majors. It has 25 first-level disciplines for master's degree authorization, 3 second-level disciplines for master's degree authorization, and 15 professional master's degree authorization categories, covering 9 categories of engineering, science, literature, economics, management, law, medicine, education, and art. It is highly compatible with the industrial transformation of Hebei Province and the development of strategic emerging industries. There are 9 provincial-level key disciplines, 1 provincial-level key development discipline, 1 discipline selected as a world-class discipline construction project of Hebei Province, and 2 disciplines selected as the national first-class discipline construction project of Hebei Province. Engineering disciplines are in the top.

It adheres to the characteristic road of deep integration with regional social development, and continuously enhances ability of scientific research and servicing society. HEBUST has successively won second prize of the National Science and Technology Progress Award, first prize of the Army's Science and Technology Progress Award, and second prize of the National Technical Invention Award for Higher Education. In the past five years, HEBUST has undertaken more than 2000 scientific research projects at or above the provincial-level and ministerial-level, including key national research and development programs and major projects in science and technology. It has obtained more than 2,500 various patent authorizations. It has won more than 70 provincial and ministerial-level science and technology awards, including 5 first prizes and 18 second prizes. HEBUST won the first prize of provincial-level natural science for the third consecutive year. It has 96 scientific research platforms at or above the provincial level. It has established 13 technology transfer branches in industrial clusters in Hebei Province, and established scientific and technological education cooperation with 377 local governments and industry organizations and research units.

College of Food Science and Biology, Hebei University of Science and Technology, was founded in 1980. Its predecessor was The Department of Light Industry Engineering, Hebei University of Light Chemical Technology. In 1996, it was renamed Department of Light Industrial Engineering, Hebei University of Science and Technology. In 1998, it was renamed Department of Biological Science and Engineering, Hebei University of Science and Technology. In 2001, it was renamed college of Biological Science and Engineering, Hebei University of Science and Technology. In 2020, it was renamed College of Food Science and Biology, Hebei University of Science and Technology.

The college has 3 teaching departments: Food Science and Engineering, Bioengineering and Life Science. There are 5 undergraduate majors in Food Science and Engineering, Food Quality and Safety, Bioengineering, Bioscience and Biotechnology. Among them, Food Quality and Safety is a national characteristic specialty. The Food Quality and Safety and Food Science and Engineering was selected into the first-class discipline in Hebei Province. Food Science and Engineering was approved by China Engineering Education. It has 4 authorized disciplines of first-level master's degree and the authorized fields of master's degree in Biology and Medicine with 3 authorized disciplines of first-level master's degree in Food Science and Engineering, Biological Engineering and Biology and 1 authorized disciplines of second-level master's degree in Biological Chemistry. It has provincial-level platforms of "Center of Fermentation Technology Innovation in Hebei Province", "Center of Excellence and Innovation in Functional Foods in Hebei Province" and "Experimental Biology and Science and Engineering Center in Hebei Province". Fermentation Engineering is a key discipline in Hebei Province.

3. Hebei Normal University of Science and Technology

Hebei Normal University of Science and Technology is listed as the first batch of national key vocational teacher training bases established by the Department of Education of Hebei Province, national science and technology correspondent entrepreneurship training base of the Ministry of Science and Technology, modern agricultural technology training base of the Ministry of Agriculture and Rural Affairs, and the first batch of national science education base of the Chinese Association for Science and Technology.

Hebei Normal University of Science and Technology was established in 1941. It began higher education in 1975 and recruited undergraduate students in 1977. It has been authorized to confer master's degree in 2006. Changli Agricultural Vocational School was renamed Hebei Changli Higher Agricultural School. Hebei Changli Higher Agricultural School was upgraded to Changli Agricultural College. In 1960 Changli Agricultural College was renamed Changli Junior

College of Agriculture. In 1962, Changli Junior College of Agriculture was renamed Hebei Changli Higher Agricultural College. In 1972, Hebei Changli Higher Agricultural College was renamed Tangshan Agricultural College. In 1975, Tangshan Agricultural College was renamed North China Agricultural University (Tangshan Branch). In 1975, North China Agricultural University (College of Mechanical and Electronic Engineering) merged into North China Agricultural University (Tangshan Branch). In 1977 North China Agricultural University (Tangshan Branch) was renamed Hebei Agricultural University (Tangshan Branch). In 1984 Hebei Agricultural University (Tangshan Branch) was renamed Hebei Agricultural University (Changli Branch). In 1985, Hebei Agricultural University (Changli Branch) upgraded to Hebei Agricultural Technology Normal College. In 1988, Hebei Agricultural Technology Normal College was renamed Hebei Vocational and Technical Normal College (Qinhuangdao Branch). Qinhuangdao Coal Industry Management College merged into Hebei Vocational and Technical Normal College in 2000. In 2003 Hebei Vocational and Technical Normal College (Qinhuangdao Branch) was renamed Hebei Normal University of Science and Technology. In 2006 Qinhuangdao Education College merged into Hebei Normal University of Science and Technology.

There are 7 provincial-level key disciplines and provincial-level key development disciplines. It has 6 disciplines of offering master's degrees (academic), 17 sub-disciplines offering master's degrees (academic) and 15 disciplines with 5 master's degrees (professional). There are 75 undergraduate programs, covering 9 discipline categories of agriculture, education, engineering, science, literature, law, economics, management and art. It has 1 national-level professional comprehensive reform pilot discipline, 20 provincial-level first-class undergraduate professional construction sites, 3 provincial-level undergraduate education innovation platforms, 6 provincial-level special undergraduate programs. It has been approved as one of the first batch of the Excellent Agricultural and Forestry Talent Education and Training Program reform pilots by the Ministry of Education.

The department of food engineering, established in 1993, was the predecessor of Hebei Science and Technology Normal College of Food Science and Technology. Its construction began with the establishment of the agricultural products storage and transportation and processing discipline in 1987, which was later known as food science and technology college in 2009. In April 2021, the Ministry of Education approved its College of Wine Technology and Viticulture as the first batch of modern industrial college. The wine college has a first-class master's degree program of food science and engineering and a master's degree program of food safety. It has 4 majors: food science and engineering, food quality and safety, wine technology and viticulture, biological engineering It has master's degree of food science and engineering (academic) and master's degree of food processing and food safety (professional).